MUIRHEAD LIBRARY OF PHILOSOPHY

An admirable statement of the aims of the Library of Philosophy was provided by the first editor, the late Professor J. H. Muirhead, in his description of the original programme printed in Erdmann's *History of Philosophy* under the date 1890. This was slightly modified in subsequent volumes to take the form of the following statement:

'The Muirhead Library of Philosophy was designed as a contribution to the History of Modern Philosophy under the heads: first of Different Schools of Thought—Sensationalist, Realist, Idealist, Intuitivist; secondly of different Subjects—Psychology, Ethics, Aesthetics, Political Philosophy, Theology. While much had been done in England in tracing the course of evolution in nature, history, economics, morals and religion, little had been done in tracing the development of thought on these subjects. Yet "the evolution of opinion is part of the whole evolution".

'By the co-operation of different writers in carrying out this plan it was hoped that a thoroughness and completeness of treatment, otherwise unattainable, might be secured. It was believed also that from writers mainly British and American fuller consideration of English Philosophy than it had hitherto received might be looked for. In the earlier series of books containing, among others, Bosanquet's *History of Aesthetic*, Pfleiderer's *Rational Theology since Kant*, Albee's *History of English Utilitarianism*, Bonar's *Philosophy and Political Economy*, Brett's *History of Psychology*, Ritchie's *Natural Rights*, these objects were to a large extent effected.

'In the meantime original work of a high order was being produced both in England and America by such writers as Bradley, Stout, Bertrand Russell, Baldwin, Urban, Montague, and others, and a new interest in foreign works, German, French and Italian, which had either become classical or were attracting public attention, had developed. The scope of the Library thus became extended into something more international, and it is entering on the fifth decade of its existence in the hope that it may contribute to that mutual understanding between countries which is so pressing a need of the present time.'

The need which Professor Muirhead stressed is no less pressing today, and few will deny that philosophy has much to do with enabling us to meet it, although no one, least of all Muirhead himself, would regard that as the sole, or even the main, object of philosophy. As Professor Muirhead continues to lend the distinction of his name to the

Library of Philosophy it seemed not inappropriate to allow him to recall us to these aims in his own words. The emphasis on the history of thought also seemed to me very timely: and the number of important works promised for the Library in the very near future augur well for the continued fulfilment, in this and other ways, of the expectations of the original editor.

H. D. LEWIS

MUIRHEAD LIBRARY OF PHILOSOPHY

General Editor: H. D. Lewis
Professor of History and Philosophy of Religion in the University of London

Action by SIR MALCOLM KNOX
The Analysis of Mind by BERTRAND RUSSELL
Belief by H. H. PRICE
Brett's History of Psychology edited by R. S. PETERS
Clarity is Not Enough by H. D. LEWIS
Coleridge as Philosopher by J. H. MUIRHEAD
The Commonplace Book of G. E. Moore edited by C. LEWY
Contemporary American Philosophy edited by G. P. ADAMS and W. P. MONTAGUE
Contemporary British Philosophy first and second Series edited by J. H. MUIRHEAD
Contemporary British Philosophy third Series edited by H. D. LEWIS
Contemporary Indian Philosophy edited by RADHAKRISHNAN and J. H. MUIRHEAD 2nd edition
Contemporary Philosophy in Australia edited by ROBERT BROWN and C. D. ROLLINS
The Discipline of the Cave by J. N. FINDLAY
Doctrine and Argument in Indian Philosophy by NINIAN SMART
The Elusive Mind by H. D. LEWIS
Essays in Analysis by ALICE AMBROSE
Ethics by NICOLAI HARTMANN translated by STANTON COIT 3 vols
The Foundation of Metaphysics in Science by ERROL E. HARRIS
Freedom and History by H. D. LEWIS
G. E. Moore: Essays in Retrospect edited by ALICE AMBROSE and MORRIS LAZEROWITZ
The Good Will: A Study in the Coherence Theory of Goodness by H. J. PATON
Hegel: A Re-examination by J. N. FINDLAY
Hegel's Science of Logic translated by W. H. JOHNSTON and L. G. STRUTHERS 2 vols
History of Aesthetic by B. BOSANQUET 2nd edition
History of English Utilitarianism by E. ALBEE
History of Psychology by G. S. BRETT edited by R. S. PETERS abridged one volume edition 2nd edition
Human Knowledge by BERTRAND RUSSELL
A Hundred Years of British Philosophy by RUDOLF METZ translated by J. H. HARVEY, T. E. JESSOP, HENRY STURT
Ideas: A General Introduction to Pure Phenomenology by EDMUND HUSSERL translated by W. R. BOYCE GIBSON
Identity and Reality by EMILE MEYERSON
Imagination by E. J. FURLONG

Indian Philosophy by RADHAKRISHNAN 2 vols revised 2nd edition
Introduction to Mathematical Philosophy by BERTRAND RUSSELL 2nd edition
Kant's First Critique by H. W. CASSIRER
Kant's Metaphysic of Experience by H. J. PATON
Know Thyself by BERNADINO VARISCO translated by GUGLIELMO SALVADORI
Language and Reality by WILBUR MARSHALL URBAN
A Layman's Quest by SIR MALCOLM KNOX
Lectures on Philosophy by G. E. MOORE
Lecturers on Philosophy by G. E. MOORE edited by C. LEWY
Matter and Memory by HENRI BERGSON translated by N. M. PAUL and W. S. PALMER
Memory by BRIAN SMITH
The Modern Predicament by H. J. PATON
Natural Rights by D. G. RITCHIE 3rd edition
Nature, Mind and Modern Science by E. HARRIS
The Nature of Thought by BRAND BLANSHARD
Non-Linguistic Philosophy by A. C. EWING
On Selfhood and Godhood by C. A. CAMPBELL
Our Experience of God by H. D. LEWIS
Perception by DON LOCKE
The Phenomenology of Mind by G. W. F. HEGEL translated by SIR JAMES BAILLIE revised 2nd edition
Philosophy in America by MAX BLACK
Philosophical Papers by G. E. MOORE
Philosophy and Illusion by MORRIS LAZEROWITZ
Philosophy and Political Economy by JAMES BONAR
Philosophy and Religion by AXEL HAGERSTROM
Philosophy of Space and Time by MICHAEL WHITEMAN
Philosophy of Whitehead by W. MAYS
The Platonic Tradition in Anglo-Saxon Philosophy by J. H. MUIRHEAD
The Principal Upanisads by RADHAKRISHNAN
The Problems of Perception by R. J. HIRST
Reason and Goodness by BLAND BLANSHARD
The Relevance of Whitehead by IVOR LECLERC
The Science of Logic by G. W. F. HEGEL
Some Main Problems of Philosophy by G. E. MOORE
Studies in the Metaphysics of Bradley by SUSHIL KUMAR SAXENA
The Subject of Consciousness by C. O. EVANS
The Theological Frontier of Ethics by W. G. MACLAGAN
Time and Free Will by HENRI BERGSON translated by F. G. POGSON
The Transcendence of the Cave by J. N. FINDLAY
Values and Intentions by J. N. FINDLAY
The Ways of Knowing: or the Methods of Philosophy by W. P. MONTAGUE

Muirhead Library of Philosophy
EDITED BY H. D. LEWIS

ABSOLUTE VALUE

ABSOLUTE VALUE
A STUDY IN CHRISTIAN THEISM

BY
ILLTYD TRETHOWAN
MONK OF DOWNSIDE

LONDON. GEORGE ALLEN & UNWIN LTD
NEW YORK. HUMANITIES PRESS, INC

FIRST PUBLISHED IN 1970

This book is copyright under the Berne Convention. All rights are reserved. Apart from any fair dealing for the purpose of private study, research, criticism or review, as permitted under the Copyright Act, 1956, no part of this publication may be reproduced, stored in a retrieval system, or transmitted, in any form or by any means, electronic, electrical, chemical, mechanical, optical, photocopying, recording or otherwise, without the prior permission of the copyright owner. Enquiries should be addressed to the Publishers.

© George Allen & Unwin Ltd 1970

BRITISH SBN 04 231002 4
US SBN 391 00025 X

PRINTED IN GREAT BRITAIN
in 11 on 12 pt *Imprint* type
BY UNWIN BROTHERS LTD
WOKING AND LONDON

To Emmi and Lance Sheppard
in gratitude for many years
of loyal friendship

PREFACE

These chapters represent the first half of a course of lectures given at Brown University (Providence R.I.) in the first semester of 1969. (I hope to produce the substance of the second half as another book in 1971.)

The lectures were designed for students who could not be expected to have a wide acquaintance with the philosophy of religion or philosophical theology, and from time to time I gave them some brief account of the existing state of a question as well as making my own proposals in regard to it. Those accounts I have, on the whole, retained in the hope that they may be of use for other such persons. I trust that more experienced readers will not find this sort of thing irritating (in any case it will not take them long to get past it); I have tried to remove all passages which, while perhaps acceptable in a lecture, might be, in a book, objectionable as irrelevances.

The arrangement of material also reflects what I take to be the needs of students. The main positions which I adopt in this first set of lectures are worked up to as rapidly as possible (this in fact involves the raising of a good many philosophical questions and even a little theology) so that they can be discussed in more detail *en connaissance de cause*. What I have to say in this book is thus said *in principle* in the first two sections of it: the other two fill out the argument, add confirmations of it and develop it. Throughout I have compared my conclusions with those of other writers in the hope of showing why certain questions have to be raised and of making clear what I am trying to contribute.

I take this opportunity of thanking those whom I had the honour of calling my colleagues in the Department of Religious Studies at Brown for the great kindness which they showed me and the generous encouragement which they gave me. Professor Wendell S. Dietrich's advice and help in a great variety of ways were particularly valuable. In case any of my pupils at Brown should come across this book, I should like to express my gratitude to them also, both for their intelligent interest and for the pleasure I derived from their company. It may be useful here to remark that they were recommended to read, as an introduction to the lectures, a little book which I produced in 1961 called *The Basis of Belief* (part of my purpose here is to amplify—so far as possible, without repeating—its brief discussions and to make

PREFACE

some reference to work on the subject which has appeared since it was written).

Conversations (now in their thirty-seventh year) with Dom Mark Pontifex have been of very great help to me. Dom Joseph Coombe-Tennant has saved me from several blunders. And I owe a very special debt of gratitude to Professor H. D. Lewis for many profitable suggestions. This must not be taken to mean (as the reader may soon discover for himself) that he would endorse all my conclusions. But it has been a great satisfaction for me to find that on certain matters of central importance, where we might have seemed to differ rather sharply, our views prove to be not so much opposed as complementary of one another.

My thanks are due to the editors of *The Journal of Theological Studies, Religious Studies, The Clergy Review, The Tablet*, and *The Downside Review* for allowing me to make use of articles or reviews published in their pages. I have also to thank Br. Peter Leinenweber for his kindness in preparing the index.

CONTENTS

Preface   13

I. A BASIS FOR THEISM
1. Metaphysics and Modern Philosophy   17
2. Awareness   29
3. Knowledge   42
4. Truth   54
5. Certainty   67

II. AN OUTLINE OF THEISM
6. Value   80
7. Transcendence   93
8. The One and the Many   107
9. The Christian Metaphysic   124
10. Evil   139

III. SOME MODERN THEISTS
11. Dr Edwyn Bevan, Dr John Baillie and Professor H. D. Lewis   155
12. Professor John Macquarrie and Professor H. H. Price   170
13. A Continental Symposium   183
14. English Thomists and the Traditional Arguments   195

IV. THEISM AND ETHICS
15. The Autonomy of Ethics   207
16. Theological Ethics   218
17. The Ethics of Professor John Macmurray (with a note on Miss Iris Murdoch)   230
18. Conclusion: Responsibility and the Significance of Ethics   241

Index   254

I

A BASIS FOR THEISM

1. METAPHYSICS AND MODERN PHILOSOPHY

The typical English-speaking philosopher would look askance at a proposal to link philosophy with theology. In speaking of the typical English-speaking philosopher here, I am not suggesting that philosophers in the English-speaking countries run to type except in a particular respect, in their general tendency to fight shy of metaphysics and therefore of any constructive philosophy of religion. I want to suggest that their attitude is based on prejudice and that it ought not to deter one from giving a fair hearing to philosophers who are concerned with metaphysical questions. The prejudice, of course, is not a conscious one. It is often simply taken for granted by the beginner in philosophy that metaphysics is no longer a live option, because everyone or nearly everyone with whom he comes in contact seems to be convinced that this is the case; a habit of mind is thus formed, and it may persist undisturbed throughout the whole of a philosophical career. Some professional philosophers, it would seem, have never judged it necessary to read metaphysical works before writing them off. And those who do read them often confine themselves to the metaphysics of Hegel and his successors; they take it for granted that there is no other sort of metaphysics deserving of their attention and it is quite natural, in the circumstances, that they should do so—even a philosopher, if he is to survive, has to take some things for granted. But it must be agreed that what is taken for granted is always open to challenge.

There are people who call themselves theologians but abolish God. They can get along in their own strange way without metaphysics, and I shall have to say a good deal about them later. But for the present I shall disregard them. Nor shall I try to vindicate any metaphysical claims for the time being, although in what follows I shall be introducing the topics with which I shall be chiefly concerned and throwing out a few hints about them. What seems necessary for a start is to vindicate my statement about the lack of interest in metaphysics among British (and, to a lesser extent, among American) philosophers. For me to claim any particular examples of this attitude as characteristic might be unconvincing. But Professor R. J. Hirst of Glasgow has edited a collection of papers that are designed as representative of British academic philosophy, and it would be unreasonable to doubt that they are so. The book, entitled simply *Philosophy*,[1] is subtitled 'an outline for the intending student', and certain passages in it will not only illustrate the state of affairs for which I am asking attention but also enable me to give some preliminary clues to the standpoints which I shall adopt at later stages.[2]

Hirst contributes the introductory paper himself. He begins by considering 'some of the wrong reasons which may tempt a student to opt for the study of philosophy'. 'Some choose it', he says, 'because they have lost their religious faith and think it will provide a substitute, while some may look to it for a defence of that faith; others think it will solve personal moral problems. . . .' He is quite right to warn them that philosophy courses in British universities will not 'satisfy the need for uplifting speculation' and to insist that one must approach the subject with an unbiased mind. But the suggestion that philosophy can have no direct bearing on questions about religious belief or about moral conduct is one which I propose to resist. Hirst does indeed emphasize that philosophy (in his sense of the word) examines the 'rational justification' of moral and religious beliefs, but he adds that this examination cannot be expected to provide reassuring answers. He does not regard metaphysical *insight* as belonging to philosophy, and, since I regard this as being at the heart of metaphysics, I must regard his attitude as anti-metaphysical. To return for a moment to the need for an unbiased mind, I should want to point out to Hirst that a convinced Christian is not biased in his approach to philosophy if he maintains that his philosophical convictions, when fully worked out, will not conflict with what he, as a Christian, has already discovered to be the case, because, first, as regards his belief in God, this belief (so I shall maintain) is based upon an awareness of God which is available for all men and therefore belongs to the philosophical sphere, and, secondly, as regards his belief in the Christian revelation, if he is genuinely convinced that

---

[1] Routledge & Kegan Paul, 1968.
[2] The dual purpose of this chapter may make difficulties for some readers. In that case they might be well advised to pass on to the second chapter, where the book's argument begins, and return to this one perhaps at the end.

he has God's authority for this, he must know that it cannot conflict with whatever he may find to be the case. There should be no question of his accepting conclusions in the philosophical sphere because they are imposed upon him by his theology. Philosophy is an autonomous discipline, and as a philosopher he remains subject to it.

Hirst goes on to say: 'experience has shown that there are fatal flaws in all ambitious speculative schemes'.[1] So an awareness of God from which wide-ranging philosophical conclusions inevitably follow would be, presumably, ruled out. We are then assured that 'a roughly similar conception of philosophy is to be found in all British universities' and that the contributors to this book 'have taken great care not to seem parochial',[2] which proves to mean that they have fully informed themselves about the condition of philosophy in British universities, and in particular that they do not stand for the dogmatic positivism which had become fashionable some twenty years ago and which claimed to prove that all metaphysics must be meaningless. It is true that metaphysics is no longer ruled out in British universities as necessarily meaningless, and that there has been in recent years a certain revival of metaphysics in some quarters. But the general position is still that it is ruled out in practice, at any rate in a form which has an interest for religious people. As Hirst remarks, 'few philosophers would claim to love wisdom any more than the next man'.[3] Philosophy, then, no longer retains its original meaning in British universities. In the penultimate paragraph of his paper Hirst mentions, but does not discuss, the possible accusation that the concentration on linguistic and conceptual analysis and on logical procedures in British universities 'conceals an empiricist prejudice (or world view even) that remains uncriticized because not explicit'.[4] By an 'empiricist' prejudice Hirst means, it seems to me, an anti-metaphysical one, and the possible accusation of which he speaks is one which I would make myself. He makes passing references in this passage to the influence of Hegel, to Marxism and to Sartrean existentialism on the continent of Europe. But there is no reference to any other kind of existentialism or to the theistic philosophers who exist not only on the Continent but in England, America and elsewhere. This attitude I must qualify as 'parochial'.

In the second of the papers in this collection, Mr D. R. Bell discusses logic and epistemology. He observes with refreshing

---

[1] 2. [2] 4. [3] 5. [4] 15.

candour that 'people can go reasonably successfully through logic courses and still argue badly'.[1] This draws our attention to the fact that an interest in logical processes is an interest in the purely general, the purely abstract. A logical process may be perfectly valid as a process although it makes reference to no concrete fact. But that is by the way. It is Bell's attitude to the question of certainty which really concerns me. Modern philosophers have commonly allowed that there are 'laws of thought' which are indubitable, although they often prove to have a conventionalist view of truth which implies that these laws are indubitable simply because the human mind happens to have developed in a certain special way. And they have commonly said that no concrete facts are indubitable. Bell, however, declares that 'while the sceptical possibility that we do not know anything to be true remains undisposed of, logic falls under the shadow of scepticism as much as anything else'.[2] That seems to me a consistent position. If no concrete facts are indubitable, we can never be sure that we have correctly followed any logical process on any particular occasion. If we could never be certain of recognizing such a logical process as a valid one on any particular occasion, we should never be able to reach the conclusion that it was in itself a valid one. My following of the argument: $A = B$ and $B = C$ so $A = C$ is a concrete fact. I claim it as a fact of my experience that I do follow it correctly and in doing so recognize that this logical process is a valid one.

It seems rather obvious that, if our own experience is untrustworthy, there is nothing else that we can trust. Bell's paper thus introduces a topic which I shall have to treat in detail before very long, the rejection of experience in providing us with the indubitable. Our typical philosophers, as we have had occasion to note, describe themselves as 'empiricists', but this does not prove to mean that thay are prepared to *rely* on experience; it means that they regard empirical knowledge, meaning by this the knowledge which comes to us by way of our senses, as the only evidence available to us—and it is evidence which may always let one down.

Bell goes on to discuss 'rationalism' as the alternative to empiricism which has been advocated by certain philosophers. He has claimed that 'the search for an indubitable foundation of knowledge in sense-experience seems as foredoomed and abortive' as the attempt to establish absolute general laws on the basis of

[1] 18. [2] 32.

A BASIS FOR THEISM

particular instances, and he goes on to say that 'it is this pessimism that has provided one of the chief planks in the rationalist platform'.[1] He then discusses the rational appeal to mathematics. 'Mathematics', he says, 'appears to afford absolutely certain and incontestable truths that are known independently of experience.' His comments on this are surprising, and I must quote two passages at some length.

The first begins: 'While one may give unstinting recognition to the certitude of mathematics, one must realize that a price is paid for this certitude. The reason why mathematical propositions are secure from refutation at the hands of experience is precisely because they are not in any sense about experience or what is found in experience....'[2] This is surprising because it seems, on the face of it, to grant the rationalist's claim to some certain knowledge but objects that this knowledge cannot be applied to the world of sense-experience, as if the rationalist were committed to the view that it can be so applied—which is not the case. The passage continues: 'The case has been cooked from the start in the sense that what the statement $2 + 2 = 4$ is about—if, indeed, it is about anything at all—is not some thing or things to be found in experience!'[3] But, if the rationalist says that there are mathematical truths, although they are not found in experience, he is not cooking a case but staking a claim. Bell, however, has now made the suggestion that these truths are not about anything, in other words that they are not truths at all, and this is presumably what he really wants to say. Mathematics, then, he will be saying, cannot provide us with certainty because it cannot provide us with truths. What I wish to point out here is that Bell has simply dismissed, and not discussed, the claims which have been made for an awareness of mathematical, supersensible realities. I do not propose to investigate the status of those realities, and they will not be a plank in my own platform. The point is that Bell expects us to agree, without discussion, that nothing is to count except sense-experience. 'It seems hardly possible to argue', he continues, 'that numbers are experienced by anyone,' and, 'in listening to four string players I do not in any way listen to, feel, see, etc. the number four.'[4]

In the second passage Bell writes that 'a rationalist seeks to establish indubitable factual conclusions on the basis of reason alone': and there will be general agreement, I think, that, in so far as a rationalist tries to deduce particular facts about the world of

[1] 52. [2] 54. [3] 54. [4] 54.

sense-experience from supposedly self-evident general principles, he is going about things the wrong way. But the sentences which follow need to be examined: 'putting it like this', Bell goes on, 'brings out the basic contrast with empiricism, which assumes that it is only by paying attention to sense-experience that we come to learn facts. Just as the price the empiricist would appear to pay in his enterprise is the relinquishing of certainty, so there is a case for saying that the rationalist buys indubitability only at the cost of ceasing to speak about experience. The history of philosophy confirms this contrast: philosophers of a rationalist cast of mind from Plato to the present day all tend to dismiss common experience as a realm of mere appearance hiding, unless we step beyond it, true realities.'[1] There are several things to notice here. First, there is the possibility, not mentioned by Bell, that we might come to know realities, whether or not we choose to call them facts, on the basis of sense-experience but not by means only of sense-experience. Clearly, if we claim to know anything, we are claiming that it has entered into our experience in some way (although we could rely absolutely on someone else's experience if our own experience could guarantee his reliability). But it is a prejudice to assume that there is no experience other than sense-experience. Secondly, it is clearer than ever that on Bell's showing there is no way of being certain about anything. The philosophers whom he represents would seem to be committed to a self-refuting general scepticism (this is a topic to which I shall return). The indubitability which he grants to the rationalist is not to be taken seriously since, in this account, the rationalist is talking about a world of ideas which has no basis in fact—that is, in sense-experience—and is therefore unreal.

But what is especially to be noticed is Bell's reference to 'philosophers of a rationalist cast of mind from Plato to the present day' which suggests that he identifies metaphysics with rationalism. I cannot here discuss how far Plato's cast of mind ought to be considered rationalistic. There have been, of course, theories which have bypassed the world of sense-experience and attempted to build systems of truths by deduction from general principles. And there have been, of course, theories which have declared the world of sense-experience simply illusory and have asserted that all is really One, the all-embracing, ever-evolving Absolute. But it would be a very great mistake to suppose that there is no other

[1] 55.

kind of metaphysics, although our academic philosophers do not often betray an awareness of any other kind. The sort of metaphysics which I shall be recommending is not an affair of abstractions. It is, in Gabriel Marcel's phrase, a 'concrete metaphysics', which is based upon, and indeed found in, common human experience.

It may be useful at this point to look back at Hirst's introductory paper. 'Philosophy', he there writes, 'is no longer (at least in British universities) the construction of imposing theories about the nature of the universe or the attempt to reveal the true reality beneath a veil of misleading appearances. . . .'[1] He has in mind, I take it, such books as Bradley's *Appearance and Reality*, which has often been the target for anti-metaphysical ridicule but is now generally accorded the respect which it deserves. When Hirst thinks of a metaphysician, it seems that he thinks of a Bradleian. I shall not be recommending Bradley's position.

The next paper in the collection, by Professor W. H. Walsh, is entitled 'Metaphysics'. It discusses the meaning of mind in its first half and the question of God's existence in the second. All that I have to say about it at the moment is that it does not envisage at any point the possibility of metaphysical *insight* with the result that (from my point of view) it reaches no interesting conclusions. (But, as we shall see later, it contains some valuable criticisms.) By a 'metaphysical insight' I do not mean a form of mental activity which cannot be promoted and defended by rational argument. It is not indeed the conclusion of a purely rational argument, but the way in which it arises can be described and cleared of obstacles, its characteristics can be indicated and the consequences of rejecting it can be drawn out. That is what I shall be trying to do later. There will be no question of reducing the world which we all know to a 'veil of misleading appearances'. It will be a question of discovering more in it than meets the eye.

There is one more paper in this collection on which a brief comment will be in place. That is Professor R. W. Hepburn's admirable account of the present position of moral philosophy in Britain. It contains in the form of a skilfully organized conversation between three speakers a most instructive summary of the current debate on determinism and freedom of the will. This is a topic of primary importance for metaphysics, and I shall be contending that the evidence for free will in the controverted sense

[1] 5.

(that is, freedom to act otherwise than in fact we do on particular occasions) is plainly the evidence of experience. Naturally, in view of their general attitude to experience, our philosophers do not accept this evidence as decisive, and Hepburn therefore leaves the question wide open when his three speakers break off their conversation.

What I have so far said about the current orthodoxy in our universities will be accepted, I think, as a report on the facts by those who are in a position to check them, although such persons may disapprove very strongly of the attitude which I am taking up in regard to them. (I must emphasize that the report is a very general one, and it may be added that the continuing inquiry into our language habits has to some extent restored a common-sense view about our knowledge of the external world.) But those who are not acquainted with the facts may hesitate to believe that there is really a philosophical 'establishment' of the kind which I have been describing. Their hesitation may be removed if I make some references to another little book, published originally in 1964 and republished (as a Pelican) in 1968, Mr E. R. Emmet's *Learning to Philosophize*. It is one of the few books recommended for further reading by Hirst and his contributors. It is addressed to beginners, and its author clearly regards himself as an exponent of philosophical views which are commonly accepted—he seems not to recognize that they are less fashionable now than they were once.

To take up again the topic of moral freedom, it is to be observed that Emmet is not content to leave this issue open. In the summary of his final chapter, he offers his own view unequivocally: 'Smith, being what he was at that moment, could not have behaved other than he did at that moment. What he was at that moment was therefore *responsible* for what he did. If you approve of what he did, it will be sensible for you to praise him, perhaps to reward him. This will make it more likely that Smith and others will behave in similar ways in the future.'[1] I shall be contending that we mean more than this when we speak of moral responsibility. Emmet, here and at some other points, is more decidedly sceptical than Hirst's contributors. He quotes with approval the following words from Sir Isaiah Berlin's *The Age of Enlightenment:* 'Propositions are either certain and uninformative or informative and not certain. Metaphysical knowledge which claims to be both

[1] 223.

certain and informative is therefore not possible. . . . This craving for a metaphysical system is one of the most obsessive which has [*sic*] dominated human minds.'[1] Commenting on these passages, Emmet remarks that when we are dealing with the world of experience, 'we can never get the complete certainty of logical necessity, though we can and do get situations in which individuals may feel a very high degree of subjective certainty'.[2] Here again we encounter the fundamental scepticism of our modern philosophers. It is to be observed that in a sense Emmet is less sceptical here than Bell, for he does grant complete certainty to logical necessity, uninformative though it be (I have pointed out already that an awareness of logical necessity in particular instances is presupposed by such a position and that acts of awareness are concrete facts, facts of experience). But what does Emmet mean by a 'subjective certainty', implying as he apparently does that the certainty of logic is by contrast 'objective'? It would obviously be a mistake to say that anything is in itself certain or uncertain. It either is or is not. It is we who are certain or uncertain. If it were suggested that logical necessity is objective in the sense that it is not in fact disputed, whereas everything else remains doubtful for some people at least, we need only recall Bell's conclusion that the shadow of scepticism covers logic too, unless we can solve the general problem of scepticism, which (according to him) we cannot do.

Emmet continues: 'It is easy to understand man's search for certainty through the ages and natural that because he was able to find it in the form of logical necessity he should think that it could be found too in a metaphysical system which would give an account of the fundamentals of experience based on a similarly solid rock and not on the shifting sands of appearance.'[3] Again we find the assumption that the business of metaphysics is to provide certainty for our experience by drawing upon some realm of reality supposed to be altogether beyond our experience. On such a showing it is easy enough to dispose of metaphysics.

One of the questions which Emmet raises for the consideration of the youthful student is: 'What is it to be beautiful?' His answer, as we should by now expect, puts the appreciation of the arts on the same level of subjectivity as (say) a taste for jam rather than marmalade at breakfast. The question about the objectivity of aesthetic judgments is often the first question to engage the

---

[1] *The Age of Enlightenment*, 180 and 190.   [2] 191.   [3] 191.

enquiring mind. If it can be shown (as I think it can be) that a consensus of informed opinion about particular instances of beauty argues persuasively for objectivity, then the ground is prepared for the recognition of objectivity in moral judgments (about which, perhaps fortunately, Emmet does not here concern himself). Conversely a complete relativism in aesthetic theory disposes the mind to relativism in all other fields of enquiry. An Oxford don once told me (in a friendly way) that from his point of view I was corrupting the young. From my point of view I must say (in a friendly way) that books like Emmet's seem likely to do so.

It emerges from all this that we may distinguish two very different approaches to philosophy. There is the approach which is still normal in English-speaking universities, for which philosophy is a highly technical business conducted with closely argued trains of reasoning on some topic which is only very indirectly, if at all, concerned with the other interests of mankind, even of academic mankind. The emphasis is upon the abstract, even in moral philosophy where the problems of practical living must be in some way affected by the conclusions reached (or, as is more often the case, the conclusions not reached). The philosopher's concern will be with the logical analysis of concepts, and he will tend to say that the adoption of moral principles and the making of moral decisions are matters for the individual about which the philosopher, as such, has nothing to do. I am not suggesting that the sort of analysis which such a philosopher conducts is without value; it is an excellent thing that we should be made to realize the implications of what we think and say in these matters. Such a book as Mr Julius Kovesi's *Moral Notions*, for instance, does remove certain confusions in a very useful (although, perhaps, needlessly exhausting) way. But it is also necessary to ask what it is useful *for*, to subject the language of morals to an ultimate (metaphysical) analysis.

The other approach to philosophy regards it as the analysis of human experience as a whole. I have already remarked more than once on the tendency in current philosophy to consider experience only in terms of sense-experience and in the context of the problem of knowledge. The sort of philosophy of which I now speak regards knowledge first and foremost not as a problem but as a fact. A good many problems arise in connection with it, but at all stages we must base our enquiries on what we have already come to *know*. We can suspect that something may be true only because we know already that something else *is* true. And sometimes we shall be faced not by problems but by what Marcel has called 'mysteries'. What we suspect to be true cannot then be worked out by a series of logical moves. We shall have to concentrate in some other way which is not to be looked down on as a *pis aller* or a lapse into the arbitrary or the irrational—into the subjective in a pejorative sense of that word. It is no more a matter of mere introspection than is the contemplation of a great work of art—this is where the importance of aesthetic theory most obviously emerges, for this contemplation is the most helpful analogy, for some minds at least, when we are speaking of metaphysical concentration. It will be immediately retorted that the appreciation of works of art, even if we accept the objectivity of the beautiful in general, is complicated by subjective factors in such a way as to make the analogy quite useless. At present I can only ask whether in fact there are not moments when we do meet the mind of the poet or of the composer in his work, when we are directly in touch with something which is undoubtedly *there* and to which we ourselves make no contribution (doubtless we shall have subtracted from it to a greater or lesser extent, failing to grasp *all* that is there). This may be called an experience of pure objectivity, however much it may be surrounded by personal associations of our own and coloured by our accumulated experience. The concentration to which I am referring is, moreover, in one sense a simpler matter, for the training which it presupposes is not that of an art-critic but that of a reflective human person. But by the same token it is more profound and so in another sense more difficult. It leads to a more profound objectivity.

It may be useful if I mention at this point a few names to suggest the sort of existentialism which I am advocating. The references to Gabriel Marcel did not imply that I think him to have all the answers. I believe that he can help one to find some of them, but I have learned more myself from others, also for the most part Frenchmen, and especially from Maurice Blondel and those who derive from him. I may be told that it is misleading to speak of Blondel as an existentialist and that the expression is in any case hopelessly vague (Marcel does not call himself an existentialist since the label is attached to such very diverse persons as Kierkegaard at one extreme and Sartre at the other). Nevertheless it does seem to me that the label has a use; it should manage to indicate that the writers to whom it is applied have a common concern with the concrete, with human action and human freedom, that they do not confine themselves to a world of abstractions or to a world of language regarded as self-sufficient. Certainly Blondel is a many-sided thinker, but if one may use 'existentialist' in the way I suggest, it is correctly applied to his teaching as a whole.

This approach to philosophy did not begin with Kierkegaard in the nineteenth century. We find it cropping up in philosophers who belong, by and large, to other camps. Descartes, for instance, is not just a rationalist in his *Meditations*. But we find it more obviously in what is called, rather vaguely and in some ways misleadingly, the 'Augustinian' tradition, deriving like most things in the thought of the West from an interpretation of Plato and passing through the Middle Ages to Pascal and to Newman. It may be considered as forming a bridge between the thought of the West with its characteristic emphasis on the physical world and that of the East with its characteristic emphasis on the life of the spirit. It may merely cause disquiet if I add that it is the way of the authentic mystics at all times in both the East and the West, but there is no need for disquiet. There is nothing fantastic or anti-humanist about mysticism, properly understood. No one is more suspicious of illuminism than the orthodox mystics. We may not feel able to follow them very far, but we may find that we have a clue to their meaning in human activities of the most familiar and apparently undevout kind.

Finally it may be asked whether this sort of thing ought not to be called theology rather than philosophy. Should one not mean by 'philosophy' what is normally meant by it in the English-speaking world? One could, of course, speak instead of 'existentialist metaphysics' if the use of the word 'philosophy' proved to make discussion impossible. But I could not agree to calling this just 'theology'. To call it 'natural theology' would indeed point to the upshot of it. But theology *tout court* is taken to mean a science based upon revelation and upon the acceptance of an authority, whereas what I am talking about here (we shall be doing some theology eventually) is accessible for the human mind (so I shall be contending) without appeal to any authority except that of our own experience. It is true that many people nowadays find answers to philosophical problems in the writings of theologians—for example, Heidegger's analysis of our situation in the world, which abolishes the sort of epistemological problem which concerns Bell and Emmet, has reached many of us by way of Karl Rahner. Indeed, the existentialist tradition has been maintained to a considerable extent by people who are primarily theologians. But this does not mean that you have to be a theologian in order to be this sort of philosopher. It points to the fact that theology throws further light on philosophical conclusions. And it may be said to take over those conclusions and so to be a comprehensive science. But it cannot tamper with them, and so philosophy—or metaphysics—remains a science and a controlling science. There must be a philosophical 'moment' in any valid approach to theology, a gateway to theology. Even the least sophisticated act of faith presupposes, logically if not temporally, such a 'moment'. But a good deal of discussion will be necessary before I can hope to make that view seem acceptable to anyone who does not already share it.

2. AWARENESS

An approach to a metaphysical standpoint has to be a gradual one in the present climate of opinion. It seems necessary in fact to start right at the beginning and to consider human awareness in its basic form. For nowadays people find it difficult to grant a peculiar status to human awareness, a status, that is, which puts it out of reach of the scientist in his laboratory. Philosophers have tried to make out that our awareness is merely the coincidence of those sense-data on the basis of which, according to them, we construct a world of objects; the mind is only a grouping of sense-data or the place where they occur. This is the abolition of the observer carried out by himself, and I venture to say baldly that it is absurd. It is flying in the face of the fact from which we must start, the fact that all human knowledge involves self-knowledge.

Descartes in his *Meditations* was not *inferring* his own existence when he pronounced the words *Cogito ergo sum*, for the simple reason that he had already affirmed 'I' in declaring 'I think'. He was distinguishing himself as a knowing subject from whatever else he was thinking about. He was discovering himself on what we may call his 'mental side'. It would have saved a good deal of trouble for later thinkers if he had succeeded at the same time in discovering himself on his bodily 'side'; it is (I shall maintain) a clear fact of experience that we are aware of ourselves as having both these 'sides'. The fact that we have a mental side as well as a bodily one leads to the conclusion that we are metaphysical animals.

Finding the distinction between our bodily and our mental activities does not prove of itself that our mental ones are of any profound significance. But it is a necessary starting-point, from which we may go on to recognize that these activities reveal us to ourselves as knowers not only of ourselves but also of what is not ourselves, a world around us. Indeed, without knowledge of the world around us we could not be aware of ourselves, because we become aware of ourselves by distinguishing ourselves from it. We cannot know ourselves without transcending ourselves. What, then, do we mean by 'ourselves'? All that is shown by the *cogito* is that all experience requires an experiencer. But it does not follow that the same experiencer must persist through a series of experiences. Is there in fact anything permanent about ourselves? Are we in any sense the same as we were fifteen years ago? We all know that we are, unless we have become muddled by reading philosophy. This is certainly a fact of experience, and a philosopher who overlooks it makes a mistake. And unless we are going to say (most implausibly) that this sameness is just an affair of our bodies, we cannot fail to see it in something of peculiar significance.

All this will have to be looked into in more detail. Let us start by considering in the most general way the genesis of thought on this planet. Once upon a time, we are assured, it contained no sensitive organisms. When they appeared something simply new was added to the existing sum of things. The fact that it was led up to gradually seems to obscure this for so many people, as if describing the process through which something happens could abolish the fact that, whereas it was not there once, it is there now. It may be just the way of the world that new things arise in it; it may not call for any explanation of a metaphysical sort for all that we can say at this stage of our enquiry—but we do need to be clear about the fact that the appearance of sensation in the world does make a real difference to the existing set-up. And when we consider the history of life on this planet we can hardly fail to conclude that another difference was made to it when a sensitive organism became what we call a man. The difference clearly lies in the nature of our mental powers. So we must distinguish specifically human powers from the sentient organism simply as such.

In forming the notion of the sentient organism simply as such we rely on what we know about the structure and behaviour of the brutes. It appears that the sensations and images which occur in our experience are to be found also in theirs. We must now face the curious fact that, in some people's view, what we call a thought is not something qualitatively different from sensations. Thought, they will say, is just an interrelation of sensations and images of a highly complex kind. First, let us note that, since the emergence of sensation must be considered a qualitative change, there can be nothing, in principle, against the contention that a further qualitative change occurred with the emergence of thought. Secondly, human awareness discloses itself to us as something more than the occurrence of sensations and images. To bring this out I shall quote from a remarkable but little-known book, *Man and Morals*, by the late Dr D. J. B. Hawkins, published in 1960. 'Animal behaviour', he writes, 'can be interpreted on the basis of the mere occurrence of sensations and images. If, then, we speak of an animal as "aware" of its environment, this is in a very different sense from what is meant by human awareness. It has to be interpreted behaviouristically, in so far as the occurrence of sensation and images enables an animal to react to its environment in a way which for a human being involves awareness as a distinctive activity.'[1]

It may be insisted that the brutes do possess the same sort of awareness as ourselves in a less developed form. But the facts point definitely enough to a qualitative difference between their powers and ours of a most radical kind.[2] And the suggestion that they possess powers of the sort which we normally ascribe to ourselves alone but that they think fit not to use them is surely a fantastic one. The reduction of thought to sensation is associated especially with Hume, for whom the self was nothing but a stream of perceptions and the ideas which we form from them. To quote again from Hawkins, 'Hume succeeded in presenting a plausible picture of a kind of mental life in terms simply of sensations and images. A great deal of behaviour which we should be inclined to regard as dependent on the *awareness* of the situation could be

---

[1] 6. Hawkins's books are published by Sheed and Ward.
[2] Dr Desmond Morris's book *The Naked Ape* indicates this in a striking way although he himself draws no such conclusion.

interpreted with reference only to the *occurrence* of sensations and images. This sort of behaviourism has been renewed in our own time with similar plausibility by Professor Ryle.'[1] Professor Gilbert Ryle's book *The Concept of Mind* (1949), to which Hawkins is here alluding, is the most important instance in our time of seeming to abolish the observer without admitting that one is doing so. This ambivalent attitude makes it possible for various views to be held about what Ryle really means; there is a considerable literature about the book. An admirable criticism of it, to my mind, is to be found in an article by Professor C. A. Campbell in a collection of essays published in 1967 under the general title *In Defence of Free Will*. It will be worth while to spend a little time on this.

Campbell points out[2] that, although Ryle claims to dissipate the usual contrast between mind and matter without absorbing one into the other, in fact he puts both into a single world of overt bodily behaviour. Some bodily behaviour he calls 'mental' and some 'mechanical'—but it is a very odd use of language to call bodily behaviour 'mental'. And Campbell concluded that *The Concept of Mind* is, at bottom, a thinly disguised form of materialism. The only difference between Ryle and the behaviourists is that the latter interpret mental happenings mechanistically and Ryle does not. They agree in confining themselves to *physical* categories. Campbell then concentrates on Ryle's ninth chapter which sets out to show that 'intellectual acts' such as judging and inferring do not take place in a private world to which only the subject of the acts has access but consist of 'publicly observable behaviour through and through'.[3] Ryle tells us that the ordinary citizen knows nothing of these supposed 'intellectual acts'. He just cannot answer at all if he is asked 'how many cognitive acts did he perform before breakfast and what did it feel like to do them. Were they tiring? Did he enjoy his passage from his premisses to his conclusion, and did he make it cautiously or recklessly?'[4] Campbell points out that these questions, 'in so far as they are answerable at all, could be answered only by a person highly skilled in introspective technique' and that none of this 'offers the slightest presumption against the occurrence of the

[1] 5. When this book was already written, the first volume of Professor H. D. Lewis's Gifford Lectures, *The Elusive Mind* (Allen & Unwin), came into my hands. His detailed objections to Ryle's positions—or rather to Ryle's oscillations—seem to me, in principle at least, unanswerable.
[2] 244.   [3] 249.   [4] *The Concept of Mind*, 292.

psychical events referred to'.¹ Indeed it is impossible to take this sort of thing seriously.

Ryle offers other arguments. One is that the meaning of an expression must be understandable by *anyone* and cannot therefore belong to a speaker's private consciousness. Campbell makes the obvious reply: 'The situation is that the speaker chooses the particular pattern of words which he hopes will excite the hearer . . . to think substantially the same thought as *he* is thinking. To that extent the meaning is, or is intended to be "public". But even where the speaker's intention is wholly successful, there is the speaker's thinking of his thought and the hearer's thinking of his thought, and the two "thinkings" remain private episodes in the respective individuals' histories none the less because the objective content of the thinking is identical in the two cases.'²

Another argument of Ryle's, which Campbell considers the crucial one, is that a speaker's meaning is really identical with the expression of it. There may be a silent speech going on in his head before he actually talks, but this is, for Ryle, 'in principle, if not in practice, publicly observable'. Here, as one might expect, Campbell has several objections to make. One is that it would not be possible, on this theory, to express the same thought in different languages. 'The King is dead' would not mean the same as '*Le roi est mort*'.³ But, most importantly, the theory overlooks a difference between uttering words, audibly or inaudibly, and such an intellectual act as seeing an implication. The words follow one another in time. Seeing an implication, on the other hand, cannot be broken up into stages. It is a single act. Ryle has given an example of what he considers to be a thought: 'the announcement to oneself that tomorrow cannot be Sunday without today being Saturday'.⁴ Campbell replies that 'the seeing that the "tomorrowness of Sunday" entails the "Saturdayness of today" cannot be broken up into a stage in which we apprehend the tomorrowness of Sunday and a temporally later stage at which we apprehend the Saturdayness of today. We should not under these conditions be "seeing the implication" at all'.⁵

Ryle seems only to underline the paradoxical nature of his contentions when he tries to explain what could be meant, in his view, by saying that a man was doing something *heedfully*. The

[1] 255. [2] 258. [3] 262.
[4] *The Concept of Mind*, 296. [5] 262–3.

explanation is that he was 'in the mood or frame of mind to do at least this one thing which was actually required'.[1] But how, Campbell asks, could such a frame of mind be publicly observable? And this is what Ryle must say if his 'one-world' theory is to stand up. There could be, of course, physical signs of such a condition. But Ryle has allowed that they are not identical with it.[2] It should be perfectly obvious that only I myself can be aware of my attentiveness or inattentiveness in certain situations.

Finally let us consider an attempt which Ryle makes to dispose of the fact, so awkward for his theory, that we do see implications. He suggests that the light does not burst upon us on these occasions—it only 'dawns'. A man does not draw a conclusion at some particular moment; he has found himself 'ready to draw it in the knowledge that he was entitled to do so'.[3] It is hardly necessary to follow Campbell's detailed analysis of this. It is so patently an evasion. For, although the conclusion may be built up for gradually, it must be at some time actually reached. Something must at some time be *seen*—and not with the eye of the flesh. I consider, then, that this most famous of modern attempts to abolish a 'dualism' between mind and body has been unsuccessful.

'Dualism', however, remains highly unpopular, largely (it appears) because it is taken for granted that any clear-cut distinction between mind and body will divide up human beings into two *things*. But there does not seem to be any good reason for supposing that a genuine unity cannot result from a combination of factors which remain distinct as factors. And our own experience, it seems to me, assures us that this is indeed the case with ourselves. We need not, I suggest, regard our bodies as inessential for us or as just places where we have somehow found ourselves locked up if we accept this sort of dualism. Plato certainly talked about man as though he were a juxtaposition of two subsistent entities. Some of the rationalist philosophers have held similar views (Descartes is commonly taken as an example, but in fact he did try to unite mind and body). Campbell pertinently enquires: 'Who among the philosophers of the last two hundred years and more who have insisted upon the different ontological status of "mind and matter" have had any interest in sponsoring a dualism of that kind?'[4] He calls his own view not a 'two-world' theory but a '*different-status*' theory. It is hard to know what to say to anyone

[1] *The Concept of Mind*, 141.   [2] *ibid.*, 138.   [3] *ibid.*, 300.   [4] 266.

who does not recognize that our thoughts and, say, our digestive processes are radically different from one another. It seems so clear that they are simply *experienced* as different. For example, there is a sense in which my body is *alien* to me as my thoughts are not (most obviously when I am ill), although my body is not one of my possessions like my clothes or my walking stick. Fundamentally the distinction seems to lie between my experiencing and an object of my experience which I call my body and which I experience as *different* from my experiencing.

More light may be shed on this situation if we return to the topic of the genesis of consciousness. A sentient organism receives a new power—or develops a new power, if anyone prefers to say so, but, as I have pointed out, we must say that it is a *new* one. Human consciousness is not a 'thing' which takes over a body and adds it to itself. We have to say that it *arises* in the body. And then we shall perhaps want to say that it is a function of body. Such language, however, is misleading. Consciousness, although not a 'thing', not a pre-existing subsistent entity, is a reality, a *new* reality, which stands in a unique relationship to the old reality, the sentient organism. When we say that it arises *in* the body, we are trying to point to this unique relationship. We do not mean that it occupies some *place* within the body. Human consciousness, it must be emphasized, does not arise except in this relationship. That is the sort of reality which it is. But it is radically different from the body. It has not the qualities of the objects of sense-perception. So we call it *im*material. It declares itself to us, and we can only acknowledge it. 'We are aware that we are aware', Hawkins remarks, 'and that awareness is an activity irreducible to anything else.'[1] It is not just an attribute stuck on to an existing thing and making no substantial difference to it. We may say that the body becomes conscious, but then it proves to be misleading to call it just a body. A body which has become conscious is a man. It is not that the body has lost anything of what it once was, unless we like to say that it has lost its previous independence. But that is only a negative way of saying that it has gained a fresh life, which makes it necessary for us to refer to it in a fresh way.

Human consciousness arises in this unique relationship and does not otherwise arise. But it does not follow from this that, when once it has arisen, it cannot develop a life of its own apart

[1] *Man and Morals*, 5.

from the body. The philosopher may have no evidence that it does so in fact, but he has no grounds for excluding the possibility. This has been insisted upon in a remarkably clear and readable way by Dr A. C. Ewing, in an article,[1] in which he quotes as follows from McTaggart: 'To argue that, because under present conditions we cannot think without the brain, we will be unable to think when we have no brain might be like arguing that, because I cannot see the sky in my study without looking through the window, I shall be unable to see it when I have gone out of the house because I shall have no window to look through.'

The relationship between body and mind is unique as a relationship between the material and the immaterial. It cannot therefore be strictly described, but this does not mean that we can say nothing at all about it. For our experience tells us that man is an individual yet that he both senses and thinks and that sensation is dependent upon bodily changes. That is to say, our experience tells us that man, despite his complexity, is nevertheless a unity in a very positive sense. The unique relationship with which we are concerned involves a unity of structure, or, in the language of Aristotle, a unity of substance. This language should not cause alarm. It means in this context only that we are talking about an organism, something which works as a unit, not just as the sum of its parts, although that is not to deny that there are also systems within it which work with a relative independence. Three more sentences from Hawkins's *Man and Morals* may make the position clear: 'Our awareness of ourselves as embodied cannot in the concrete be separated from our consciousness of sensation . . . to describe the sentient psyche as a higher form of the organism and as composing a substantial unity with it is only to do justice to the unity of body and sentient consciousness. . . . But in self-consciousness, the reflective awareness of the sentient self, thinking is in the concrete inseparable from sentience. Hence we must extend to man what we have said of the animal psyche in general and hold that the human soul is a substantial form of the organism.'[2]

I would add that, although thinking is inseparable from sentience in so far as awareness is built upon sentience and in so far as it is always accompanied by sentience in our present condition, we may still hold that it is not confined in its operation, even in its present condition, to bearing only upon sense-presented

[1] Published in *Philosophy*, April 1954. [2] 16–17.

materials. We may accept Aristotle's conception of the mind or soul as the form or organizing principle of the body, but we are not therefore obliged to say that it can have no function save that of being this form. That is not to say that there is more than one soul in man. The suggestion is that the same soul has different functions, that it is not only sentient and conscious as the form of the body, but also spiritual. It was one of the merits of St Thomas Aquinas to have insisted that the soul is a single substantial principle. We may recognize this without postulating, as he does, 'prime matter', and without abolishing, as he does, all subordinate forms, sub-systems which, although animated, presided over by the soul, function in their own way with a sort of local autonomy.

The topic on which we have been engaged is of such fundamental importance that it seems desirable to go over the ground again from a different starting-point. This time I propose to consider some features in Professor Walsh's account of it (in the article, already referred to, contributed to Professor Hirst's *Philosophy*). He considers the question whether the pain of toothache occurs in a mind. If I suffer from toothache, am I in a mental or a physical state? Many philosophers, he tells us, 'would agree that the pain in question is normally occasioned by physical circumstances such as decay in the tooth or exposure of a nerve, but refuse to allow that there is more to it than that'. He continues: 'We might ask them by way of comment whether the very concept of this sort of pain does not merely presuppose a physical setting but also involve a physical condition: a pain of this sort is felt *in one's body*—it is not a happening in a spirit loosely attached to some body.'[1] It will be clear, I hope, that I am in agreement with Walsh so far. Pain in human beings is an awareness of a sensation, and in that sensation we are aware of our own bodies as being in a certain condition. Thus it involves both a mental and a physical condition. But Walsh does not offer that explanation. Instead he goes on at once to mention difficulties which he thinks to arise when we attempt to make distinctions between the mental and the physical:

'We may ask further, here following Wittgenstein, the most penetrating of recent writers on the subject, whether sense can be made of the idea of a pain which has no natural, external expression. . . .

[1] 67.

Of course people can and do feel pains which they contrive to keep to themselves. . . . But would physical pain be what it is if our feelings under this head had no natural expression of any kind; if it was just a matter of chance that men cry out when they are hurt, the cry having a purely incidental connection with the pain? Yet, if we once agree that having a toothache and, say, drawing breath may be two aspects of a single situation we are once more landed with something which is mental and physical at once.'

I shall not venture to comment on Wittgenstein's own view on this matter, for I cannot claim to understand what it is. I shall only express the opinion (despite much controversy on the issue) that, although the word 'pain' could not have come into existence if it were not for certain observable, public, happenings, it refers nevertheless to experiences which are private. The paragraph in which the passage just quoted occurs begins as follows: 'It is arguable . . . that the whole attempt to sort out human activities into watertight classes, mental, physical and mental-cum-physical is a mistake.' Walsh's own conclusion, however, given in the next paragraph, is that 'experiences and human activities, mental and physical alike, are to be attributed to persons, a person being something which is neither exclusively mental nor exclusively physical, nor for that matter a strange amalgam of the mental and the physical "conjoined" '.[1] I am not sure what to make of this passage. It would appear to presuppose a distinction between the mental and the physical; and if both sorts of activity belong to the person, I do not see why they should not be described as 'conjoined'. Perhaps Walsh means only that they should not be described as an 'amalgam' with the implication that they cease to be distinct. In that case I should agree with him. But Walsh's discussion of pain is part of an argument for saying that the Cartesian assumptions need to be rethought and especially the assumption that 'the terms "experience" and "mental activity" carry with them no reference to anything physical'. He denies that they could 'properly be applied to pure, i.e., unembodied, spirits'. It is true that 'mental activity' in its standard use refers to embodied persons. But there has been no proof that it *must* carry with it such a reference, that it could not be meaningfully used in reference to pure spirits if one entertained the hypothesis that

---

[1] 68.

there are such spirits. And there seems nothing to prevent one's entertaining it.

Walsh now considers Ryle's theory as an alternative theory to that of Descartes, and in this connection he makes some very useful points. He agrees that it seems to rule out consciousness. 'How', he asks, 'can a view which, to put it crudely, reduces mind to character and capacities account for consciousness?',[1] and adds that, if we accepted the theory, we should be apparently unable to use the common-sense method of distinguishing human beings from computers. Ryle's attempts to meet this objection are then considered. He can indeed make certain distinctions between human beings and computers. But he cannot make the fundamental distinction. For, as Walsh puts it, he 'is never tired of denouncing the theory of "privileged access", according to which only the owner of a mind can properly pronounce on what is going on in that mind. . . . Take for example an occasion on which I am silently turning over some matter in my mind, and you ask me what it is: might I not claim to be in a uniquely favourable position to answer this sort of question? . . . But if this is so, privileged access is in effect preserved and with it an important part of the traditional account of consciousness.'[2]

Walsh then asks why so many philosophers should be unhappy about admitting 'privileged access'. He mentions the suggestion that 'they are deeply prejudiced against the inner life' and he goes on to mention as a difficulty in their eyes that in any form of the traditional view 'the "I" will be dual-centred, in so far as it will present itself in one way to the person concerned and in another to others: I shall know some things about myself directly, others will have to find out about me by studying my behaviour. What then becomes of the unity of the person.'[3] This seems to me a most odd objection. Of course, if one rules out from the start any kind of dualism, a distinction between my public and my private lives becomes impossible. But there is no difficulty about it if we are prepared to accept the evidence of common sense. There is nothing whatever to prove that I must appear to others in all respects as I appear to myself. Why should I not have a private life? And obviously the knowledge which others have of me does not endanger the unity of my person. Their knowledge of me belongs to them; it is not a part of me. What is required for the unity of my complex person is that it should appear to function,

[1] 70.   [2] 72.   [3] 73-4.

in my experience, as a unit. And so it does. What others make of it is irrelevant.

In this connection Walsh considers an anti-dualist theory, especially associated with a group of philosophers in Australia, on which he makes some illuminating comments. It is known as the 'identity-hypothesis' and is the subject of vigorous discussion. What it amounts to is that, when I am said to be thinking, something is going on which presents itself to me in one way and to the scientific observer in another. When I am said to be thinking of my dinner, I am having sensations of a certain kind, but this appears to the observer simply as a certain sort of brain activity. These two aspects of one state of affairs are, according to one form of the theory, irreducible. According to another form of it, our thoughts and feelings are nothing more than electrical charges in the brain; in Walsh's account of it, 'the immediate experience is subjective and elusive, but science shows (or, as it develops, will show) the true cerebral nature of mental events'.[1] That seems to be pure behaviourism and to contradict our experience in the plainest way. The form of the theory which preserves both aspects intact is a more subtle one. But it seems exposed, so far as I have been able to understand it, to a fatal objection. An object may have a number of qualities and, in different circumstances, may reveal different qualities. But, if we knew only those different qualities, we should not know that they were possessed in fact by that one object. We must also know the object itself if we are to know that. In the present case we seem to be told that we can know the different appearances of a single state of affairs which is itself unknown.

To my knowledge, the most vigorous defender of dualism in our time is Professor H. D. Lewis. In his Presidential Address to the Aristotelian Society in 1962, published in the volume edited by him and entitled *Clarity is not Enough*, he has stated a view which so emphasizes the distinction between body and mind as to make it seem that the unity of the person really is endangered. He is discussing Mr P. F. Strawson's problem (in *Individuals*[2]) that we can ascribe states of consciousness and physical characteristics '*to the very same thing*'. Lewis rejects the problem. 'The truth seems to be', he writes, 'that we do not ascribe corporeal characteristics and mental characteristics to the same thing. When, for example, I say "I am tall", I am not saying anything about my

[1] 75.   [2] 89.

mind but only about my body which of course affects my mind in a great many ways. My mind has neither height nor length nor breadth. . . . The much maligned Descartes was obviously right in maintaining that it was distinctive of minds not to be extended.'[1] So far this should be altogether acceptable. But a little later we we find the following passage, analysing the meaning of the statement 'I am bald':

'The strict truth is not that *I* am bald, although that is a perfectly clear way of putting it for normal purposes, but that my *head* is bald . . . if the baldness is ascribed to me, that is only to me as a complex being having a mind as well as a body or being dependent on a body; it is not ascribed to me in any further sense which requires physical and mental characteristics to belong strictly to the same entity. I should also wish to add that my real self is my mind, and that it is only in a derivative and secondary sense that my body is said to be myself at all. In other words, in the strict sense I am not bald at all, and cannot be; it is only part of my body that can be bald, my body is not something that I *am* but something that I *have*. . . .'[2]

This does seem to make the body a mere appendage to the mind, and most of us would want to say, I think, that it is no less proper to say 'I am a body' than to say 'I am a mind', even though we should recognize that the mind has an importance which the body has not. But, if what I have said earlier is true, it is my awareness which constitutes me as a man; my body is the body of a man only because it is united with my mind in a unique relationship. In this unique relationship mind and body may be called the same entity in that they function as a unit. Lewis is not to be taken as denying this relationship when he points out that mind and body are distinct even in their union, and, when they are regarded from this point of view, he rightly calls them distinct entities. He claims that my real self is my mind on the ground that without it I should not be myself, whereas there is no evidence that I should cease to exist if I ceased to have a body. This we might accept, but to say, as he does, simply that I *have* a body seems nevertheless not to give a satisfactory account of my complex being. It appears that there can be no satisfactory description of a unique relationship. For example, to say that body and soul

[1] *Clarity is not Enough*, 385.   [2] 387.

are *parts* of our complex being is to use a mere metaphor. So we want to say, I think, not only that we have bodies but also that we are bodies. We try to point to the unique relationship by using both these expressions and playing them off against one another.

Before we leave this topic it may be remarked that in the Thomist system there is said to be a relationship to the body which persists in the disembodied soul. There is an incompleteness about the soul until it is united once more with the body at the general resurrection. I do not propose to investigate that doctrine here, although it may be well to remark in passing that the theologian is not entitled to give us any description of a 'glorified' body—it can be the same as the body of the present life only, I suppose, in the sense that it is informed, organized, by the same soul. My purpose in referring to this question at the present juncture is simply to draw attention to the fact that for Christians the relation in which body stands to soul is not one which can be permanently broken. The suggestion is sometimes heard among Christian thinkers that it is in fact never broken, that there is no interval of time for the soul between death and bodily resurrection.

3. KNOWLEDGE

In embarking upon the general topic of human knowledge we must first look more closely at the relation in which human awareness stands to our sensations. My proposal has been that the brutes have sensation but not awareness. Admittedly this will at first sound odd. But we must have some word to refer to what is fundamental in our experience and what, by all appearances, is not shared by the brutes. We may find it impossible to imagine sensation in the absence of awareness because, normally at least, we are in fact aware of, conscious of, our sensations. But are we always aware of them? The question may seem absurd. But are there not occasions, I would ask, when we register our sensations in a curiously impersonal sort of way? One wakes up sometimes in the morning with a vague feeling that something has gone wrong. Perhaps the fact that one has cramp has not at this stage risen to consciousness; there is only a sort of question-mark which seems to have nothing to do with us. In the second stage of the waking process we feel discomfort and realize that something will have to be done to alleviate it. Or consider our hearing the striking of the clock *after* it has struck. Is it possible that we were not attending to our sensations when in fact it struck and that when our minds are more receptive a moment later we recapture these sensations? Conceivably the *déja vu* situation might have a similar explanation —our sensations had already put us in touch with the situation before we brought our minds to bear on it. And what about dreaming? If there is anything in these hazardous suggestions, we may have a foothold on such occasions in the world of the brutes, the life of pure sensation.

I have spoken of awareness as fundamental in our experience. That is to say, not only is it the distinctively human characteristic, but all other forms of experience, such as being afraid of something, are dependent on it. What we as human beings mean by 'pain', for instance, is something which requires a consciousness. And we have not two consciousnesses, one connected with our senses and another connected with our minds. Our experience has different functions, but that side of us which does the experiencing is one side, not two. It was necessary to make this rather obvious point because a distinction is sometimes made between sense-knowledge and intellectual knowledge which would seem to imply such a dichotomy. And if we embarked on a discussion about human knowledge with that notion in our minds it might well prove an obstacle. All human knowledge, then, belongs to the awareness of mind or intellect, which works on different levels. When it is working on the level of the senses (that is to say, when it is bearing upon our sensations) we may call this sense-knowledge provided that we understand what should be meant by it.

In an important respect, then, I do not mean by sensation what Aristotle meant by it. For, according to him, sensation is itself an awareness, an awareness of particular, singular, things, and intellectual knowledge begins with the abstraction of universal essences. Aristotle has not wholly freed himself from the Platonic doctrine that true knowledge belongs to a world beyond the senses and not at all to the sensible world. In my view our intellective awareness bears directly upon the singular. It is not, however, confined to the apprehension of particular things in their particularity. I quote again from Hawkins's *Man and Morals*: 'It belongs equally to awareness to be capable of various sorts of differentiation of attention, among which must be included the observation of similarities and the ability to think in universal terms. But thinking in universal terms is not the whole story of thought; it presupposes that simple awareness of fact which is the primary form of thought ... Aristotle over-intellectualized sensation and failed to grasp the full nature of thinking.'[1] That is, our sensations are worked on and worked through by intellect; but sensations in themselves do not provide what we as human beings mean by knowledge.

We must now consider in more detail what this 'primary form of thought' does for us. I have maintained that in our awareness of our sensations we are aware of our own bodies; we are aware of ourselves as embodied. We must first face the fact that this apparently obvious conclusion has been overlooked by philosophers so regularly that there is now a very strong prejudice against it in many quarters, although this prejudice is being steadily overcome in our time largely through the work of the phenomenologists. It may seem very plain to common sense that our sensations, although not themselves occupying space, reveal themselves to us as belonging to a physical organism that does occupy it. But it will be remembered that Descartes discovered himself in the *Cogito* on his 'mental side' only, not also on his bodily one, and a brief account of the effects of it on his successors will give some indication of the importance of the topic and of the need to emphasize it in our own time.

Descartes had inherited from a decadent scholasticism a notion of representative 'ideas' as connecting the mind with material objects. He was, not unnaturally, suspicious of these ideas. We might easily be deceived about them. And so in his *Meditations* he doubts the experience of the material world, his own body included. He satisfies himself eventually only by arguments purporting to show that God exists and that God would not have given us so strong a tendency to believe that the material world exists if in fact it did not do so. These arguments have not given much satisfaction to subsequent philosophers. The heritage of representative ideas was passed on from Descartes to John Locke who only succeeded in making clear to his successors how hopeless the position had always been. One of the few things on which epistemologists are agreed with virtual unanimity is that a 'copy-theory' of perception is self-contradictory. The argument against it is very simple. If all that our experience provided us with were copies of some reality, a sort of photographs, then we should not be in touch with any reality. We should have no right to maintain

[1] *Man and Morals*, 6.

that there were any realities. You cannot infer the existence of something previously unknown from the behaviour of the things which you know if the behaviour of the things which you know is *all* that you know. If all the things we know were a sort of photographs, we should not be able to know them as such. You cannot even talk about photographs unless you have at some time encountered something which is not a photograph but an original. When Locke realized that some of the 'ideas' (by which he meant sense-impressions or sensations) certainly did not 'represent' (the 'ideas' of taste and smell are the most obvious cases), one might expect that he would have thrown over the whole theory. But in fact it was left for Berkeley to point out that a sensation can be *like* nothing except another sensation. And this left the way open for the Humean world of interrelated sensations. The basic fact that we know ourselves as embodied was, as it were, forgotten about. So British empiricists in our own century are still found talking as though the only basic fact were the experience of a disembodied mind or, when they are unwilling to talk about minds, the experience of a disembodied experiencer or, when they are not willing to talk even of an experiencer, simply a disembodied experience.

We may now ask an important question about our knowledge of our own bodies (it is plainly a fact, and this brief glance at the consequences of overlooking it may have underlined it). Is it properly to be called a direct acquaintance with our bodies? We are directly aware of our sensations; we experience them and in such a way that we might be tempted to say that we have experience in them and not also of them. This, I have tried to show, is not the case for human experience, human awareness. But a body simply as such has no sensations. Sensation arises *from* the body in the evolutionary process; it is not an essential activity of it. We have to say, I think, that, when we are aware of ourselves on that side of us which is itself non-experiencing, we *are* directly aware of it *as* non-experiencing. We are aware of it as being, simply as body, on all fours with inanimate objects which come in contact with it. We are, then, directly acquainted with it as a matter of fact. We are aware of it and of the bodies in contact with it as simply bodies. And we recognize sensation as something which depends for its occurrence on changes in the body and which reveals the body to us.

At this point we encounter another prejudice. It has seemed to some minds that we can have no direct acquaintance with a material, extended world because there is thought to be too great a difference between mind and matter. To this it can be replied in the first place that an interaction of mind and matter is plainly evident in the fact that we can move our limbs at will. Secondly, if we were to try to build a bridge of some kind between the material and the immaterial, we should find ourselves committed to the 'copy-theory' of knowledge. This is the route by which some scholastic thinkers found themselves developing such a theory. There is in fact no good reason for objecting to the conclusion that we know our own bodies directly; for there can be no general principles which apply to this situation and there is no sort of contradiction to be found in the conclusion itself. The difficulty, so far as there is one, is a difficulty for the imagination. The 'primary form of thought' must itself be thought, not imagined. But it may be helpful to recall that we think of matter nowadays as a kind of energy and of mind as another kind of energy. They are radically different in status, but this need not mean that they have nothing at all in common.

The analysis of our intuitive awareness of the body, of our own bodies and of other bodies in interaction with them, has been conducted by Hawkins in a condensed but extremely lucid way in his book *The Criticism of Experience*, published in 1945. He points out that 'when we have a feeling, as we say, in the head or arm or any other part of the body, we are unmistakably conscious not only of the feeling itself, but also of a region of the body, whether smaller or larger, connected with it'.[1] 'A feeling of warmth', he continues, 'is more or less intense, but it is not in itself extended.... Yet, even when the intensity of the sensation is the same, there is a quantitative difference between the warmth of my finger held near a candle flame and the warmth of my whole body in front of a fire. This difference, while it is not a difference in the sensations themselves, which are not voluminous, we can recognize, on reflection, to be due to a difference of volume in the regions connected with these sensations. This latter difference of volume, when we are conscious of the sensations, also naturally rises to consciousness.' Hawkins describes this awareness of one's own

---

[1] 54. Throughout this discussion of human awareness I have been heavily indebted to the author of this book, a distinguished epistemologist who has remained comparatively unknown because he makes no concessions to lazy readers or to philosophical fashions.

body as 'a primitive consciousness', 'the purely internal consciousness of a mass whose parts and limits have not yet been explored'.[1] To define and compare different areas of the body we require also visual acts. But before we can begin to make such differentiations we must have 'an internal apprehension of the mass simply as mass'. We can increase our knowledge of our bodies by looking at them, but unless we had first apprehended them in this primitive fashion we should not have registered them as bodies at all. Hawkins points out that, although this apprehension 'accompanies the consciousness not only of organic sensations and of feelings of temperature but also of every kind of sensation . . . the attention so tends to be concentrated on their external significance that we might overlook the bodily consciousness accompanying them, but it is undoubtedly discoverable if we care to reflect'.[2]

'We are conscious of the parts of the body', he writes, 'as a mass, or volume with density, in a state of mechanical tension'[3] and 'it seems evident . . . that the part of the body of which we become conscious in sensation is the part in which mechanical changes transmit the stimulus to sensation.'[4] I continue to quote: 'Since the primary notion of the body is that of mass, it seems likely that the clue to the perception of other bodies will be found in this consciousness. And surely it does provide the answer to our question. For it is in the experience of contact and mutual pressure that we find an intuition of other bodies for which sensation by itself affords no foundation. When I press my hand against the arm of my chair, I am conscious of a certain tactile sense-quality which belongs to me as a sentient subject. I am also conscious of part of my hand as a mass which is being compressed. And at the same time I am aware of another mass, which is in fact the arm of the chair, with which I am in active contact. These three factors in experience are distinct.' It follows that 'since mechanical change is necessarily due to external causes, the consciousness of any part of the body is always accompanied by the intuition of a corporeal mass external to it, whether this be another part of the body or a completely external thing'. And so, 'since . . . all sense-consciousness . . . is accompanied by the perceptual intuition of a body external to the sense-organ', we are able 'to refer . . . the data of sight, hearing, taste and smell to the action of external bodies', although 'the perceptual intuition which

[1] 55. [2] 56. [3] 108. [4] 57.

occurs in connection with these senses is only of material things in contact with the sense-organ'. Thus 'our customary employment of the senses for the discrimination of relatively distant objects is an instance not of intuitive perception but of perceptual inference'.[1]

This view that what we directly know of the world around us is confined to that part of it with which we come into direct contact must not be taken as suggesting that we can make only hazardous inferences about distant bodies. It is true that I can mistake a piece of stage scenery representing a bookcase for an actual bookcase. But I have no doubt about the bookcase in which I have just replaced some book. My justification for such an assurance will be considered later. For the moment it must suffice to stake a claim that this account of perception accords with common sense. It is an account not easily discovered in the works of epistemologists. Hawkins remarks kindly: 'Since the intuitive basis of what we call perceptual experience is comparatively small, it is not so extraordinary that many philosophers have overlooked it.'[2] I submit that his elaboration of common-sense notions, while coping with those problems of illusion with which theories of sense-data try to cope, is not exposed to the objections which lie against such theories. He makes clear that sense-impressions are in themselves purely subjective. The redness which I experience is a sense-impression which as such belongs simply to me as a sentient subject. The pillar-box is, in certain conjunctions, the cause of this sense-impression. This is what we prove (after a minimum of reflection) to mean by saying that it is red. We have intuitive knowledge of external bodies because they are present as causes of our sense-impressions. The cause is present with and in its effects. We are aware of our sensations as activities of a sentient organism, and so we are aware also of that organism. We are aware of it not only as sentient but as a body. And we are aware of some other body which is acting upon it or of some part of our own body acting upon some other part.

This theory, or rather this fact, of causal presence will be of decisive importance at a later, metaphysical, stage in our enquiry when I shall be no longer in agreement with Hawkins. It will be useful perhaps to point out at once that the knowledge of a cause which is present in its effects may be called a direct knowledge which is nevertheless a *mediate* one. A distinction between the

[1] 108-9.   [2] 110.

direct and the immediate is one that has commended itself to a number of modern thinkers, working, in some cases at least, independently—for example, it is to be found in Professor J. E. Smith's *Experience and God* and in earlier works of his, although he does not make use of it in quite the same way as I do. Knowledge of the effects of a cause I shall call *immediate* knowledge. We are immediately aware of sense-impressions. It requires a degree of attention to be aware, or at least to be explicitly aware, of the body in which they arise, of the body (external to the sense-organ) which is their cause, and of the self which is the owner of the body and its awareness. Our knowledge of these bodies and of this self is obviously a very restricted sort of knowledge. In an obvious sense it is obscure. Nevertheless it is unmistakable (unless, like Hume, we can contrive, or suppose that we can contrive, to overlook it). Since it does not fulfil Descartes' requirement for knowledge that it should be 'clear and distinct' we must conclude that he was mistaken in making this requirement. We must take experience as we find it and not lay down rules for it in advance.

At this point it may be instructive to turn back to Emmet's and Bell's remarks on our present subject in their writings to which I referred in the first chapter. Emmet tells us that 'to say that material objects exist out there ... is merely a convenient way to group our experiences ... scientists are coming more and more to the conclusion that the material object is not a useful postulate'.[1] I have expressed the view that Emmet's standpoint is becoming old-fashioned, but it is still very much something to reckon with, and this passage shows not only the length to which scepticism has gone among epistemologists but also the tendency to regard the hypotheses or working-models of the scientists as philosophical definitions. A scientist may find it convenient to discuss material objects in terms only of mathematics, but we are not bound to follow him in this. Indeed, as philosophers, we cannot do so.

Bell adopts a somewhat similar position. When he considers the view that 'experiences are *caused* in us by objects acting upon our senses',[2] his first criticism is that 'it complicates the relation between the perceiver and the perceived in a way which has no warrant from experience itself'.[3] He is thinking of sense-data theories which, it should be obvious, are very different from the

---

[1] *Learning to Philosophize*, 192–3.
[2] *Philosophy*, 44.   [3] 46.

theory which I have been advancing, which introduces no such complication. Then he remarks that 'we cannot equate any single experience with the cause of the experience' and declares that therefore we could never know the cause. I have tried to show that we apprehend the cause directly, that the intellect bears upon it *in* the effect—there is no question of an illegitimate inference from knowledge of an alleged effect to knowledge of its cause.[1] Bell implies that we have nothing but sensations at our disposal for the perception of material objects. He does at one point consider the contention that 'we are necessarily conscious of our sense-experiences'; his comment on this is that 'the certainty *that* one is hearing or seeing does not imply certainty about *what* one is seeing or hearing'.[2] But we are never just hearing or seeing; we always hear or see something, and we know that something is there, although we may, of course, make mistakes about it. Again Bell seems to suppose that if anyone appeals to sense-data in any way he must be committed to constructing a world which consists only of sense-data, and he concludes that 'once more the certitudes of common sense dissolve under the persistent questioning of the epistemologist'.[3]

Let us now ask a further question about these acts of awareness that put us 'in touch', as we say, with our own bodies, with other bodies and with ourselves as persons, as substantial units with their two sides, the side of awareness and the side on which awareness bears. What does 'in touch' mean here? Just as the relation between mind and body is a unique relationship, considered as constitutive of the human person, so the activity of mind in relation to body is a unique activity when it is aware of the body. Knowledge cannot be, in the strict sense, described. We cannot jump out of our experience so as to compare it with something else. But we can talk about it, and we all do. We talk of 'seeing things', and not with the bodily eye. We talk about 'being enlightened'; things 'come to light', we have to say, in our minds. Knowledge presents itself as a beholding. It would be misleading, perhaps, to say that such expressions are metaphors. It has been maintained by Mr Owen Barfield, if I understand him correctly, that, if we mean by metaphor the transference of a word's mean-

---

[1] Bell remarks that 'Locke and other upholders of the causal theory' leave us 'with a cause of experience which is not itself experienced but merely *inferred*' (48). The 'copy-theory' is not the only kind of causal theory.
[2] 49.   [3] 52.

ing from one sphere to another, then the expressions to which I have just referred are not metaphors. For men live on two levels at once, and they have always used such expressions to refer, with equal propriety, to either level according with the requirements of the context.[1] And unless we take up with an anti-intellectualist philosophy which imposes on us a special language, we cannot help talking about a union between subject and object in the activity of knowing. A fly settles on my nose while I am asleep. I do not notice it. It is present only on my body. Then I wake up and notice it. It is now present to me in another way. Its presence to my mind means that it may be said to enter into me in some sort. Aristotle was talking about this when he made his famous remark that the mind is in a kind of a way all things. But obviously this makes no difference to the things. The fly is unaffected by my awareness of it if I am content to leave it in peace. Nor do I become in any way confused with the fly. 'Union' seems the right word for describing the situation, because it imports that each party to it remains distinct.

It is tiresome to have to expatiate on what should seem so obvious, but in fact it is not obvious to important persons. Professor A. J. Ayer, for example, deprecates the sort of language which I have just been using. Speaking of certain philosophers, he writes that 'starting from the premise that consciousness, in the sense of cognitive awareness, must always be consciousness *of* something, they have perplexed themselves with such questions as what consciousness is in itself and how it is related to the things or facts which are its objects. It does not seem to be identical with its objects, yet it does not seem to be anything apart from them. They are separate, yet nothing separates them. When there is added to the further premise that consciousness is also self-conscious, the problem becomes more complicated still.'[2] It does not seem to me that these statements are hard to understand. When we make them, we are pointing to *facts* about our experience. If they seem to us strange, it may be interesting to ask what criteria of strangeness we are employing, for, again, we cannot get outside our experience and compare it with something which might seem to us not strange. The facts might be called mysterious, however, because they seem to have implications which we cannot as yet pin down.

[1] *Metaphor and Symbol*, edited by L. C. Knights and Basil Cottle, 55.
[2] *The Problem of Knowledge* (Pelican Edition), 23.

That is perhaps why Ayer dislikes them so much. Philosophy, he believes, must not entangle itself with the mysterious. Everything must be clear and distinct. Ryle was avoiding these same disagreeable facts in concentrating upon an aspect of Aristotle's thinking which considers knowledge as a disposition, 'knowing-how' as opposed to 'knowing-that'. It is certainly true that we do speak of knowledge in this sense. To say that a man knows French is to say that he can read books in French and so forth. He has certain capacities. But that is not all that is meant by the statement. The man must have contemplated certain marks on paper, listened to people speaking and realized, *seen*, what the French equivalents are to the words in his own language. I return to that topic here because we hear much talk about an Aristotelian as opposed to a Platonic approach to the question of knowledge. It refers to these attempts to ignore the basic character of knowledge, its intuitive character, which was stressed, very properly, by Plato.

Since knowledge is basically a matter of *seeing* things, arguments, reasoning processes, are of secondary importance—and this not only because without direct awareness or apprehension no processes of thought could get under way at all, but also because the point of these processes is to promote further apprehensions. We apprehend particular things. We explore the world which we inhabit piecemeal through the information which comes to us through our senses. But it must now be noted that we at once proceed to classify the things which we come to know. Our thinking proceeds by the employment of universal concepts which refer to all members of a class. Everyone knows that Aristotle brought Plato's forms down to earth and made them into the 'essences', the class-concepts, which the intellect abstracts from sense-presented materials. If we had supposed, as Aristotle did, that this was the primary activity of intellect, then we should have had to face the question of universal concepts before we could claim knowledge—the awareness of things as they are—for the intellect. Does anything in the real world correspond to these concepts? Might it not be that it is our minds which construct universal ideas? Then we might have to say with Kant that concepts without percepts are empty, and if we also held with him that percepts without concepts are blind we might be led to say that we have no knowledge of reality at all. For if percepts do not themselves put us in touch with it and if concepts are just a way of arranging percepts, then the world of our experiences is a world not of reality but of appearances—whatever that might mean.

If, however, in fact we encounter reality in the form of the material concrete thing, we need not be much worried by the problem of universals. Here I should like to make only a brief suggestion about it. The problem, reduced to its simplest terms, seems to lie in attributing to a single thing a character which belongs at the same time to a number of other things, to all the other members of the class. If this tree has 'treeness', how can all the others have it too? A common move at this point is to say that such talk treats 'treeness' as if it were itself a 'thing'. But it may still remain a difficulty to see how it can be any sort of objective reality. Perhaps some light can be thrown on the situation by considering how we are using the word 'same' when we talk about the 'same' treeness. We are not using it in the sense of numerical identity. When an actor reappears on the stage in a fresh part it is the same numerically identical man who comes before us. When two actors appear in the same clothes, there are two sets of clothes involved. Provided that we keep this second sense of 'same' distinct in our minds from the first, we may perhaps find that there is after all no difficulty. For this second sense refers to that relationship in which a member of a class stands to all other members of it, and we know perfectly well what we mean by talking about members of classes. It is another case, I suggest, of a unique situation. If that is so, all we have to do is to avoid confusing it with other situations.

There is no need, then, to suspect that our universal concepts impose a sort of grid over the real so that it always suffers a distortion in the process. Indeed such a notion is surely incoherent, for it implies that we *do* know what is real—because we could not otherwise discover that we were distorting it. That last remark is an instance of the sort of reasoning which has great importance for philosophy—although only a negative importance. In practice a great deal of philosophizing consists in untying knots, which need never have been tied in the first place, by pointing out the implications of what someone has said. If you want to say X, then you will find that you are really saying Y as well, and Y is incompatible with X.

But what about the 'laws of thought' which we are using when we go through a process of that kind? Are they realities which we just see? Or are they not rather imposed on our minds quite apart from experience? Taking the case of the law of non-contradiction, I should reply as follows. Suppose you are talking to a friend and a messenger informs you that this same friend is asking for you on the telephone. If you have really satisfied yourself that the person in question is there before you, then you just know that the messenger has got it wrong. The law of non-contradiction, we may say, is in operation. But that does not mean that one is appealing here to an abstract rule which may not be broken. The empirical fact is that we are simply unable to reject a piece of evidence so long as it is actually before our minds. The law of non-contradiction is simply the generalization of this state of affairs.

Later we shall have to consider the persistent denial that anything is 'really' evidence. But the intellective character of our awareness may have already emerged sufficiently to provide some answer to this. The results of this discussion are largely summed up in two passages in another of Hawkins's books, *Crucial Problems of Modern Philosophy*, a set of essays published in 1957 in which his theory of knowledge is set out in final form. In the first passage he writes that we tend to confuse human consciousness with sensation because 'sensations and their complementary images serve as indications of the state of the external world and of our own bodies. On the purely sensory level they are not apprehended as signs. For the apprehension of a sign as a sign belongs to thought, but they are no less behaviouristically efficacious as signs.'[1] It will be recalled that the activities of the brutes are to be accounted for on those lines. The second passage reads: 'We cannot understand true awareness, the awareness of thought, as anything but an original and irreducible energy in the universe of reality, not simply accompanying certain elements in it, but laying hold of and assimilating the real as far as it may.'[2] What makes us men, therefore, is our power of knowing the truth. Theories of truth must be the topic of the next discussion.

4. TRUTH

A certain sort of theory about truth can be most conveniently considered by referring briefly to Mr John Hartland-Swann's book *The Analysis of Knowledge* (1952).[3] Hartland-Swann regards himself as an exponent of authoritative opinions, and these

---

[1] 128–9.   [2] 131.
[3] In *The Basis of Belief* I have discussed it in some detail.

opinions have been, in fact, widely accepted. The most fundamental of them is that the philosopher's task, or at least one of his most important tasks, is to show up the alleged mysteries of human life as pseudo-problems. Problems which cannot be resolved by the analysis of language or of concepts are treated as non-existent. Hartland-Swann has no use for such accounts of *knowing* as that which I have been offering. He claims that 'knowing-that' is always reducible to 'knowing-how'. And his theory is that when we claim to know something, we have simply *decided* that something is the case or accepted a decision to this effect made by other people. This proves to mean that we consider ourselves to have sufficient evidence for saying that something is the case. What we have decided is that there is this evidence. But this never means, according to Hartland-Swann, that the evidence is in itself decisive. We are entitled to say that our decision is a 'correct' one when it is supported by the general agreement of those who have examined the evidence. But further evidence may always turn up which will bring this general agreement to an end, and it would then be 'incorrect' to persist in the original conclusion.

The object of Hartland-Swann's exercise is to avoid a situation in which anyone is directly *aware* of anything, for he rightly suspects that this would be a situation with metaphysical implications of a far-reaching kind. But it is surely the case that we must be aware, directly aware, of *something* in order to make any judgement about evidence; for example, if it is said that general agreement on some question is brought to an end by the appearance of fresh evidence, it must be that the persons concerned have become aware of certain facts as having some relevance to the matter in hand. Unless *something* has been simply *seen*, theories about general agreement cannot be even begun. To put it in the simplest way, Hartland-Swann is saying that nothing is ever more than probable. This position, it seems to me, has been decisively refuted often enough. To say that something is probable is to say that something else is evident and that *this* something suggests a further something. The clouds are there and the rain is to be expected. If nothing is evident nothing can be expected. Even if we say that we base our expectations only upon certain regularities in the behaviour of objects, regularities on which we can never rely, it still remains that we have *observed* regularities up to date. We cannot have evidence *for* something without having had evidence *of* something else. Hartland-Swann, however, writes that 'all correct empirical statements, like the dominant decisions on which they are based, are at least capable of being revised', and he adds that 'the difficulty we sometimes experience in saying with assurance that *this* is the correct account about so and so may well depend upon our being unable to find a decision which we can really regard as dominant'.[1]

It seems to follow that everyone depends upon everyone else for the conclusions to which he comes and that nobody *sees* anything for himself. 'Correct' is surely being used in a very peculiar way in the passage just quoted. Most of us, I venture to say, would not feel ourselves entitled to assess the 'correctness' of any statement if there were nothing more than a 'dominant decision' in its favour. We should say, I think, only that it was a commonly accepted statement. The point is that to consider all correct empirical statements revisable is to deny that they are ever *true* in that sense of 'true' which is plainly the normal sense. It might always prove to be incorrect, according to Hartland-Swann, to say that the cat is on the mat, but it will be correct to say it so long as most other people do. If we want to talk about 'truth' at all, in his opinion, *that* is the only sort of situation to which we can apply the notion. It seems to me that this is just to abolish it. But I must leave for a later and more detailed discussion the deep-seated prejudice that no empirical fact is indubitable and pass on to consider other accounts of truth.

Some philosophers speak of necessary propositions as true by linguistic convention. For example, it is necessarily true that a red thing cannot be green all over, but the necessity is really a matter of our language habits. As Professor William Kneale remarks, in an article entitled 'Are Necessary Truths True by Convention?',[2] it is difficult to see what can be meant by this. As he puts it in a summing-up, 'If conventionalism is the doctrine that we might have adopted other rules for the use of the sounds and marks we use as symbols, it is platitudinous. If it is the doctrine that we could vary all the rules of usage of our symbols while leaving their meaning unchanged, it is absurd.'[3] To make clear what the second of these doctrines amounts to I quote another passage from Kneale's article: 'Sounds and shapes [that is, words spoken or read] acquire meaning only by being made subject to restrictive rules of usage, and an alteration of the rules must alter

---

[1] 23.   [2] In *Clarity is not Enough*, ed. H. D. Lewis.   [3] 137.

the meaning. If I decide to allow inference from "this is green" to "this is red" (that is, if I lay it down that "this is red" must be denied, when "this is green" is asserted), I adopt a new code in which one or other of the sounds "green" and "red" no longer has the same meaning as in English. If, on the other hand, I decide to use these sounds with the meaning that they have in English, I am not at liberty to change the rules which govern their usage. I cannot, for example, abandon the rule which forbids their use in conjunction.'[1] That seems to me unanswerable. Kneale remarks at the end of his paper that the 'conventionalist' is trying to avoid the dangers of talking about intellectual intuition. But he is doomed to disappointment, for 'whenever he hopes to get clarity and determinateness by setting out his rules and considering their implications, he will find that he is forced to rely once more on intellectual intuition, although this time it may be only insight into logical connexions'.[2]

There is also an article in *Clarity is not Enough* by Dr A. C. Ewing on 'The Linguistic Theory of *a priori* Propositions'. How do we come to learn, Ewing asks, that a statement that a red thing is also green all over is inadmissible? If the truth of this statement depends on rules of language, this question could be answered by referring to them. But it should be apparent that there are no such rules. We have indeed to learn that the words 'red' and 'green' stand for certain qualities. But we can know that the statement in question is untrue only 'by knowing that the qualities . . . are incompatible, which is not a proposition about language'.[3] The argument which I have just reproduced from Ewing's article seems to be just as unanswerable as Kneale's (it is in fact the same argument at bottom). He also points out that necessary propositions are not uninformative, as the 'conventionalists' sometimes allege. For the statement about red and green tells us that a certain state of affairs is impossible and this is to tell us something about the world in which we live. I take one more point from Ewing's article. If the man who entered the house at midnight was the murderer of B and if A was the man who entered the house at midnight, then A is guilty of murder. This would prove, on the linguistic theory, only that 'well-educated people will use the word "murderer" of A under such circumstances'. 'Why,' asks Ewing, 'should A be hanged because of a linguistic convention?'[4]

[1] 136. [2] 145. [3] 163. [4] 167.

Let us consider next Professor Leslie Dewart's much discussed book *The Future of Belief* (1967). In an assessment of his book, which appeared in a collection of such assessments called *The Future of Belief Debate*, I have drawn attention to the theory of knowledge and consciousness which is fundamental to his whole case about our knowledge of God and of revelation. So far as I can understand it, it goes like this. The brutes have knowledge as well as ourselves, but what distinguishes us from them is that we do not just objectify ourselves in knowing—I do not know myself as 'other'. The point about consciousness is 'the presence of being to itself which constitutes the self'. 'So', Dewart writes, 'if truth is the relation of man's intellectual life to his world, and if that relation is not established in the act of a faculty of man, but in the very constitution of man's being . . . that truth cannot be a mental faculty's conformity to things. . . . Truth is . . . the adequacy of our conscious existence.'[1] And it follows from this requirement that whatever truth a man may acquire must be 'continuously surpassed'.[2] The development of the self, Dewart tells us, can occur 'only to the degree that the world is objectified, that is, conceptualized, systematized, organized, *lived with* and *made meaningful* for our consciousness', but this does not mean that 'truth depends upon an external reality's *fiat* to the effect that the mind must conform to its requirements regardless of what the mind may need . . . for its own existence and being'.[3] I quoted these puzzling passages in my review of the book. I quote them again because I want to develop my comments on them and to compare them with other comments made by other writers in *The Future of Belief Debate*.

At first we might have the general impression that Dewart is only pointing out the supreme importance of the development of consciousness, and that this 'presence of being to itself' is bound up with a knowledge of the world outside which must itself develop into new forms. Both these claims are acceptable. But the theory that truth does not depend upon conformity with external reality seems to mean not merely that such conformity is only a condition for the mind's development but that such conformity is not recognized as necessary at all for the attainment of truth. In fact it seems to be disallowed. It seems that, on Dewart's view, we have no knowledge at all (in the sense in which I use the word) of the external world, for what we make of it by our conceptualiza-

---

[1] 91–2. [2] 95. [3] 93–4.

A BASIS FOR THEISM 59

tions has no permanent truth-value. It is not just that we get to know more about it. Dewart indeed emphasizes that he is not using 'true' in the 'traditional' sense—which I should call the 'ordinary' sense. He speaks of 'the substitution of consciousness for assimilative knowledge' and adds that with it 'the distinction between language and thought disappears'.[1] 'Assimilative knowledge' refers to the union of subject and object in which, I have maintained, we penetrate or assimilate reality. If Dewart reduces our awareness of external reality to conceptualizations, then, I should say, he has failed to appreciate its nature. Anyone who sees no distinction between language and thought must certainly have done so. Moreover I should say that conformity to external reality is not only *a* condition for the mind's development: it is *the* condition of it. It is only by being submissive to the facts that we can increase our stature.

This will become clearer, I hope, when we consider our knowledge of God and how this knowledge lies at the root of all our knowledge. But it should seem clear enough at the present stage. Dewart has proposed that the mind needs by nature 'for its existence and being' something more than the conformity to external reality. Certainly it needs an increasing conformity with God. But Dewart is led to reject any kind of conformity. I cannot avoid the conclusion that the notion of truth as absolute is excluded by his account, and it is satisfactory to find that other writers in *The Future of Belief Debate* have reached similar conclusions.

Professor Frederick Wilhelmsen quotes Dewart's statement that 'a concept is true *to the degree* that by its elevation of experience to consciousness it permits the truth of human experience to come into being', and remarks that 'thus he has apparently discovered a "truth" beyond the truth'.[2] He points out that this is, in effect, to reduce truth to the conceptual order and to overlook judgements of existence. A passage from Fr Bernarde Lonergan's criticism must now be quoted: 'Objectivation... consists in acts of meaning. We objectify the self by meaning the self, and we objectify the world by meaning the world. Such meaning of its nature is related to a meant, and what is meant may or may not correspond to what in fact is so. If it corresponds, the meaning is true. If it does not correspond, the meaning is false. Such is the correspondence view of truth, and Dewart has managed to reject

[1] 104. [2] *The Future of Belief Debate*, 56.

it without apparently adverting to it ... he overlooked the fact that he needed a correspondence view of truth to mean what he said.'[1] Lonergan also quotes Dewart's remark that the correspondence view of truth is contrary to both logic and observation, 'as if we could witness from a third, "higher", viewpoint the union of two lower things, object and subject'.[2] Lonergan is equally opposed to this talk of a 'higher viewpoint', but he points out, if I follow him, that reflective awareness is a single act, not to be broken up into an act of knowledge followed by a subsequent act of introspection. Lonergan's own view I find somewhat elusive, but that, at any rate, is what I should say. His second comment, however, is clear enough: 'The union of object and subject is a metaphysical deduction from the fact of knowledge, and its premise is the possibility of consciousness objectifying not only itself but the world.' Even Mr Brian Wicker, in an otherwise laudatory article on Dewart's book, draws the line at the doctrine that the only valid criterion of truth is the intensification of consciousness.[3] It is curious that the editor of *The Future of Belief Debate*, Fr Gregory Baum, refers to this doctrine in his own contribution to the volume but seems not to think it requires any defence. It is still more curious that Dewart, who contributes an 'Afterword', should not have discussed it at all.

The notion of absolute truth is unpopular in many quarters because people have a feeling that immutability of any kind must be a bad thing—it strikes them as a denial of what they mean by life. That is what I would call prejudice. Associated with it is the feeling that one must not be *committed* in any final way, but to universalize the need for holding off, which is obviously desirable in a great many circumstances, is no more rational than commitment to a cause on the ground that commitment is always a good thing. Such questions must be approached without preconceptions.

At this point it will be convenient to turn to the work of the Dutch theologian, Fr Edward Schillebeeckx. His collected essays are being published in English under the general title of *Theological Soundings*; the second instalment, which, in my opinion, contains much of great value, is called *The Concept of Truth and Theological Renewal*. The first essay in that volume, written several years before the appearance of Dewart's book, is highly relevant

---

[1] *The Future of Belief Debate*, 73.   [2] *The Future of Belief*, 95.
[3] *The Future of Belief Debate*, 143.

to it. It might seem at first that it lends support to Dewart's main thesis. 'Present-day thought', we read in its first paragraph, 'is clearly reacting on the one hand against idealism, according to which human thought creatively produces its contents and therefore truth, and on the other hand against the "representational realism" of scholasticism, which regards the content of our concepts as an exact reflection of reality without any reference to a human act which confers meaning.'[1] Those last words might seem to fit in with what Dewart is saying. But we may readily allow that the human mind is not a mere reflector of external reality, and that our concepts do not reproduce reality apart from any reference to our own circumstances and requirements, without coming to the conclusion that these concepts do not reveal this reality to us at all. The fact that we know the external world only in its activity upon ourselves does not mean that we cannot distinguish it from ourselves. On the contrary, it means that we do make this distinction. Apart from ourselves there can certainly be no *meaning*. But it does not follow from this that the criterion of truth is the intensification of consciousness, as Dewart seems to suppose.

Schillebeeckx goes on to say that 'the reaction against these two trends of thought (idealism and scholasticism) moves clearly in two directions. On the one hand, it tends in the direction of phenomenology, one of the basic affirmations of which is that the world is essentially a "world-for-me". In other words, reality has no independent, absolute meaning, but many different significations in relation to man, and these significations vary according to the standpoint from which man approaches or deals with reality. Indeed, according to many phenomenologists, the objective signification of a reality can be found only in the meaning that this reality has in relation to man.' I am not alone in finding it very difficult to understand what this sort of phenomenology is really saying. If it is not merely saying that we know the external world only in terms of its activities directed upon ourselves, it must presumably be saying that we cannot distinguish at all between ourselves and it. Schillebeeckx, at any rate, must understand this doctrine as sometimes constituting a denial of absolute truth, for he proceeds to contrast it with a second trend of thought (instancing Fr de Petter, whom we shall meet again), according to which there is an absolute meaning in reality *implicit* in the relative meanings given to it by man. But I have to ask in what way it is

[1] 6.

implicit. If all our meanings are relative meanings how can we know that an absolute meaning is implicit in them? How could we talk about relative meanings if we could not compare them with an absolute one? The old anti-sceptical argument seems to force itself on us once again.

Schillebeeckx does himself use this sort of argument a little later on, as the following passage will make clear, especially in its final sentence: 'From a finite, limited, constantly changing, and historical standpoint, we have a view of absolute truth, although we never have this in our power. In this sense, we cannot say that truth changes. We cannot therefore say that what was true before is now untrue, for even our affirmation of truth does not change or become obsolete. The standpoints from which we approach truth, however, are changing continuously and our knowledge is thus always growing inwardly. The whole of our human knowledge is, in its orientation towards the absolute, also coloured by these standpoints. It is, however, at the same time apparent from the fact that we are aware of these perspectives from which we view absolute truth that we rise above relativism.'[1] What Schillebeeckx seems to mean when he speaks of an absolute meaning as 'implicit' is that God, the transcendent absolute, presents himself to us as that to which our human knowledge is orientated. For the human mind could not be aware of having an orientation except through some acquaintance with what is orientating it. And I shall be proposing that, when we make a valid claim to know the truth about *anything*, we are in fact looking at it as established in its reality by God. The knowledge of the truth involves knowledge of God. But that is to anticipate.

The passage just quoted from Schillebeeckx continues: 'We do not possess a *conscience survolante*, an awareness which is able to transcend all relative standpoints and then survey objective reality. Yet this is the view held in many scholastic theories with regard to truth.' In the light of what Schillebeeckx has just told us, we must take this to mean only that our knowledge of absolute truth and our relative standpoints are not incompatible with one another. We can gain absolute truth only on the basis of viewpoints which themselves are changing. We cannot jump out of our own skins and view absolute reality in isolation from our own consciousness. That is what Schillebeeckx must mean when he rejects a '*conscience survolante*'. And that is presumably what he meant by his

[1] 7–8.

earlier statement that we never have absolute truth 'in our power'.

In another passage Schillebeeckx speaks of 'the school of de Petter' to which, he tells us, he himself belongs. According to this school, he says, 'a non-conceptual aspect is the basis of the validity of our conceptual knowledge'.[1] The topic here is our knowledge of God, but the principle is applicable to all human knowledge. De Petter is quoted as saying that the concept is 'a limited expression of an awareness of reality that is itself unexpressed, implicit and pre-conceptual',[2] and Schillebeeckx adds that this 'pre-conceptual awareness is in itself not open to appropriate expression'. I would say myself that our awareness, whether of God or of material objects, although we have to talk about it in conceptual terms, is not in origin conceptual. Schillebeeckx holds that our concepts can give 'inadequate and limited expression'[3] to our pre-conceptual awareness. I must leave until later the question whether our pre-conceptual awareness of God can be properly described as expressible at all and, if so, in what sense. As regards our knowledge of material things, I should want to say that our conceptual knowledge is not merely an unsuccesful attempt to express our pre-conceptual knowledge but also a further stage of knowledge. We must make contact with things before we conceptualize, but when we do conceptualize we classify things, and this marks an advance in knowledge. The fact that we classify them from our own point of view and for purposes of our own need not mean that we must falsify them in the process. But the important point here is that we have pre-conceptual knowledge, which, though limited, is nevertheless, as far as it goes, an absolute knowledge, a knowledge which is absolutely true.

Let us now consider again Sir Isaiah Berlin's statements that 'propositions are either certain and uninformative or informative and not certain' and that 'metaphysical knowledge which claims to be certain and informative is therefore not possible'.[4] The point which needs now to be noticed is that these statements imply an identification of knowledge with the enunciating of propositions.

---

[1] 18.   [2] 19.   [3] 19.

[4] It is also often maintained that what is true must be in principle falsifiable. That a green thing cannot be red all over is a proposition that is not conceivably falsifiable, but we must not be forbidden to call it true. And we have seen that it is not just a matter of language and not uninformative. In ordinary language we say that things and facts are true when we mean that they are the case. We are not necessarily confined to ordinary language in philosophy, but we have no good reason for departing from it here.

Certainly when we know something we make a judgement—that is to say, we tell ourselves, as it were, that here *is* something. But behind the judgement there is surely a simple awareness of fact. Even if we wanted to say that judgement is the basic act of intelligence, there would still be the question whether a judgement must always be formulated in words or with some reference to words. And even if we agreed with Berlin that the discussion should proceed with regard only to propositions, it would still be the case that, if $A = B$ and $B = C$, then $A = C$, and this is not uninformative. Of itself the conclusion that $A = C$ seems, indeed, to tell us nothing about the external world, but the fact that the conclusion follows from the premises is certainly a fact about the workings of our minds. Could it be a fact *only* about our own minds? Dr Ewing, we have seen, has shown that we cannot account for inference in terms of linguistic convention. Could we explain it in any way which avoids an intuition not only about the way in which our minds have to work but also about the realities with which they come in contact?

The conclusion which we reach when we say that $A = C$ is undeniably the right one in some sense. If anyone fails to draw this conclusion when we have presented him with the premises we should certainly say that he has been too lazy to hold them together in his mind or that he is almost incredibly stupid. But when we say that the conclusion is the right one, could we mean simply that it is the conclusion which a normal person, some one possessed of the standard equipment, will in fact reach? On what basis should we have formed this notion of a standard equipment? We could perhaps say that this method of thinking proves to be serviceable in practice and that anyone who fails to employ it is inefficient, sub-standard. But this is a desperate expedient to adopt in the attempt to evade a fact. For it is a fact, if we care to notice it, that when we draw this conclusion, $A=C$, we know that we are thinking as we *ought* to think, that this method of thinking is imposed upon us not by the peculiarities of our mental make-up but by the nature of reality in general. Here again we have a statement which seems pregnant with implications, perhaps of a disagreeably metaphysical kind, but one which, for all its vagueness, we cannot properly deny.

Two considerations may underline this contention. They involve some repetition, but they are sufficiently important to warrant it. The first is that abstractions, such as 'A', 'B' and 'C', depend, as I have tried to show earlier, upon an intuitive awareness of those extramental particulars which we call material objects. From a genuinely empirical point of view, we have to say that abstractions cannot arise in our minds without a basis in concrete fact. For a philosopher who is employing the technique of methodical doubt the emergence of a conclusion from premises may be more immediately evident as an instance of true judgement than the judgement that there is a world of material objects of which his own body is a part. Nevertheless it may seem to be infected with unreality if it is not linked up with the claims of the latter judgement. The two judgements may reinforce one another if either seems in need of reinforcement. The process of inference reveals to us that we are capable of valid thought processes: the awareness of a world of bodies assures us that we have something to think about. For minds which have been conditioned by a fashionable scepticism these conclusions may prove acceptable, if at all, only when taken in conjunction. And of course they are conjoined in our experience if we allow it to develop without inhibitions. In discovering material objects, we discover that they are members of classes and that there are wider and narrower classes, so that if all men belong to the wider class of animals, then Tom, Dick and Harry do, for they belong to that narrower class of man which lies within the wider class.

The second consideration is a form of the general argument against scepticism which Croce has called somewhere 'the schoolboy's argument'. The fact that it is comprehensible to schoolboys is no reason for looking down on it. It consists in pointing out that we cannot get away from absolute truth because we are always presupposing it. If we suggest that our processes of inference are just the ways in which our intelligences happen to work but that they are not revelatory of reality, we are suggesting that what we think about things is not the *truth* about the things themselves, that there *is* a truth about things themselves but that we are unable to attain to it. How could we know this unless we could attain to it? And in any case we can hardly avoid the claim that our own theory is a true one. We can *say*, of course, that to talk about truth is only a way of talking about our experiences and that these are purely subjective, and we could then declare it meaningless to say that such a theory itself makes any claim to truth. We can *say* this, but I find it difficult to conceive how anyone can really *think* it. There is also another attempt at evasion which is sometimes met with. It amounts to saying (the issue is often obscured by ingenious irrelevance) that, although we must sometimes know the truth, for otherwise (it is admitted) we are in a difficulty about the notion of a mistake (implying, as it does, that we can contrast a mistake with what is not a mistake), nevertheless we can make mistakes at any time. We can never be sure that we are knowing the truth on any particular occasion. But how could we be possessed of a notion of truth except on the basis of particular occasions when we are *aware* of knowing the truth? Again we must insist on the implications of a genuine empiricism. A knowledge of what truth means in the abstract in the absence of all awareness of truth in the concrete is surely out of the question.

It may be impossible to avoid the notion of truth, someone may say, but must we say that truth is always absolute? The answer seems very plain. To say that a statement is not absolutely true is to say that it contains some truth—and that the rest of it is false. The part which is true is just true, and the part which is false is just false. Moreover, to say that it is true seems to mean not only that it corresponds with the facts but that its truth is knowable for any knower who has access to it. Truth is not relative to particular minds, and it seems that it could not be relative just to human minds if we are prepared to entertain the hypothesis that there might be non-human ones. And truth is absolute in the further sense that something once true cannot become false. 'Caesar is crossing the Rubicon' might indeed be true at a particular time and then only, but, if it is a fact that he did cross it, then this apparently would always remain a fact even if there were one day no minds to contemplate it. Truth seems to have an eternal quality. It is not perhaps surprising that, in the eyes of some philosophers, an eternal fact has seemed to be an impossibility without an eternal mind to contemplate it. There is no possible demonstration along those lines of an eternal mind. But what the notion of truth does for us, when we are properly apprised of it, is to open up metaphysical questions. To say that things are true is to say that they exist independently of our minds. Existence is indeed not a predicate in the ordinary sense. But we cannot say that for a thing to exist means only that we are aware of it.

Is the independent existence of things just a 'brute fact' which leads nowhere? There is Wittgenstein's remark in the *Tractatus*: 'Not how the world is, is the mystical, but *that* it is.' Moreover, the fact that all things are in principle knowable does seem to suggest that they have some kinship among themselves. But it is the *absoluteness* of our knowledge which seems to make it especially difficult to regard the fact of knowledge as a 'brute fact'. There is nothing else about us which is at all like this—to which it may be replied, sensibly enough, 'why should there be?' So we might try again to explain what we mean. When we just *know* something, when we encounter reality without doing anything with it, we (some of us, that is) come up against 'otherness' with a certain kind of shock. What kind of shock? Well, the more we consider things simply in their independent existence, the odder their 'otherness' becomes. It seems to be not *their* 'otherness' at all. That is to say, their existence seems no longer an independent one. 'Otherness' seems to come to us from beyond them. And the absoluteness of our knowledge seems to come from beyond us. But this is a metaphysical insight which may take a long time to develop.

5. CERTAINTY

Before trying to make any advance on metaphysical territory, I propose to discuss, under the general heading of certainty, questions about our knowledge of our environment which may seem to be still outstanding. Some topics already touched on require a fuller treatment in view of the present preoccupations of philosophers. And in particular it seems necessary to consider in more detail the fashionable doctrine that no concrete fact is indubitable. But, although in what follows we shall not be breaking any really fresh ground, it may be hoped that this further scrutiny of the fact of knowledge may help to develop a metaphysical insight into its true significance.

Let us first discuss the question of indubitability in an informal way and without reference to particular philosophers. It is incontestable that we are often without doubt about certain facts. We simply take them for granted and should be prepared to say that we were certain of them. It is also incontestable that we sometimes find that we were, after all, mistaken about them. This may lead us to suppose that 'certainty' means nothing more than an absence of doubt. For if we can even feel certain about something and then find ourselves mistaken, then for all we know this may always be the case. There is no such thing, we may think, as a certainty which could not be somehow overthrown. We can *feel* certain, but there is no sense in talking about *being* certain as though that meant that we were in touch with a fact which declared itself to us, irrevocably, as a fact.

A classical illustration of this is found in the experience called dreaming. You may tell yourself that a certain experience is too vivid to be a dream. You may then, in this experience, test that out by sticking a pin into your arm, feeling the pain (or so it seems), and satisfying yourself that you are really awake. Then you wake up. You told yourself that you were 'really certain', but it proves that you were not. If this sort of thing can happen at all, then, for all we know, we may say to ourselves, it may always be happening. It is of the essence of a mistake that we are not aware of making one at the time—so we may be making mistakes all the time. I have already suggested that we could not talk of making mistakes if we did not know what it was *not* to be mistaken. And it can be maintained in the same way that we could not talk about dreaming if we did not know what it is to be awake. But we must now face the fact that such arguments are not always decisive in practice.

It is possible for a sceptic to say that although he does entertain such notions as those of waking and dreaming, he is not committed to saying that they stand for objective realities. He may refuse to commit himself to any statement or even to any theory about statements which would involve him in making a claim to know the truth. He may not allow that he is really certain whether or not he is certain of anything. This, of course, lends to an indefinite regress, but, if he wants to go on with this curious performance, there is no way of stopping him. The only way of settling the matter is to *exhibit* the fact of absolute certainty. If anyone is unwilling to look at it, that is his affair.

So the claim that I want to make is that there is, as a matter of experienced fact, a difference between being merely without doubt and being certain. 'Being certain' is not just a feeling; it is *knowing*. We are always knowing something, although we might be hard put to it sometimes to say just what it is. Let us first consider being without doubt. I have no doubt as I enter my study that there is a light-switch just inside the door. I put out my hand to where it ought to be and discover that for some reason it is not there. Perhaps it has been removed for repair. It did not occur to me that this might have happened. There is no reason why it should have occurred to me. Indeed there is an excellent reason why it should not have occurred to me. If we spent our time envisaging this sort of possibility, we should never get things done. We cannot be always testing out the possibility of the poisoned pancake or the skilfully concealed mantrap. We are right to take it for granted that things will go on as they usually do. When they do not, we should not say, I think, that we had made a mistake, for that would be to imply that we should have taken precautions. But we were wrong in supposing that the poisoned pancake was wholesome. So we were not certain of it. If we are to talk of certainty as opposed to just being without doubt, we must mean by it a state in which doubt is consciously excluded in the sense that we know that no doubt in the matter is *possible*. We need a word for this state, and so to confine the word 'certainty' to the description of it is not to take unjustified liberties with ordinary language. It is a clarification of language for which we have good reason. It can be misleading to say that we are certain when we mean simply that we happen to have no doubt.

'Being without doubt' is sometimes called 'practical certainty', because we rightly treat it as if it were certainty for practical purposes. At one time I used to call it 'pragmatic certainty' in the hope of making this clearer. But it now seems to me that, in this sort of discussion, it should not be called any kind of certainty. For we have either excluded the possibility of doubt or we have not. We are either certain or uncertain. So long as we find ourselves hesitant, even in the smallest degree, we are uncertain. It hardly needs to be added that we can make a judgement which is in fact perfectly correct without being certain of it. In such a case we may be *said* to know the truth. But we are only supposing something which in fact is true. We 'know' it only in a certain sense of 'know' which can be just as misleading as it is to say that we are certain when we merely have no doubt. So we are justified in using 'know' in the same strict sense in which we have used 'certain'. In that strict sense, knowledge is always certain.

At this point questions break out. How, then do I propose to deal with the difficulty about dreaming that one is awake? Surely any claim to infallibility must be paradoxical? What in fact do we know in this proposed strict sense? I shall take these questions in order. When we are dreaming we are not capable of certainty. We cannot make the judgements which we can make when we are awake. We may *tell* ourselves that we are certain, but this is very different from *being* certain. When we are asleep, we are on the way to the condition of the brutes, or perhaps in it. We cannot stand back from the situation and bring our minds to bear on it with that sense of control and finality which we have in our waking moments. The fact that we make mistakes in our dreams is perfectly compatible with the claim that we are not making them when in fact we *know* ourselves to be awake. But we must remember what that means. It means that we have excluded the possibility of mistake, not just in word but in deed. This does not require necessarily a deliberate reflection on our mental activities. For instance, to use Samuel Alexander's language, we can simply 'enjoy' the experience of being persons, of being in some way continuous with the child in the old photograph, without deliberately adverting to it. If anyone asks us whether we do 'enjoy' it, we advert to it at once because it is always present, waiting, as it were, to be adverted to. We were certain of it already before adverting to it. And we can be sure that we are awake before any question about it is raised—but not always. Speaking for myself, at any rate, in some circumstances I should be unable to decide at once whether I was really awake. It might be necessary to ask myself whether in fact I was using that power of definitive judgement which goes only with full consciousness. Putting such a question to myself might have the effect of restoring me to full consciousness.

The claim to infallibility, which we have next on the list of questions, is only a modest one. It is only a claim that we have *some* certainties. But it does seem to commit us to saying that we can always avoid mistakes if we are careful. For, if we have any certainties, we can distinguish them from mistakes, and why should we not just stick to them and dismiss all uncertainties from our minds? Mistakes arise only when we draw conclusions which are not warranted by our evidence, by what we are certain of. The answer to this, however, has already emerged. It was allowed that it would be possible in principle to avoid drawing any inferences about the goings-on of material objects—but it also appeared that this would bring life to a standstill. We must here explore the implications of this more fully. In our practical dealings with the world of material objects we rely (according to the view which I have offered) on perceptual inference. We are directly aware of material objects as causes of effects on ourselves. An object which has produced certain effects in the past may have invariably produced certain others also. We classify objects as productive of all these effects. What affects our sense of sight in certain ways we shall suppose to be capable of affecting our other senses in certain ways—we shall suppose that we could feel it with our fingers. This looks like a tree. When at this stage we call it a tree, we are making an inference; we are inferring that it is capable of producing all those effects which qualify it for being what we call a tree. But it could be a representation of a tree. What we are committed to saying is that we could always avoid being taken in by some representations if we cared to take the trouble. And this conclusion seems to stand. We could prevent ourselves from performing any perceptual inferences from this moment onwards, but to succeed in so fantastic an undertaking we should have to avoid all commerce with the world of objects. We should be aware that it was there, but we should be quite unable to cope with it. The policy would be literally suicidal.

To deal with the last question on our list (what do we really *know* in the strict sense?) we must first return to the notion of direct experience and its rejection by many modern philosophers. It is often argued that when we are perceiving we are always interpreting and that there is nothing which is just 'given'. The notion of interpreting, so it seems to me, implies that there is something 'given' to be interpreted and that we can make *some* distinction between it and our interpretation of it. At least, I suggest, we are aware of something which is sheerly 'given' in our awareness of bodies not our own. But there are other objections to be considered. It is often said that the notion of a 'given' implies that we see only coloured shapes and so forth, never *things*, and that this is an absurdity. Such an objection may hold against certain sense-data theories, but it seems to have no relevance to my present contentions. It may be wise to insist again at this point that I am not suggesting a theory of perception according to which we construct a world of objects out of our sense-data or make an inference from them to a material world. I am suggesting that what we know is the interaction of our own bodies and other bodies, and the fact that we know this in terms of our sensations would make it possible to call this view a 'sense-data theory'. But it is quite different from what modern philosophers are objecting to when they object to sense-data theories. The existence of sense-data, they sometimes say, is just a hypothesis which has been thought up to account for illusions and to provide some indubitable foundation for knowledge; we can point to nothing which can be properly called a sense-datum. This may be the case for some theories—it depends on what they prove to mean by sense-data. But the sensations which were the starting point for Hawkins's analysis can certainly be pointed to, and illusions can in fact be accounted for on the basis of it. To show in some detail that this is so (it has been established already in principle) will constitute part of the answer to our question about what we can be said strictly to know.

A brief anecdote will introduce the topic. A friend of mine was once walking with a friend of his along the bank of a river. It became very hot, and they conceived the desire to swim. They had no equipment for swimming, but there was no one about, so they took off their clothes and went in. As they returned towards the bank, they observed certain figures, not far from their clothes, which they immediately identified as nuns. The only thing to do was to go on swimming around until the nuns took it into their heads to go away. But this they showed no signs of doing, and at last the swimmers were forced to approach the bank—uttering warning cries. As they approached, they became aware that the 'nuns' were black and white cows. What had the swimmers actually seen? What objection would there be to saying that what they had been directly aware of was visual sense-data?

Nevertheless, I should want to say, they were also directly aware of certain bodies. Were these the bodies of the cows? It may be held that they were, on the ground that one body can be said to act upon another when there is causal activity set up by it and passing across the space which divides it from the other body. Nevertheless we could not say that the sense organs of the swimmers were in direct contact with the bodies of the cows. The perception of distant bodies is an affair of perceptual inference. What these people were directly aware of was, then, what was in immediate contact with their sense organs. I do not know what to call it.[1] But a material sense organ must be affected by something in contact with it which belongs to the material world. No doubt the scientists would be able to give us an account of it. But they might want to say that nothing is ever in absolute contact with anything—that this is an unsophisticated notion which is opposed to the facts of science. From their point of view this is true, I dare say, but I am talking here of our basic human experience (on

[1] 'Light-rays'? Bits of stuff? (Would there be *nothing* in what we call 'empty space'?)

which even scientists have to rely in the last analysis); this is logically prior to anything discoverable by the special sciences and cannot be disproved by them.

The swimmers, then, I shall say, were directly aware of some bodies affecting them in certain ways. Their conclusion that there was a causal connection between these bodies and certain distant bodies was just as much a perceptual inference as the conclusion that these bodies were the bodies of nuns. They could have been mistaken about any such inference: they might have had just 'spots before their eyes' and taken them to indicate bodies on the bank. The ground on which such inferences are based may be called 'sense-data' if it is understood what this means in the present context. And we should then conclude that which we really *know* about the material world is only 'sense-data'.[1]

Such a conclusion, however, is exposed to a serious objection. Some of us, at least, would say that we were simply certain about the presence of distant objects (for example, of the books which we replaced a few minutes ago in the bookcase at the other end of the room). But on this showing, we should have no right to be certain. Hawkins discusses the matter as follows in *The Criticism of Experience*: 'As I look round the room, I am fully persuaded that it contains a desk, chairs, and bookcases, but their existence can only be an inference from my visual data. If I had nothing but such data from which to infer, the belief that they were caused by external bodies would be an unrefuted but quite gratuitous hypothesis. It is because I have a genuine intuitive awareness of the chair in which I am sitting, and because I have at various times been in contact with the familiar objects in my room, that I am able so unhesitatingly to rely on my sensations as indications of real bodies surrounding me.'[2] This brings out the reasons for regarding the inferences in question about distant bodies as in the highest conceivable degree probable and reliable, but it is not a claim to *certainty*. Hawkins is 'fully persuaded' of the presence of these bodies; he relies 'unhesitatingly' upon his sensations as indications of them. But he is not directly aware of them. He has not, it seems, excluded the possibility of doubt in regard to them, although in fact he has no doubt. Can we be satisfied with this?

[1] Objections to talking about 'sense-data' are often based on J. L. Austin's *Sense and Sensibilia* (1962). It seems to me that Austin disposes only of certain theories about sense-data. The tenth chapter of this book, it may be added, contains an excellent account of the *fact* of certainty.

[2] 110.

Speaking for myself, I have to say that in such circumstances I am just certain that the books and the furniture are present. I confess that I find it difficult to account for this. But I do not see how the possibility of doubt can arise; I give it every chance to arise, and it fails to do so. It is just not conceivable that something might occur later to prove that I was wrong. I have satisfied myself that I am awake. I have a distinct recollection of replacing those books a minute ago. I know that no change has occurred in the room which might have affected the question of their presence, and so on. This situation has been analysed so admirably by Professor Norman Malcolm in his paper 'Knowledge and Belief' (to be found in his book *Knowledge and Certainty*, 1963) that I am constrained to quote from it a whole page:

'Now could it turn out to be false that there is an ink-bottle directly in front of me on the desk? Many philosophers have thought so. They would say that many things could happen of such a nature that if they did happen it could be proved that I am deceived. I agree that many extraordinary things could happen in the sense that there is no logical absurdity in the supposition. It could happen that when I next reach for the ink-bottle my hand should seem to pass *through* it and I should not feel the contact of any object. It could happen that in the next moment the ink-bottle will suddenly vanish from sight; or that I should find myself under a tree in the garden with no ink-bottle about; or that one or more persons should enter this room and declare with apparent sincerity that they see no ink-bottle on this desk, or that a photograph taken now of the top of the desk should reveal all of the objects on it except the ink-bottle. Having admitted that all these things *could happen*, am I compelled to say that if they did happen then it could be proved that there is no ink bottle here *now*? Not at all! I could say that when my hand seemed to pass through the ink-bottle I should *then* be suffering from hallucinations; that if the ink-bottle vanished it would have miraculously ceased to exist; that the other persons were wishing to drive me mad, or were themselves victims of remarkable concurrent hallucinations; that the camera possessed some strange flaw or that there was trickery in developing the negative. I admit that in the next moment I could find myself under a tree or in the bathtub. But this is not to admit that it could be revealed in the next moment that I am now dreaming. For what I admit is that I might be instantaneously transported to the garden, but not that in the next moment I might *wake up* in the garden . . . nothing that could happen to me in the next moment would be accepted by me now in proof that I now dream.'[1]

On the next page Malcolm points out that he might come *later* to believe that there had been no ink-bottle, but that this has nothing to do with his certainty about it here and now. I ought to make clear that Malcolm might disagree with much that I want to say about certainty. But we are in agreement about the way in which the fact of it ought to be described in reference to physical objects before our eyes.

But there are other circumstances about which, I think, we have to reach the same conclusions. What about our awareness of other people, of other beings with minds? The problem of the existence of other minds has exercised modern philosophers (in particular Wittgenstein, Wisdom and Malcolm himself) in a very big way. I am not proposing to unravel the complications which they have found in it. I am concerned only to suggest that we are certain about other minds although we have no direct access to them. In *The Criticism of Experience* Hawkins takes the view that 'there are occasions when we have genuine intuitions'[2] of them. But if we are not prepared to say this, as I am not, what are we to say? Without going into details about the sources of our evidence for their existence, I would say that the evidence for it is overwhelming. Some of us at least cannot doubt that there are other minds. The question which faces us is that of our justification for certainty in such matters. The difficulty will be most clearly illustrated perhaps if we take the case of a certainty about the existence of some place which one has never visited. It so happens that, although I have never visited Moscow, I find myself unable to doubt the existence of it, and I fancy that others who have never visited it would say the same.

The suggestion which I now want to make is that in the absence of direct awareness there can yet be evidence which is absolutely conclusive and that some explanation of this state of affairs is possible. In a tentative way, then, I suggest that the nonexistence of Moscow can be seen by us simply to make no sense. If in fact Moscow did not exist, there would have to be a worldwide conspiracy to persuade us that it did. I can contemplate the

[1] *Knowledge and Certainty*, 66–7.   [2] 119.

possibility of such a conspiracy and conclude that I must definitely reject it. It is perhaps worth making the further suggestion that such a conclusion has a concealed major premiss to the effect that the world is not a nonsense world. Is it perhaps the case that those who are uncertain about Moscow's existence may be people who have not accepted that premiss, in other words that one's attitude in this matter is affected by more general considerations of a metaphysical or anti-metaphysical kind? We might consider in this connection the problem of induction. Reduced to its simplest terms, it is the problem about the universal rules which are commonly taken for granted, the rule, for example, that a kettle must in due course boil when you have lighted the gas under it. This is what has always happened in the past and it is assumed that it must always happen in the future. Despite the many ingenious attempts to justify this assumption, the obstinate fact remains that what has happened in the past can be no absolute proof of what will happen in the future. These attempts indicate, I believe, a belief that the world does in fact work to some definite plan or set of plans. It may be remarked incidentally that there is no reason why one such plan should not be subordinated in particular circumstances to the requirements of another plan of wider scope. That is what is or should be meant by a miracle.

We have not yet considered that form of the argument against certainty which consists in maintaining that no statement can be incorrigible. Although our evidence is not confined to statements, it is worth considering how such a statement as 'I am in pain' could be corrigible. Someone could misuse the word 'pain' in the sense of not conforming to the established usage through ignorance of the language; and he could use it with intent to deceive. Otherwise the statement 'I am in pain' must surely be true. In the symposium *Prospect for Metaphysics* (1967) the editor, I. T. Ramsey, then Nolloth professor at Oxford and now Bishop of Durham, considers the suggestion that 'I'm angry' is corrigible. He concludes that 'we know something incorrigibly, to which corrigible descriptions are inevitably applied'[1]: 'Corrigibility', he adds in a footnote, will never 'reach zero, without a word changing its logical character from a description to a proper name', and in a reference to my own views on the matter he remarks that I should 'no doubt reject this antithesis'. My reason for rejecting it in the cases of 'I feel pain' and 'I'm angry' is that I can be certain that I

[1] 175–6.

am not misusing these words, but here it is to be noticed that my evidence for that statement has the same sort of complexity as my evidence for the existence of Moscow.

In my own contribution to Ramsey's symposium I was concerned with Ayer's book *The Problem of Knowledge*, and above all with his denial that 'there are, or can be, any mental states of intuition which are such that their existence affords an absolute guarantee that one really is, in this sense, seeing what one thinks one sees'. 'It must always remain possible', Ayer concludes, 'that one is mistaken.'[1] I shall not repeat the comments which I made on this statement in *Prospect for Metaphysics* except to remark that, if certainty means that we have excluded the possibility of doubt, the only criterion of certainty is the awareness of having excluded it, an awareness which is, of course, at the same time an awareness not only of a state of mind but also of some fact of which one is aware. But the doctrine that 'it must always remain possible for one to be mistaken', although I have dealt with it at an earlier stage, is important enough to be dealt with a second time. It has become a sort of philosophical dogma against which I have been protesting for some twenty-five years, and I was delighted to find in Malcolm's *Knowledge and Certainty* a full-scale attack upon it.

Malcolm considers the dogma as part of the 'verification argument' to which the first paper in his book is devoted, running to fifty-seven pages. Various forms of the argument are subjected to a patient and skilful analysis, but the conclusions to which Malcolm comes seem to me to stand on their own feet without this massive support. According to the verification argument in its most general form, we can never be certain of the truth of any empirical statement because we should have had to conduct a series of tests which are infinite in number. In other words, if a certain material object is really present, it will react under tests in certain particular ways. But there is no end to the tests which we can conduct, and so we can never know that one of them might not break down. That last statement is equivalent to the doctrine that 'it must always remain possible that one is mistaken'. Malcolm now considers in a further exhaustive analysis the various meanings which could be given to those last words, with special attention to the word 'possible'. To give two examples: they could mean that the contradictory of a perceptual statement is not self-contradictory

[1] 22 (Pelican edition).

(which is irrelevant to the question about the statement's truth), or that, since some perceptual statements are false, it is not certain that any particular statement is true (which is just bad reasoning). We must conclude, Malcolm says, that the statement 'it is possible that any perceptual statement is false' can only mean that 'the grounds for accepting any perceptual statement are never conclusive'. What follows must be quoted in its entirety:

'As I have said, I believe that the grounds which one could offer in behalf of any perceptual statement do not entail that the statement is true. It does not follow in the least, however, that the grounds are not perfectly conclusive. I can produce enormously good grounds for accepting my perceptual statement that I saw the phrase "the stream of thought" on page 224 of James's book [*The Principles of Psychology*] yesterday. The best way to show that those grounds are not conclusive would be to offer *some evidence* for saying that I did not see that phrase yesterday. But no philosopher is prepared to do this. Therefore the philosophical claim that those grounds are not conclusive does not rest upon *evidence*. On what does it rest? On a confusion, I believe. One is inclined to argue that "It is not conclusive that a perceptual statement is true because it is possible that it is false". But an examination of this statement shows that the words "It is possible that it is false" do not mean that there is *evidence* that it is false. They mean that it is *logically possible* that it is false. But the fact that it is logically possible that it is false does not tend to show in any way that it is not conclusive that it is true.'[1]

At the end of his paper[2] Malcolm adds that proponents of the verification theory say the truth of an empirical statement can be practically certain but not 'theoretically certain'. He points out that on their view an infinite number of acts of verification would be required for what they call theoretic certainty. But that is impossible even in theory. They are in fact identifying theoretical certainty with absolute certainty. It follows that to say that it is absolutely certain that a given statement is true 'would *entail* the proposition that someone had performed an infinite number of acts'. And therefore such a statement as 'It is absolutely certain that Socrates had a wife' would have to be self-contradictory. And that is patently not so.

[1] 49.   [2] 55–6.

I had been accustomed to making the point, thus elaborately established by Malcolm, in the following short form. The question at issue is not a question of logic. It is a question of fact. (As we have seen, without some knowledge of facts we can perform no logical processes.) It is logically possible that the cat should not be on the mat. But this has nothing whatever to do with the fact that I am aware of the cat on the mat. The fact that I cannot prove it to myself is not merely irrelevant. To allege it would be to show a complete misunderstanding of what is being talked about. For (if I may say it once more) we require to prove something only when we are uncertain of it. Certainty is its own proof. Evidence, as such, is self-guaranteeing. That, as we shall see, is commonly denied in contexts of greater importance than those with which we have been so far dealing. Hence the necessity to establish it on the ground floor of knowledge.

Finally I should like to refer to a passage in Ayer's *The Problem of Knowledge* which I have not discussed on a previous occasion. He is considering what may happen when I am shown two lines of about the same length, drawn parallel, we may suppose, on a piece of paper. He reaches the conclusion that one could be making not merely a verbal but a factual mistake in saying that one line *looked* longer than another. He suggests that it might not look the same to other people and that 'the fact that the report given by these other people disagrees with mine may have some tendency to show that I was making a mistake'.[1] But how could I be mistaken about how the line *looked* to myself? Ayer does say a little later that 'there is nothing fallible about the experience itself' and that 'what may be wrong is only one's identification of it'.[2] But if the mistake about the lines is not only a verbal but also a factual one, this seems to mean that we can never register for certain even our own sense-impressions. Such are the strange consequences of trying to avoid the indubitable.

[1] 66 (Pelican edition). [2] 67.

II

AN OUTLINE OF THEISM

6. VALUE

We may now at last leave the topic of our acquaintance with material objects and pass on to topics of superior interest. It seemed necessary to spend so much time on these preliminaries because otherwise I should have been constantly exposed to the objection that I was simply assuming a certain theory of knowledge without even saying what it was. There may be many objections to what I have said about knowledge. But I suggest that they would constitute not a disproof but just a denial of it. For I have been trying not to prove something but to show something, and, although the performance may have seemed unconvincing, I do not see what can be alleged in disproof of what I have tried to show. In brief, I have been concerned to show that human awareness is a special sort of fact, that we are directly aware of bodies at any rate and of our own 'selves'. It is possible for someone to say that he just does not see what I am talking about when I talk about human awareness in this way. But it is not possible, so far as I can see, for anyone to prove that there is no such thing. I have been arguing against certain theories of knowledge, but I have been not so much arguing in favour of anything as trying to show that certain facts are the case. Philosophers have often maintained that they were not so much evolving theories as simply defending common sense. Berkeley, perhaps, is the most famous instance of this—but he overlooked that awareness of body *as* body on which I have insisted at some length, and so I may make the claim, I think, with more justification than he had.

So far nothing much has been said about our knowledge of our own 'selves', except to claim that we have it, that we are aware of ourselves as continuous in a more than physical way, in what we may therefore call a metaphysical way. This metaphysical fact may now be looked at more closely. It is a commonplace to say that we know very little about ourselves, and the remark would often be taken to refer, at least in part, to what is called the 'unconscious'. But I am referring to the *obscurity* of our knowledge of ourselves. We are never aware simply of ourselves and of nothing else; our knowledge of ourselves is always, as it were, interfered with by knowledge of something else. This gives it an elusive quality. Hume managed to avoid it altogether, for philosophical purposes, by concentrating upon the succession of sense-impressions and images; he seemed to suppose that the self should present itself, if it existed, in total isolation or, as it were, on a plate. We come across the self *in* an awareness of interacting bodies. Such spatial metaphors as 'in', as I remarked earlier, have to be used when we are talking about mental operations, which are not themselves spatial.

We know our own minds or souls only in their particular activities, but this is not to say that we have no direct knowledge of them. Some philosophers have maintained that the first object of our knowledge is an external body and that we know our own minds only as secondary objects or indirectly. I find it difficult to understand what can be meant by calling knowledge of one's own mind an indirect knowledge as contrasted with our knowledge of bodies. Human awareness, it seems to me, is essentially self-awareness. I have spoken of knowledge of our own bodies as direct but also as 'mediate' because we know them only in our sensations and we come across our sensations immediately. In the same way we know our minds directly but mediately. Immediately we know their particular activities.

Philosophers have been known to protest that to speak of knowing oneself is to speak of a subject which is also an object and that this is unintelligible. It is true that subject and object are distinct in all other circumstances. But our experience compels us to say that in this instance the subject becomes its own object. Once again we find a state of affairs which is a unique one. And why should we not do so? A prejudice against the unique is a frequent by-product of a training in the natural sciences. We do not mean in this instance what we mean when we speak of subject and object in other contexts. But we can point to what we mean, if we need to do so, only by using such language.

We have been pausing on the threshold of human experience. As soon as we step over it, we observe that our experience is very much richer than philosophers in a certain empiricist tradition have tended to suppose. We have seen that they have commonly assumed that they are disembodied minds. They seem also to regard themselves as just spectators. In fact we do not find ourselves just looking at things and wondering what, if anything, we know about them. We find ourselves wanting things or wishing them out of the way. We find ourselves in contact with other human beings, some of whom we like or love, some of whom we dislike. We find ourselves always engaged in some sort of plan or project which makes all the difference to the ways in which we react both to persons and to things. Our experience is not only retrospective but also prospective, anticipating the future not only by a process of guessing at its contents by analogy with the past but by an awareness of our own undeveloped capacities which gives us a real insight into what is possible for us if we care to pursue it. We are aware of ourselves in a state of progress—or perhaps of regress.

It is the recognition of this very obvious complexity about human experience which should be considered, I think, the distinguishing mark of the existentialist philosopher. Such a philosopher is in reaction against regarding man simply as a knower. His problem is not the problem of knowledge but the problem of life. The existentialist need not and should not deny that awareness is the distinguishing mark of the human being. But his awareness does not function in a vacuum. It promotes and is profoundly affected by his feelings, his desires, and his choices. It is his *choosing* which usually impresses the existentialist more than anything else. We are in a situation which forces us to choose. It may seem a very odd state of affairs. Sartre, as everyone knows, thinks it an absurd one. But Sartre is, nevertheless, a moralist, holding forth about 'bad faith', for instance. If you once start talking about projects, even if you declare them absurd, you find yourself inevitably facing the question of *value*.

By speaking of the value of anything, it will hardly be contested, we mean what makes it worth while. Let us consider the implications of this notion. I shall suggest that it does more than merely hint at metaphysical questions: it raises the ultimate ones. Someone who disagrees with this may say that what is worth while is for him simply what ministers to his personal convenience. This statement cannot be proved self-contradictory, but it is just as desperate an expedient as the statement 'I am uncertain whether I am uncertain whether I am uncertain *ad infinitum*', which is equally secure against logical attack. On such a view it would have to be maintained that, since most people enjoy certain things, for example, an expensive sort of dinner, our language reflects such common agreement and that thus a language about what is worth while has grown up which we call the language of morality (this is the counterpart in the field of moral theory to the 'conventionalist' view of truth). On such a view, then, 'I ought' will be reduced in meaning to 'If I want something, this is the way to get it' or 'This is what the people around expect of me, and if they don't get it they may make themselves unpleasant'. I have called this a desperate expedient, but it may not be clear that it is so unless a better answer to the question becomes clear. It should be clear already, however, that the answer just mentioned is at least very difficult to justify. It seems to rule out everything which has seemed most worth while to the man in the street and to the philosopher in all ages up to our own, and, in regard at least to the man in the street, including our own, for the great movements of thought (or should I say of feeling?) which are going on among us, movements for the unification of classes and of races, are certainly not based on the philosophy of egoistic hedonism. It will be much more to the point to consider what answer can be given to our question by the secular humanist.

Secular humanism has many different forms, but it always implies the production of some kind of programme for mankind, however vaguely described. The secular humanist is often prepared to go to much trouble in the interests of other people's happiness. How is he going to explain to himself why he regards this as worth while? He will be forced to ask himself the question, it may be, because he wants co-operation in his project but finds that other people do not always regard it as worth while. 'Why', someone may say to him, 'should I have to bother, as you do, about other people's happiness if in fact I am disinclined to do so?' Our humanist may reply that one cannot achieve one's happiness without aiming at that of other people. He will not mean by this what the egoistic hedonist means by it, that you have to use other people as a means to your own happiness. The sort of humanist whom I have in mind, at any rate, will mean that other people's happiness is worth while because other people are worth while in the sense of having value in themselves, and that one cannot be truly happy unless one is aiming at what is worth while. He may not put it in those words, but that must be in fact his position if it is to make sense as something different from egoistic hedonism. He will not be able to gain co-operation for his project in some cases until he can persuade someone to take his view about what 'worth while' ought to mean. And 'ought' now becomes the operative word. The notion of value is bound up with the notion of obligation. To say that people are worth while, that they have value in themselves, is to say that there is something about them which makes a demand upon us, that we *ought* to make them part of our own project, identify ourselves with them in some sort.

Again this is something which has to be *seen*—it cannot be proved by a coercive argument starting from premises which everyone will accept. But it is not possible to deny it, I should wish to say, without making nonsense of human living. Our humanist might try to avoid talking about moral obligation because he might feel (and rightly) that it does not fit into a view of things which is purely secular. He will perhaps say that, although things are valuable in themselves in some mysterious way, some people see them as such and some people do not. Some people find fulfilment in giving themselves up, so to say, to aesthetic objects, to works of art, other people in giving themselves up to moral objects, to various causes. They just happen to be sensitive to the cause of social justice or whatever. Naturally you like people to co-operate with you for the causes which you espouse, but there need be no question of anyone's having any *obligation* to do anything. It should be obvious that the humanist is now slipping into the position of the egoistic hedonist. In the end, he will find himself saying, it is just a question of what you personally happen to like. But some secular humanists, at any rate, will not fall back on this position. They are ready to devote themselves to the interests of future generations, to give up their comfort and convenience for the happiness of those whom they will never see. They will have to say that it is the acknowledgement of what is worth while, simply as such, which is the motive force of their lives. But nothing can be a motive force for us unless it makes an appeal to us, unless it is something that we *want*. I propose to say that the awareness of obligation is an awareness of God from which, unless we reject it, happiness derives and not only beyond the grave but on this side of it. It is hardly necessary to say that happiness then proves to mean something very different from material comfort and convenience.

So sudden an introduction of the name of God may seem startling and gratuitous, and it will take some time to explain it.

It will not seem justified, perhaps, until other aspects of the general problem of human experience have been investigated. The point which I want to repeat for a start is that the secular humanist of the self-sacrificing kind seems to be asserting an absolute unconditional obligation in fact whether or not he cares to describe what he is doing in those terms. He declares by his actions that the welfare of others (however one may envisage it) *ought* to be aimed at, whatever the cost. And can we regard the acknowledgement of moral obligation, absolute and unconditional obligation, as just a brute fact which requires no explanation or as a fact which can be explained in a naturalistic, non-religious way? If I found myself faced with it as a brute fact I should find it such an odd one that I should take it to a psychiatrist. If we are to make sense of it, we must ask ourselves how it can exercise the appeal which it undoubtedly does exercise. Why do people get a certain satisfaction from following their consciences and a dissatisfaction from not doing so, people who, as secularists, do not suppose that any religious sanctions attach to not following one's conscience? The secular humanist may be willing to say that he 'feels called upon' to adopt his course of action. My suggestion is that this is precisely the case. He is responding to the call of God. What he is aware of is God calling him. But his rejection of religion (probably based on unfortunate experiences with pseudo-religious people) makes it impossible for him to interpret this in terms of religion (of religion as he supposes it to be).

His acceptance of the call, however, is in fact an acceptance of God. There has been a real contact with God, and it is strengthened, indeed transformed, by his response to it. This is what he would be referring to if he spoke of the satisfaction which he gets from following his conscience. But probably he will not refer to it at all, for there is a natural reserve about such matters. He is more likely perhaps to refer to the dissatisfaction which he would feel if he went against his conscience. Would his situation make sense if he were not destined to a clear knowledge of God beyond the grave? A Christian will say that it will not make complete sense except on that condition. But it can make sufficient sense to get on with for the secular humanist. So far as he is concerned, following one's conscience is worth while for its own sake; it is something that he values, something that he *wants*. What he does not know is that the human project makes better sense than just this.

The general view which he takes of the world does not dispose him to recognize the human project for what in fact it is. Let us consider what his view of it presumably is. It is that the world is not the product of an intelligence, but that it has itself somehow produced intelligence. Here we meet another position which cannot be refuted by mere logic. To say that it is just the nature of the world to produce intelligent minds and that no explanation of it is called for may seem to be unreasonable (as indeed I think it is), but it is not in any way to contradict oneself. To go on to say that a world which began with no purpose subsequently acquired one (which is what the secularists' gospel implies) is surely even odder. But this, too, is irrefutable in just the same way. To say that some splendid future lies ahead for the spirit of man, which is the sort of thing which the secular humanist must say, seems very hard to believe if the spirit of man is itself some sort of cosmic accident. It is very near to saying in the same breath both that the world has not an overall purpose and that it has one. It may sound plausible at first to say that we ourselves can give the world and ourselves a purpose. But although we can give ourselves purposes in the sense of choosing this or that particular project, to bestow a project for life as a whole upon a world entirely devoid of projects should seem a hopeless task. How could we invent our own framework?

It will be useful to keep such considerations in mind, but of themselves, of course, they do not settle the problem of God. That can be settled, I shall say, only by the awareness of God. The case which I am beginning to develop is that this awareness is to be found in the most fundamental form (but not by any means exclusively) in our moral experience. One needs to talk about the awareness of God to people who are without it or, more probably, suppose themselves to be without it because they do not understand what it is. An egoistic hedonist seems to be without it; he has perhaps rejected it. A secular humanist, if he is not an egoistic hedonist in disguise, is really a theist in disguise. So I began by considering these two types of person because they are the people to whom talk about this awareness is naturally addressed. Those who have it already do not need to be considered for present purposes. But there are also those who are quite uncertain whether they have it or not. They have just a suspicion of God. They need to know how such an awareness grows up out of a suspicion. So far I have only suggested the area, so to speak, of our experience in which, I think, it most obviously does so, the area of our moral experience.

Before analysing our moral experience more closely, I want to make clear that I am not proposing an argument from conscience according to which an inference is made from the existence of a law to the existence of a lawgiver. What I am proposing is an interpretation of our moral experience. I argue that other interpretations of it are implausible, but the inferences which can be drawn from that conclusion will not prove of themselves that my interpretation is the right one. Again, it is something which has to be *seen*. To interpret something for anyone is only to put him in a position from which he can, if he will, see the answer for himself. Whether he sees it or not is up to him, not to the interpreter.

There is an obstacle ahead of us which, I must confess, I find rather baffling. It is the fact that a good many theists have little use for the claim that our moral evidence is evidence for God or, as I should prefer to put it, evidence *of* God. If a theist believes that God enters into our experience, it seems very strange that he should not enter *basically* into our awareness of ourselves as moral beings.[1] (And if someone who calls himself a theist denies that God enters into our experience in any way, I do not know what he means by calling himself a theist.) One more point must be emphasized before I move on. I am not suggesting that the moral evidence declares its full meaning to us in a flash. As with all metaphysical conclusions, in which the central conclusion about God is always implicit, there may be for some time, perhaps for a very long time, a stage in which there is only a suspicion that we are in fact faced with evidence of God. For one thing, it may seem to lead to conclusions which are unacceptable, perhaps contradictory of truths which we cannot deny. The only way to turn such a suspicion into a certainty is to take a long cool look at what is offered to us as evidence. By a 'cool' look I do not mean a detached one, a mere spectator's look; it is *our* situation which we are examining.

When we start to look at ourselves engaged in a human project, we come to realize that there must be some project which is

---

[1] The theists whom I have in mind would allow that our moral experience *can* be seen as evidence for God. But they have little use for the claim because, according to them, *everything* can be so seen and moral experience in itself has no basic significance, no special importance as evidence.

proper to us as human beings, a project which is *the* human project. We do mean something by talking about a human being. We must mean that we have certain powers which we are capable of developing, mental ones as well as bodily ones. A determinist will say that what this means is simply that we shall in fact develop in those particular ways which circumstances will dictate. If we accept that view, then the present discussion stops. Let us consider again what it would imply. It would imply that it would be an illusion to believe that we can at least sometimes, of our own free choice, direct our minds to some particular topic, excluding from it some other topic which presents itself to our attention. At the present moment I am thinking about the question of moral responsibility. A question about my holiday arrangements might be competing for my attention. I propose to say that I am simply *aware* of my ability to exclude it—at least to the extent that I can go on thinking about moral responsibility. If I allowed that question to disappear from the field of my attention, I should be morally responsible for abandoning my present project. I am free to choose in the sense that at this moment my decision is not the inevitable outcome of my history up to date, as the determinist would have it. I claim to be aware that it is my choice here and now which will decide the outcome and that this choice is not itself determined. No ingenious sophistry can overthrow this fact of experience.

If I recognize my moral freedom in regard to particular projects, I shall recognize it also in regard to *the* human project. And by *the* human project, I must mean the development of my own powers. The human project is a project of self-development. I am not compelled to develop my powers. I could decide to take no interest in them. I could pack up on the whole business by taking an overdose of something. What I am proposing is that, if we take a long cool look at our human powers, we can come to the conclusion that they *ought* to be developed. This is, I believe, the way to trace the notion of moral obligation to its deepest root in experience. We discover *value* in our human powers because we do not feel entitled to throw them away. Our own experience shows itself to us as possessing a value without which nothing else would seem valuable to us. It has value already, but this value needs to be developed. And this value is not something which we have produced by ourselves. For the value of an experience derives from *what* is experienced. We may say that we have a capacity for experience and that this is itself a value in a sense, a potential value. But even so it would remain that what is *actually* value is something which we receive. Such, in brief, are the considerations which lead me to say that the acknowledgement of value is the awareness of God's summons. It is a summons to accept value and to go on accepting it as it reveals itself to us more fully. We *have* value because we receive it from a source of value. That is what I mean, for a start, by God. We know him as giving us value. That is why the demand upon us to develop ourselves is an absolute, unconditional, demand. It is a summons to the absolute, the unconditioned. We are free to resist it (it is in our awareness of moral freedom that we become aware of it), but the demand is still there all the same. God's attitude to us never changes, although we can ignore it.

If this way of looking at things can be at least entertained, it will be seen to fit in with a good deal which might be otherwise very puzzling and in particular with what was said earlier about the value which people and things have in themselves. We found that a secular humanist recognizes people as having value in themselves; he recognizes an absolute obligation to aim at their welfare. Would such an *absolute* obligation make sense if we regarded other people simply as objects of our thought, our interest and our love, just these particular objects (in a world full of other objects) who happen to be connected with us in various particular ways? There is nothing absolute about people regarded simply in that fashion. An adequate explanation of this state of affairs will have to be a metaphysical one; it will have to lie behind people regarded simply as finite beings with no relationship to the infinite. Why should I be obliged to devote myself to the interests of other people if we are all on the same level and have no link with any other level? If, however, created persons and created things stand in a relationship to God of such a kind that we may call them 'reflections' of him, and if they are part of a divine plan, then, it would seem, we have an explanation or at any rate a clue to one. This is a topic which I shall be probing from various angles for some time to come.

On these lines it would be possible also to shed more light on the absoluteness of knowledge. We are in touch with absolute reality through derived reality. To talk of persons and things as values derived from absolute value must mean that they owe the whole of themselves to it. Their value is not a *part* of themselves;

it refers to everything that they have. In all true knowledge, then, we are penetrating to the ultimate absolute reality on which everything else depends. Without realizing what we are doing, when we contemplate the derived realities which we directly encounter we also encounter their source. What we know is absolutely true because it is grounded on the absolute. When we affirm it absolutely we declare it established in being by the source of being. Philosophers have often expressed this conclusion by saying that, whereas creatures *have* being, God *is* being. This language, it seems to me, does not sufficiently indicate that the source of being and the beings which derive from it are incommensurable. We cannot put them together within any sort of bracket except in so far as we claim to have knowledge both of the source and of the beings derived from it, and that does not mean that the source itself has anything strictly in *common* with its 'reflections'. What derives from it does not emanate from it as a part splits off from the whole to which it belonged. In all circumstances the source remains unchanged (that is the topic of the next discussion, the topic of transcendence). What I want to emphasize here at once is that I do not propose to say with the Thomists that 'being' is an analogous concept because that might suggest a scale of being with God as the top member of it. And God cannot be a member of any class. If I had to talk about the concept of 'being', I should suggest that it is properly a double one, that it refers both to the finite and to the infinite in that it refers to the finite in its relation to the infinite.

This is perhaps the right point for the remark that there is no contradiction in the claim to knowledge of the infinite made by a finite being. We do not *become* what we know in the word's ordinary sense. We are in a unique way united with it. That we should have a knowledge of God which is dim and fitful, yet capable of indefinite development, is perhaps highly astonishing, but if it happens to be a fact there is no logical ground for objecting to it. Nor is there any valid objection to speaking of God as an object of our knowledge. Obviously, it is not to say that he is an object in the sense of a particular object, or to say that our knowledge of him is on all fours with our knowledge of a particular object. It is just a piece of language which we cannot conveniently avoid if we are going to say that God enters into our experience. And, I repeat, I do not see how a theologian, at any rate, can fail to say that.

These rather breathless metaphysical excursions seemed unavoidable even at this early stage of the enquiry because, as soon as the name of God is mentioned, a whole crop of misapprehensions commonly arises and until something is done about them further discussion may be useless. But we shall be returning frequently to the topics so hastily touched on. To simplify matters in the course of this exposition I have passed over a number of objections which, though important, did not seem to demand immediate attention. I shall conclude by saying something about them. As regards the question of moral obligation, it might be objected that I have spoken of it as a general obligation to develop our human powers, but that it presents itself to us in fact as the obligation to help our neighbour in this particular difficulty or in some other specific way. I am not denying that this is the sort of context in which the notion or rather the fact of it presents itself. It is, no doubt, the claim which our neighbours make on us which makes us first suspect what it really is to be a moral being. What I am saying is that it is the awareness of ourselves as summoned to self-fulfilment which leads us, in the last analysis, to accept the fact of obligation as a real fact. It may also be objected that I have hardly touched on the arguments so often advanced by positivists to show that the fact of moral obligation is a sociological phenomenon needing no religious explanation. My answer is that, if we once satisfied ourselves that it was the result of historical accidents, we should then be able to free ourselves from its bondage, and we should have to take up with egoistic hedonism. And I have said as much as it deserves about that. In any case, as has often been pointed out, to push back the problems of moral obligation into a distant past is not to abolish it. In the end, however, it is, as usual, our own awareness of it which is decisive. When I accept an absolute obligation, I am aware that so far from lapsing into the determinisms of history I am emerging from them, exercising my personal freedom in the completest way.

It may also be objected that, although the recognition of other people as 'reflections' of God would certainly explain their value, it would not follow from this that we should have to devote ourselves to them if this meant neglecting our own interests. The answer to this, I take it, is that what we prove really to want (to put it with all simplicity) is just God himself, but that this means that we also want his plan for the world. His will is our peace. And thus it does not prove to make sense to talk about our own interests and the interests of other people as though there could be in the last analysis a conflict between them. That we are all in it together is something which the present generation sees more clearly than its predecessors, although what that really means is not often appreciated. That is why a further objection is likely to break out now. You are telling us, someone may say, that we ought to love people for God's sake. That is just what we do not want to do. We want to love them for their own sakes. And to that I reply that to love people because they are creatures of God, 'reflections' of God, is the only way to love them as they really are. To say that they are God's creatures is not just to mention an interesting fact about them. It is the essential truth about them. They have value indeed in themselves, but only because God gave it to them. Unless we saw God in them as the source of value, we should not *really* see that they had it. But I have also put forward the view that we do not in fact really see value until we see it in ourselves, that is, until we are aware of God's action on ourselves.

But the most strident of the objections, I suspect, will be made against my bland assertion that the value of an experience comes from *what* is experienced. *We* give meaning to things, it will be said; *we* are valuable ourselves. I am not denying this if it means what it ought to mean. What ought to be meant by our giving meaning to things is that they are meant for us to know. By acting on us they are doing a job, and they need us in order to do it. But we do not alter them by knowing them. When it is said that we are valuable in ourselves this should mean that the value which we receive is our living substance. The fact that we receive it does not mean that we are passive to it in the sense of being just kicked around by it. It means that it is given to us, making us what we are. When you listen to music, if you do it properly, you simply attend to it. It makes you what you are for the time being and very nice too. It *makes* us active in a very big way, but only on condition of our submitting to it. If you start interfering with it, you can't properly enjoy it. To say that our value comes to us from God is obviously only another way of saying that he creates us and not just when we start to exist but all the time. A theist, if he is to be consistent, must say this. Yet people who call themselves theists are constantly harping upon the way in which religion concentrates on God and abolishes man in the process. If you regard religion as obedience to arbitrary commands, that would indeed be the case. But that is completely to misunderstand the relationship in which we stand to God. We are made for him in the sense that he is for us. He fulfils us. That means that we become fully active. But for this to happen we must first listen to him, attend to him and receive from him. To say that we are in our whole being gifts of God is not depress our status but to show its true dignity.

I may be allowed perhaps to add, by way of appendix, two very brief reflections. One is that academic persons who detach themselves as far as possible from all general questions about human existence may find the present topic especially uncongenial to them. But in their less guarded moments they may be heard to say that the claims of truth are sacrosanct—even in regard to some remote item of research with which they happen to be concerned. Why, we might then ask them, and how does truth really matter? And their shocked silence might be the occasion for the suggestion that there is more in life than the peaceful pursuit of an academic hobby has so far revealed to them. Secondly, it seems to me a remarkable thing that people should be content so often to go on wobbling between two directly opposed views about the human condition. The real issue for the thought of our time is manifestly whether man is just one of the higher animals, much more complicated than the others but not fundamentally different, or whether he has a meaning—and, if we decide that he has, this must be our ultimate concern. Philosophy, as I understand it, is concerned fundamentally with this issue. And I shall be concerned with it here for quite a long time before raising any question about God's revelation to us in Christ.

7. TRANSCENDENCE

Since 'transcendence' means simply 'going beyond', it can be used in a variety of contexts. In this context it will refer to the way in which God is 'beyond' the world. Here is another of those inevitable spatial metaphors which can be misleading. The Bishop of Woolwich was perhaps right to say in *Honest to God* that it is better nowadays to speak of God as being 'down there', in our depths, than to speak of him as 'up there'. But he seemed not to realize that it can be totally misleading to speak of him in either way. To say that he is 'up there', however, is a perfectly natural way of talking about the difference between the finite and the infinite. But it has to be understood that he is 'up there' in a sense which does not prevent him being also at work 'down here'. And nowadays this is often not understood. God is both transcendent and immanent. If he were only transcendent he would have nothing to do with the world. If he were only immanent, he would be confined to it.[1] It is just because he is transcendent, not confined in any way, that he can be immanent everywhere in the world. That is, he is active everywhere. He is immanent in us in our knowledge of him—we know him as the cause *in* what he effects. In knowing him we know him as not only immanent but also transcendent, for the cause is 'beyond' those effects in which we know it.

I have suggested that the concept of 'being' is really a double one in that it refers both to creatures and to the relation in which they stand to God and in that way to God himself. But it thus refers to him not as a being nor even as Being but as the source of being. This use of language avoids the danger of seeming to put God and his creatures within a single class. The word 'existence', I think, should be used in the same way. In ordinary English we mean by the existence of anything not just something about it but the whole thing, with an emphasis on the fact that it is really there and not a figment of the imagination. By speaking of the 'being' of anything we also mean the whole of it. Philosophers often use these words in technical senses, and they often become confused, so it seems to me, in consequence. I propose to use them in the sense (which I would call the ordinary sense) in which they both refer to the totality of persons, or of things. We have to be careful not to use 'existence' of God in a way which makes him seem to be a member of a class, for just the same reason which makes us avoid using 'being' of him in that way. We must not use any words of God in a way which suggests that we are using them in the sense in which we use them of his creatures. If we are going to say that creatures 'exist', we must not say that God 'exists'. We might say that he is the source of existence, but at once we have to point out that the word 'is' in the sentence 'he is the source of existence' is not being used in the ordinary way. What it means is that we are *affirming* God as the source of existence. Even this is not entirely fool-proof

---

[1] And thus confused with it. Unfortunately so many people prove to mean this when they speak of God's 'immanence'. It would be deplorable for Christians to give up using the word for fear of being thought pantheists.

language, because 'source' here could be understood in a finite sense. So it emerges that we cannot *describe* God at all. Nevertheless to call him the 'source of being' will at least avoid the unnecessary confusions which result from calling him 'pure Existence' or 'pure Being'. Some writers, mystics especially, have thought to safeguard God's transcendence by calling God 'being' and creatures 'non-being' or God 'non-being' and creatures 'beings'; this certainly asserts the difference between them, but it is a very unnatural use of language and is therefore liable to special misunderstandings.

That we should not be able to describe God at all is thought to be an objection to the theist's case by a great many modern thinkers. This seems to me extremely odd. From the point of view of anyone who really believes in God, he is necessarily indescribable. That does not mean that we cannot talk *about* him—it means that we cannot build up a knowledge of him out of familiar, finite, materials. It is the element of the indescribable in our experience on which we have to concentrate if we want to turn a mere suspicion of God into a definite awareness of him. By 'the element of the indescribable' I do not mean something for which we cannot find just the right words; I mean something which does not seem to be communicable at all in words. It is just different—and all-important. The question is whether it is really there or only seems to be. In the long run, when all the arguing is over, all we can do, what we have to do, is to concentrate on this suspected 'beyondness' or 'otherness'.[1] This sort of concentration requires that we should free ourselves from the tangle of thoughts which normally hold us up. It may prove difficult at first because we also have to let ourselves be *acted upon*; in other words, it involves what I can only call letting ourselves go, perhaps an unfamiliar and even alarming business. I am not talking—yet—of mystical prayer, but I think that this is where prayer begins. This is not introspection—retiring into the fortress of self-consciousness—but precisely the opposite.

The object of this exercise is to make us realize that the negative language which is used about God has a positive meaning. To say that God is infinite will not necessarily convey more than the

[1] Those theists who do not see any special significance in the moral evidence would agree about 'otherness'. My contention is that, until this 'otherness' becomes all-important for *us* (and we are essentially moral beings), we are not sufficiently 'in touch' with God to claim *knowledge* of him. Professor H. D. Lewis allows me to say that he is not without sympathy for such a contention.

denial than he is finite. For the theist it points to what is super-positive about his experience. But what is to be done if somebody tells one that he has no 'suspicion' of God, that the whole topic is utterly meaningless to him? Unless he can be brought to *recognize* something as a suspicion, one can only point to the difficulties in his own position and embark on a process of general education. But he will very probably not realize what is meant by such a 'suspicion'. I have suggested that he is most likely to realize it if one talks to him about moral obligation as an instance of how 'suspicion' arises. When there is knowledge of God, it does not in fact normally present itself as something quite new, totally unfamiliar. It is regularly a matter of recognition. We cannot remember when the first unrecognized contact occurred because it occurred in the dawn of our thinking. God offers himself to us in the very principles of our thought. Naturally our awareness of him begins in great obscurity. We know him as acting on our minds and we know them only mediately, so we know him, if I may so put it, more mediately still. But we know him *in* them, and so this too is a direct knowledge, a knowledge of the cause in its effects. And to say that we come to know ourselves as totally dependent on him is a way of asserting his own independence—another negative word which now points to what is super-positive.

Am I saying that we can satisfy ourselves about God's transcendence only through religious experience? It depends on what is meant by religious experience. It is often talked about as an affair of the feelings rather than of the mind, and it should be clear that I am not talking about that kind of thing. The awareness of God will not be accompanied necessarily by any comfortable feeling. It may even be accompanied at first by a strong feeling of distaste, for it may carry with it unwelcome requirements. If the awareness of God is welcomed, then there will be an appropriate feeling-tone about the situation. But it need have nothing to do with what is called 'sensible devotion', which is perhaps another name for religious sentimentality. It has become a commonplace of the philosophy of religion to say that one can put no reliance on 'religious experience'. It is a purely private, subjective, affair, and in philosophy, it is said, one must appeal to common ground. The sort of appeal which I make to common ground has been illustrated by the discussion of absolute obligation. But when it comes to the question of one's own eventual conviction, talk about common ground is out of place. This is simply the old contention that we must see things for ourselves. Nobody can do it for us. The supposition that it is the philosopher's business to produce an objective proof of God in the sense of a purely logical development of explicit ready-made notions shows a complete misunderstanding of religion. All our judgements are subjective in the sense that they are *ours*. But a judgement is not subjective in the pejorative sense just because it is not achieved by everybody. A judgement of value, for instance, can be perfectly objective—that is, we can be certain that it is a true one.

In a discussion of this sort one has to approach the same issue first from one side, then from another, in the hope that, as Plato put it, light may sometime break through. This inevitably rambling procedure is normal in the so-called Augustinian (ultimately Platonic) tradition. So I now turn to consider the views of certain contemporary writers in the hope that my position may become clearer if I compare it with theirs. I shall begin with Professor John Macquarrie's book *God-Talk* (1967). Macquarrie regards 'encounter' with God as the best ground for asserting his existence, but he does not regard it as solid ground—it cannot give us certainty. At the end of the book he sums up his findings as follows: 'St Paul has had many successors in the use of a language of existence. . . . They talk an intelligible language with a recognizable logic. They steer theology away from the objectifying language of myth and from the abstruseness of metaphysical language. Theological talk becomes in the main existential talk, that has a secure place within the total field of meaningful discourse.'[1] It is a pity that Macquarrie uses 'metaphysical' in a pejorative sense; he is talking in fact about the claim to metaphysical knowledge and saying that it makes sense. 'But', he continues, 'we keep coming back to the difficulty which has dogged our steps throughout these investigations. Can intelligibility in theological language be gained only at the price of a complete subjectivizing? . . . The description of religious attitudes and states of mind is certainly something of value, and it is something that must be taken into account if we are to understand what a religious faith is and to estimate its claims. But theology is commonly understood to be more than a psychology of religion, and faith is more than a state of mind.'

We cannot here consider the question about belief in specific

[1] 241–2.

doctrines, for that introduces the question of revelation. But Macquarrie's difficulty also bears on the question of an encounter with God, our present concern (but I do not much care for the *language* of encounter; it suggests that God's dealings with us are always of a dramatic nature). He refers to Rudolph Bultmann's view that 'all existence is encounter, so that the God-talk which proceeds existentially is talk about a real Other that stands over against the self in encounter'.[1] And it is Macquarrie's comment on this which brings out clearly his own position:

'Frankly I do not suppose there is any way in which one could prove that the assertions of faith and theology do refer to a Reality (God) that is independent of and prior to the experience which we call "experience of God". In order to prove that there is encounter with a real Other, one would somehow need to get behind the experience, or to find a second route to what we know in the experience, and this is not possible. Yet on the other hand the conviction that there *is* a real Other is extremely deep-rooted.'

It may now become clearer why I spent so much time talking about certainty. I have claimed it as a fact that experience, strictly as such, always gives us certainty: only the inferences which we draw from it can be uncertain. It does not, of course, follow from this that what is claimed to be experience of God is in fact experience, strictly as such. And that is Macquarrie's point. But he must not be allowed to say that it is of the nature of experience that we could have no certainty about an experience of God. He adds that we may 'compare the conviction of the independent reality of God to the conviction of the independent reality of the world or other selves' and believes that it would be 'impossible to *prove* the reality of either'. In any case, he says, this would be 'little more than an academic exercise', for it is not in serious dispute. He misses the point which I have made that a proof of the world's independent reality is in fact ruled out because we are always in touch with it anyhow (we only prove to ourselves what we are uncertain about). Instead he continues: 'But how far could we claim that religious experience of God, the encounter or confrontation or whatever we may call it, provides a roughly parallel case?' As to this, I should say, everyone must speak for himself. But I can see no reason why such a claim should be

[1] 244.

disallowed in advance. The main point here is that Macquarrie seems not to recognize the self-guaranteeing character of experience as such. This principle, on which I have had to insist so often, may now perhaps reveal its supreme importance. The failure to grasp it is the great obstacle to progress in the philosophy of religion. Time and again in this most important of all contexts a philosophical prejudice intervenes and darkens counsel.

Plainly it is true, as Macquarrie goes on to emphasize, that knowledge of God and knowledge of the external world are not parallel in all respects. But there is nothing to show that certainty is impossible for either case. There can be an awareness in which doubt is excluded in either case. Macquarrie also writes: 'Belief that there is a real river flowing outside my window is confirmed by everyone who looks out and sees it; but there is no such universal agreement about the reality of God, and no simple way of testing the belief.'[1] True again, but it still does not follow that I cannot satisfy myself about God's reality. It is not as though I were claiming to see a river which nobody else can see. In that case I should certainly consult a psychiatrist. And I can explain to myself, reasonably enough, why some people call themselves atheists and why they may indeed, in certain cases, really lack any awareness of God. I should leave a false impression of Macquarrie's book, which contains so many excellent things, if I failed to quote his remark that 'the whole trend of our study . . . has been leading us towards an increasing confidence that God-talk is well-founded'.[2] So far, so good; but I think it not enough.

My admiration for Macquarrie's work as a whole (although I shall differ from him later on other important points) led me to adopt this piece of advice which he offers in this book: 'no self-respecting theologian should now talk glibly of a "self-authenticating encounter" unless he has read Hepburn's acute analysis of this conception, and found some answers to his strictures'.[3] He is referring to the third and fourth chapters of Professor R. W. Hepburn's *Christianity and Paradox* (1958). In the first of these chapters Hepburn discusses Martin Buber's famous distinction between an 'I-It' relationship and an 'I-Thou' one, and also the views of Professor H. H. Farmer as expressed in his book *The World and God* (1935). Hepburn points out that, according to Buber, 'conviction of God's existence is not the result of any process of argument',[4] but he nevertheless goes on to complain at

[1] 246. [2] 246. [3] 110. [4] 27.

some length that the argument from the analogy of encounter with another human being is an unconvincing one. There is nothing in this that need detain us, but it should be emphasized perhaps that all analogies are unconvincing in the sense that they are only 'pointers'; they cannot be guaranteed to work. Hepburn now asks whether knowledge of God as personal 'can be entirely self-authenticating, or whether there is room here (and even likelihood) of error and illusion'.[1] Of course there is plenty of *room* for them. And no one is expected to accept other people's claims.

Hepburn has no difficulty in showing, although he takes a long time about it, that an 'I-Thou' encounter, an encounter with a person as opposed to an encounter with a thing, is not at all easy to establish. Buber's account, he says, means that we can detect a peculiar element in personal relationships which is not to be explained in terms of knowledge *about* them or knowledge *that* something is the case. The peculiar element, according to Buber, would appear in its pure form in our knowledge of God. Hepburn's argument against this is summed up in the following passage: 'If we seriously try to conceive circumstances in which we might claim to have done away with all behavioural checks in communing with someone, we will find either that we have in a peculiar way failed to maintain the separate identities of the two persons concerned, or that we have no means of knowing whether we are in *rapport* with someone or not which do not ultimately rely upon the behavioural checks themselves.'[2] A later passage takes up again the topic of analogy: 'To ask someone to think analogically is to ask him (*a*) to imagine some familiar item of experience ... and (*b*) to give him directions how to *modify* this item of experience so as to increase its resemblance to the unknown and to diminish its inadequacy.'[3] Now I agree that we cannot build up a knowledge of the infinite by starting with a knowledge of the finite and just *modifying* it. So, if Buber is to be understood as recommending that, he is wrong. But I cannot see that Hepburn has said anything yet against a 'self-authenticating encounter' with God. He tells us that a theologian might give up 'the analogy between meeting human beings and meeting God' and 'choose to make a last-ditch stand'. He could make it 'by staking all on that sense of utter uniqueness that is involved in all genuine *I-Thou* relations'.[4] I am not proposing to say that. I would say that there is a 'sense of utter uniqueness' about our awareness of God. But this is not, so

---

[1] 30.   [2] 36.   [3] 38.   [4] 37.

far as I am concerned, a 'last-ditch stand'. That is to say, I have not been driven into this position because I have been driven out of others. I have never occupied any other. This is the only position, as I see it, in which a theist should ever want to find himself. But he is not confined just to insisting on this uniqueness. There is a good deal to be said in preparation for making the assertion of it and a good deal to be done by way of unpacking it and defending it.

The relationship in which we stand to God is found to be a personal relationship because it is one in which we as persons stand to him, and we discover him in it as the source of personality, as a super-person. Once we have discovered him in this relationship, we realize that personal relationships between human beings are a created echo of this fundamental relationship. But that is a topic which I cannot develop at present. The point about it at the moment is that these human relationships have not in themselves that character of uniqueness which attaches to a relationship with God.

When Hepburn turns to Farmer's book he does find himself faced with the sort of claim to which I have just referred. He quotes from him: 'The religious man is aware of a certain peculiar type of resistance being set up within the sphere of his values and preferences: the resistance, namely, of absolute, sacred, unconditional values . . .'; and again: '[experience of God] in the nature of the case *must* be self-authenticating and able to shine in its own light independently of the abstract reflections of philosophy, for if it were not, it could hardly be a living experience of God as personal'.[1] Hepburn has some objections to make about Farmer's identification of absolute values with the *will* of God; this introduces a subject which will concern us in a later connection but which has no bearing on the present issue. Apart from this, all he has to say is that 'it is by no means sure that the assertion of unconditional values does require the idea of some divine bearer'.[2] He seems to make it an objection that if any experiencing is self-authenticating it must be enjoyed by everybody which (as I have tried to show) is not at all the case. And in the last section of this third chapter he refers to certain 'numinous' experiences of his own, set off by his dreams, which were eventually explained by memories of childhood. I cannot see anything damaging to my own position in any of this.

---

[1] *The World and God*, 23, 158, quoted by Hepburn, 40, 44.   [2] 43.

Later we are offered a dialogue in which an unbeliever addresses a believer in the following terms:

'Here is the crux. You wish at all costs not to distort your *I-Thou* encounter with God. This pushes you towards excluding any descriptive element from the word "God". But if you do exclude them, you cannot also consistently claim "directness" and "immediacy" for your judgements that the one you encounter is Father, Creator, and so on. What you are doing is giving an *illusion* of immediacy through oscillating between descriptive and propername uses of the word "God".'[1]

This is the only passage in the fourth chapter which seems to raise any real problem which I have not discussed in principle already. First it must be made clear that insistence upon the *indescribableness* of God is not a device to avoid being entangled in the snares of descriptive language—it is a necessary statement of what is in fact the case. Secondly, this indescribableness is not that of a blank but that of an indescribable fullness. Thirdly, we may use such words as 'Father' and 'Creator' on the basis of this indescribable experience because it reveals to us the source of being, although in the sense in which they apply to that source they may not be intelligible to others (that is, they are, for them, *not* descriptive words).

It will not be irrelevant if before I leave Hepburn's book I take the opportunity of making a reply to certain strictures of his[2] upon a passage in a book of my own, published some fifteen years ago. He quotes as follows from *An Essay in Christian Philosophy*: 'That I should be constantly slipping away from reality . . . that my actions of five minutes ago should be (as it were) *dead*, and my life confined to the evanescent point which I call the present—this produces in me a spiritual vertigo if I cannot lay hold of an eternal somewhat to save the world from absurdity, from utter unreality.'[3] I am not particularly attached to that passage and should now agree that it is rather rhetorical. But it is given by Hepburn as an instance of faulty reasoning about time. 'What I call the present', Hepburn writes, 'is normally *not* an "evanescent point".' He thinks that I was trying to prescribe 'some one philosophically correct concept of "The Present" ', and this, he says, 'is to fall victim to an abstracting vice that has received just

[1] 56–7.   [2] 182–3.   [3] 67.

castigation from a variety of recent philosophers'. The past, he goes on, can be anything but 'dead' to us (it makes a continual impact upon the present). And the unbeliever can make good sense of his past without postulating an 'eternal somewhat'. In this passage, it will (I hope) be clear, I was not in fact presenting anything which would be called in the ordinary way a reasoning process. I was trying to point to a phenomenon of consciousness (not, I think, altogether uncommon) and to suggest that there might be found within it an awareness (or a suspicion) of something beyond it. Of course in other contexts one can talk about 'the present' in other senses. Of course there is a sense in which the past is still very much alive. Of course the unbeliever is not threatened with vertigo if he sticks to, say, linguistic analysis. I was trying to suggest that if he thinks about the transitory character of our experience he may come to realize that it is not self-explanatory. But what makes all that worth mentioning is the fact that Hepburn has extracted this passage from a book which makes the same sort of claims as those which I have been making here and seems to think it unnecessary to refer to them. In order to knock something down, he puts up a straw man.

Finally I shall consider a remarkable theory put forward to explain religious experience by Mr C. H. Whiteley in his book *An Introduction to Metaphysics*.[1] He introduces the theory with certain proposals about the relation between body and soul:

'The body is a system of vital activities outside the person's consciousness, but intimately connected with his conscious activities . . . body and soul form a single purposive system. . . . The body is not and cannot be completely under the control of the soul. . . . The relation between soul and body is like that between the administrative and executive grades of an organization. The general direction of policy is the concern of the soul. . . . But the routine maintenance of the organism's life, and the detailed execution of my general intentions, are matters which I leave to the body to carry out by itself. . . . My body is made up of many millions of cells. . . . In a sense the man *is* his cells. And yet he is quite unaware of the very existence of all these separate lives which together sustain his life. . . . It is not unplausible to attribute a kind of conscious experience to each individual cell. . . . But these cell-consciousnesses certainly do not combine to constitute the

[1] Methuen paperback, 1966.

total consciousness of the human person; he is unaware of the matters which must constitute the main concern of any consciousness which the cell may have.'[1]

This account of the human person as a 'one-in-many' is, I think, in principle acceptable and helpful except for the suggestion that the individual cells have consciousness, which does not seem to be plausible. Let us see what use Whiteley proposes to make of this conception. He considers that 'if we are to suppose that the human soul is not the highest form of personality in existence, but that there is a divine soul, or more than one, far exceeding our own in knowledge and power . . . this is the most promising analogy we can use for understanding the relation between him and ourselves'.[2] He continues:

'Applying the analogy, many suppose that there is a vaster vital activity, to which the life of men and animals contributes, a more comprehensive purpose which our actions may help to fulfil. . . . But the divine plans are effected through the acts of subordinate beings; there are no separate "acts of God", as distinct from the acts of his creatures. The activity of the creatures is to some extent independent of the will of God; thus the control of God over the world, like the control of soul over the body, is imperfect. . . . And we might suppose that, besides the superficial level of consciousness in which the individual is aware of his own distinct identity, purposes and circumstances, there is a deeper level in which he is aware of his own ultimate identity with God, and through him with all other creatures.'

'Such a theory', Whiteley concludes, 'fits fairly well the testimony of religious experience.' And he also remarks: 'That we are the vehicles of purposes broader and more far-reaching than our own may be made known to us in the sense of obligation. . . .'[3] The great advantage of this theory, in his eyes, is that the problem of evil no longer presents itself to us as it does for the orthodox theist. There is no question of having to explain how an infinite, all-knowing and all-loving God can permit evil in his world. That is a question which we shall be facing before long. Whiteley gets rid of it by postulating a divine being who (if we are to take strictly the analogy with the soul and the cells of the body) is not

[1] 161-2.   [2] 163.   [3] 170.

even aware of the existence of some of his creatures. And although Whiteley calls them 'creatures', he supposes that 'particular finite minds . . . branch off from the universal mind as the vehicles of particular projects; it is in them and through them that the cosmic purposes must be realized'.[1] That sounds like emanationism. (And what are we to make of the statement that 'there are no separate "acts of God", as distinct from the acts of his creatures'?) What are these cosmic purposes of which Whiteley speaks? He talks in explanation of this about 'spiritual progress' as 'an advance from a narrower to a wider sphere of experience and action, in which, as we attain the opportunity of a richer and finer goodness, so we run the risk of a grosser and profounder evil'.[2] He has found a way of freeing God from responsibility for evil, but he has to accept it as a brute fact. A Christian, as we shall see later, can at least offer an account of *how* evil arises which claims to be intelligible.

But what is this 'wider sphere of existence' of which Whiteley speaks? Presumably his answer is to be found in his further statement that 'in the profoundest experiences of religion we know our ultimate oneness with God'.[3] But 'if there is one mind giving impetus and direction to the whole process of terrestrial life, it is a mind which changes, develops and learns'.[4] So the questions arise: What does this God learn? What is the good or goal to which all this process is supposed to be leading? What gives it meaning and value? We are supposed to be in process of self-development to a knowledge of a God who is also developing, for he is just that mind which is the ultimate stuff of the developing system. This mind, which is a finite mind and not therefore what is in fact meant by 'God' in our vocabulary, learns, it would seem, by developing itself. It brings into being the goal to which it moves. I submit that this is not intelligible. A mind can be led onwards only by what is not itself. Whiteley's 'divine mind' cannot be of value to us because it does not itself make sense. It cannot, for the same reason, explain our experience. It is not necessary to consider the various assumptions which Whiteley has to make in the construction of his system or to speak of those features of religious experience which it cannot accommodate. It is sufficient to show that it breaks down.

This is an issue of importance for our time. With the development of secular humanism in a variety of forms there is a certain

[1] 170. [2] 171. [3] 171. [4] 170.

recrudescence of pantheistic or quasi-pantheistic theories. It seems to me that the principle just enunciated, that a mind cannot be led onwards except by what is not itself, is the ultimate answer to all such theories. But of course it is possible to reject it. It is a general statement about our experience—that is to say, there is no possible appeal to anything beyond it, and if anyone does deny it there is nothing in particular that one can do about it. I can only say that the rejection of it seems to me plainly the result of a confusion. To see that it is a confusion requires, I should say, only a modicum of attention. But to apprehend infinite value in finite value does require more than a modicum of attention. It is one thing to see that Whiteley's theory is an incoherent one, but quite another to find a positive answer to his question.

The issue, in fact, for clear-minded people is that between theism and atheism. If the world has a purpose or meaning, we must not be fobbed off with a self-developing God. Unless we apprehend the infinite in the finite, we have no good ground for belief in such a purpose or meaning. If we are asking ourselves whether we can really believe in God, we must ask ourselves whether we can really believe that the world has no purpose or meaning. If we can believe that it has not, we can still get a certain sort of enjoyment out of it. We can even take up with causes which appeal to our feelings. But we shall have decided that it is fruitless to ask questions about our state of affairs in general. It makes no sense, and so one sort of nonsense about it is about as good as any other. I should like to suggest that it may be a good thing to take a long, cool look at that conclusion. It can be a way of coming to realize that the alternative conclusion is, after all, inevitable.

There is a good deal more to be said about it. But before going on to do so I think it best to say something about those difficulties or apparent contradictions which may seem to threaten if one accepted the theistic conclusion. Until this has been done it may be impossible for some minds to give serious consideration to the hypothesis that there is an infinite source from which we derive and to which we must return. The difficulties which I shall discuss concern the notion of creation and the relation in which the created world stands to its creator, and his management of the world, that is, the problem of evil and the notion of providence. It will be impossible to discuss these topics without some reference to Christian doctrines, but they will be presented as hypotheses to be entertained for purposes of argument. The next three discussions in fact will exhibit the outlines of a world-view, a *Weltanschauung*, as academics like to call it, the framework of a metaphysical construction (the sort of thing which makes most modern philosophers shudder), or, more simply, a manifesto of my convictions about our state of affairs and its ultimate significance. At any rate this should have the limited advantage of showing the workings of my own mind and making it easier to follow what I shall be saying at later stages.

8. THE ONE AND THE MANY

Metaphysical intuition is a sort of spreading light which reacts upon its earlier stages, confirming them. My claim is that it develops into an explicit apprehension of God. The recognition of our spiritual powers as spiritual develops into the recognition of the Infinite Other. A 'suspicion' of God will not become a certainty until this process has reached a point of development which we must call the entrance to faith because it is not only a point of intellectual achievement but also one at which a decision, or commitment, is required of us. That is, we must accept the love which is offered us, which we are now aware of, by our own self-surrender to it. (Although we know that it is offered to us, the mysterious fact is that we are nevertheless able to reject it.) I shall pursue that topic not in the present discussion but in the following ones, and I mention it now only because it may help to make the claim to an awareness of God seem more credible. For, unless we look at it in the context which I have just hastily indicated, we may feel that it does not fit the facts of experience and that its connection with what we mean by religion is by no means obvious.

What I propose to do at the moment is to consider one of the important difficulties which may seem to arise out of an acknowledgement of God. It concerns the relation in which the created world (and that includes ourselves) stands to its creator. But as a preliminary we shall have to consider the objection that we have no business to talk about a creator at all if we are not already presupposing the Christian revelation. And we have not yet come to the question about that revelation. The doctrine of creation, the objector will say, is a Judaeo-Christian one; the philosopher as such, that is, the philosopher who has not yet become a theologian as well by accepting revelation, cannot discover God as creator. It is quite true that the philosophers of the ancient world, to speak very generally, show few signs of grasping this truth with any firmness, although it is difficult not to think that Plato, for example, is trying to express it in certain famous passages of *The Republic*, and there are the theistic philosophies of the East, Hinduism in particular; a Christian theist could hardly maintain that there was no genuine knowledge of God in pre-Christian times except for the Jewish people. What, then, are we to say about this? We must certainly say, I think, that without revelation the explicit knowledge of God as creator is difficult to come by. One of the functions of revelation is to turn what might otherwise be only suspicions into certainties. But I think we should also say that the men of the ancient world did make a genuine contact with the one true God by their following of conscience, their pursuit of ideals and their reverence for truth, although certain philosophical notions, their notions of cosmogony especially, I suppose, clouded their minds and prevented them from realizing, at least in any articulate way, that what they were in contact with was in fact the source of being.

Nowadays what is meant by God in our Western civilization is the source of being. But it may be recalled that I started by speaking of an absolute demand made upon us, a summons from a power beyond ourselves, as the foundation of theism. If that is so, then we may say that these men of the ancient world whom we have been considering may be called at least rudimentary theists. They had not our problems, by and large, about the notion of creation because they were not operating with that notion or not in a way sufficiently explicit to enable them to appreciate these problems. But a thinking man today, faced by the question of God, will often feel that there is an incoherence about the notion of a God who freely creates, a God who, it is said, need not have created. That is what 'God' means to us today, in the Western world at any rate, and this is the chief problem to which I shall address myself in the present discussion. It may be noted, in passing, that the notion of a universal source is one to which nearly everyone nowadays can attach some meaning. When an unbeliever says to a believer that he has no idea what he is talking about when he talks about God, the unbeliever really means that he has no personal contact with this alleged source and no evidence that the idea of the infinite corresponds in fact to reality. He cannot literally mean that the idea of a universal source, an Infinite Other, has no meaning for him. A notion of it is present to his mind, but he believes it to be a human invention. This seems to me a very difficult position for anyone to hold, but I am not concerned with that here. The present point is that the unbeliever does entertain some notion of the Infinite and that this involves for him some notion of a Creator. Let us now consider what he has to say against its being a coherent notion.

The universal source, he will say, if indeed it is a reality, must be independent of everything else, for without it there *is* nothing else. If it is infinite, it must be complete and therefore immutable. But this independent God is also said to be free either to create or not to create. Obviously he cannot be made to do so by anything outside him. But if he had not created he would have lacked a certain character or quality which he has in virtue of being the creator. He would have been a *different* God. So the notion of a universal source leads to a contradiction. This may seem a remote sort of difficulty when one comes across it for the first time, but it is one which has been felt very keenly by serious thinkers, people who deserve to be taken seriously, and to examine it will have the special advantage of introducing us to certain questions about the relation in which the world stands to God which are of the greatest importance in themselves. There is also this importance about the objection that it has been regularly glossed over, in particular by St Thomas and those who are content to follow him, so that it constitutes (in the precise sense of the word) something of a scandal. There is a marked tendency here for theologians to take illegitimate refuge in mystery, and certain ecclesiastical pronouncements have made it difficult for them to offer a clear answer.

Let us begin by considering how the difficulty is stated in Arthur O. Lovejoy's well-known book *The Great Chain of Being*, which is often prescribed for undergraduates (both on the arts and on the science sides) in English-speaking universities. Lovejoy remarks that St Thomas 'is under the necessity of affirming the freedom of the absolute will';[1] it would be heterodox to say that God acts by 'necessity of nature'. And so, according to St Thomas, 'though the divine intellect conceives of an infinity of possible things, the divine will does not choose them all; and

[1] 74.

the existence of finite things is therefore contingent and the number of their kinds is arbitrary'.[1] Yet on St Thomas's general principles we should expect him to say that 'nothing less than the sum of all genuine possibles could be the object of the divine will'.[2] How could he leave a possible good unrealized? What Lovejoy has called 'the principle of plenitude' (that God creates all possible varieties of things) is irreconcilable, we are told, with the requirements of orthodox theology. Professor John Hick in his recent book *Evil and the God of Love* has drawn upon Lovejoy and repeated his argument with emphasis. It is very much a live issue.

It seems to me that there is only one answer to this: to say that there are *no* 'possible' worlds. There is simply *the* world. But this needs a good deal of explaining. I shall offer the explanation in the form of an imaginary dialogue between a conventional Catholic theologian and a Christian of a more critical cast of mind.[3]

Criticus: I have come across a passage in C. S. Lewis's *The Problem of Pain* which I should like to read to you: 'With every advance in our thought the unity of the creative act and the impossibility of tinkering with the creation as though this or that element in it could have been removed will become more apparent. Perhaps this is not the "best of all possible" universes but the only possible one. Possible worlds can mean only "worlds which God could have made but didn't". The idea of that which God "could have" done involves a too anthropomorphic conception of God's freedom. Whatever human freedom means, Divine freedom cannot mean indeterminacy between alternatives and choice of one of them. Perfect goodness can never debate about the means most suited to achieve it. The freedom of God consists in the fact that no cause other than himself produces his acts and no external obstacle impedes them—that his own goodness is the root from which they all grow and his own omnipotence the air in which they may all flower' [p. 123]. Tell me, Scholasticus, do you regard this as a defensible position in Catholic Theology?

---

[1] 75.
[2] P. 74. Lovejoy quotes the *Summa Contra Gentiles*, 1, 75 and 1, 81 together with the *Summa Theol.*, 1, 19, 4.
[3] This appeared in its original form in *The Downside Review*, Spring 1948, 'A Dialogue on God's Freedom'. It contains a few technical terms, but their meaning should be plain in the context, even to those who are unfamiliar with this sort of scholastic language; and it also throws out some hints about theological themes which will receive fuller explanation later on.

Scholasticus: I do not. Surely you know that Abelard was condemned for saying that God can do only what in fact he does and that the Vatican Council condemned Guenther for teaching the necessity of creation.[1]

Criticus: I thought you would say that. You will agree that it is often not so much what is said in a condemned proposition as why it is said that is the reason for the condemnation. But before we discuss that, I wish you would explain to me the metaphysical principles on which you base your own position. For I suppose you don't just take the answer 'on Faith'. Let me say at once that I don't find the 'necessity of creation' in Lewis, if by this we mean that the created universe contains within it the reason for its own existence. That is plainly a contradiction, for God is that reason.

Scholasticus: I have here Fr Boedder's manual of Natural Theology which contains a comment on a passage of Victor Cousin's. Cousin, as you will see, took a line which is substantially the same as Lewis's. Here is the passage: 'The creative act is a necessary act because it results from the nature of a cause which needs must act, and it is free, for it proceeds from the proper, independent, primitive spontaneity of a cause which acts by itself, which determines itself, so that its determination, though necessary, is nevertheless its own, and is not under any influence from without.'[2] Fr Boedder's comment is as follows: 'Against these assertions we maintain that God has created only because He freely willed the existence of creatures, being equally free not to will had He pleased' (p. 136). Cousin's words, Fr Boedder considers, imply that 'creation was a necessity required to supply some deficiency in God'.

Criticus: I don't see that. Cousin's doctrine as given by Fr Boedder seems to me not only intelligible but inevitable. He is saying, surely, that without the act of creation God would not be God, because (as all agree) he *is* his acts. It is meaningless, then, to envisage the possibility that there could have been no such act. And it does not even begin to follow that the *term* of God's Act,

---

[1] Denzinger, 374, 1805.
[2] Quoted on p. 135 by Boedder, who refers to Alleux, *La Philosophie de M. Cousin*, 19-20.

'creation' in the sense of the created universe, adds anything to God. It is a commonplace in this connexion that you cannot *add* chalk to cheese. Lewis is not suggesting that God and his creatures add up, when he rejects the use of the conditional mood in statements which have God as their subject. Indeed, I find it hard to see how the transcendence, the immutability, of God, is to be safeguarded on any other showing.

Scholasticus: There is of course a difficulty, and I can show you a passage in which Fr Boedder deals with it. He distinguishes the necessity of Pure Act from that free will to create which is yet the same Pure Act looked at from a certain point of view. He says, you see: 'the internal act of [God's] will, which is really identical with the essence, can without change involve or not involve that relation to an object which we call *choosing* and willing'.[1]

Criticus: I don't find that thinkable. I can think of *choosing* only as a response in face of a state of affairs upon which the chooser is in a sense dependent. If God is described as choosing, this can mean for me only that he finds himself faced with 'possibles' soliciting his will and therefore in a certain respect acting upon him and so making him dependent on them. Besides, I thought it was good Thomism not to allow that there are *relations* in God to creatures, but only in creatures to God.

Scholasticus: I admit that this language of relations has its drawbacks. But you seem to suppose that, just because we cannot conceive of an act which combines freedom of choice with freedom from external solicitation, we cannot allow that God's act of creation is of this kind. You are dragging God down to your own level.

Criticus: We are always doing that. All I can say is that it is the attempt to avoid it which causes my dissatisfaction with the usual Scholastic treatment of this question. Try as I may, I cannot reconcile the notion of alternative courses with what I know of God, and I observe further down on this page of Fr Boedder's book the following sentence: 'The will of God in its relation to creatures is absolutely necessary in its entity (i.e. in its internal actual state) but not in its *term* (i.e. it does not necessarily bear to

[1] *op. cit.*, 304.

creatures that relation which we call volition).' This is the regular Scholastic formula, isn't it? Now to say that the will of God is not necessary in its term is perfectly acceptable if it only means that God's creatures do not enjoy his necessity. Creatures stand in a unique relation of total dependence upon God. This relation in which they stand to him is such that he is other than they, utterly transcendent: yet at the same time they have a mysterious 'likeness' to him. This is what we *find* in our experience; and we cannot *justify* it except by showing that we do find it. My difficulty is that the Scholastics seem to introduce this lack of self-sufficiency, which is the mark of God's creatures, into the creative act which is God himself.

Scholasticus: I don't think you fully grasp the Scholastic position. It may help if I contrast it with your own. Your own is, I think, that it is the nature of God to create. God's nature is necessary.[1] Therefore his act of creation, which is identical with his nature, is also necessary. But I say that it is not so simple as that. It is just as much God's nature to create as not to create. By which I mean that his simple perfection is indifferent to creating or not creating; it includes both. It is his nature to create or not to create at his pleasure.

Criticus: God created because it was his will to do so; and his will is free. But the meaning which you give to 'free' seems to set up a contradiction in God. How can we avoid the conclusion that if God had chosen not to create there would have been something 'unrealized' in him? You may say that I am obliged to accept your meaning by the condemnations to which you referred. But it is not unreasonable, I think, to suggest that those condemnations bear simply and solely upon an error which inspires the condemned propositions, the error, namely, that creation is necessary in an 'emanationist' sense, that God is incomplete without creatures. The condemnation which controls the Scholastic discussion I take to be that of the Guentherist proposition that God created with the necessity with which he loves himself,[2] which certainly leads to a confusion between God and creatures. For it suggests

---

[1] This use of 'necessary' must be distinguished from that in which philosophers speak of the (logical) necessity of propositions. It means simply that there is no question of God's being other than he is.

[2] Denzinger, 1805.

that there is a relationship between God's will and his creatures of the same kind as that between God's will and himself. If we work in these terms, since we must say that there is a relation of identity between God's will and himself, we must say that there is this same relation between himself and his creatures. Naturally Rosmini was also condemned for saying that there is a 'moral necessity' for God to create 'because he loves himself in creatures'.[1] And Abelard was condemned for saying that God 'can do things only as he does them in fact'[2] because in the light of his other statements this seems to be setting bounds to God's omnipotence. But all I am saying is that God would not be God without his act of creation.

Scholasticus: But are you not involved in these errors? For you find it inconceivable that God should exist without creatures.

Criticus: It is his nature to be generous, to give, to produce what is *not* himself, not because he requires us.

Scholasticus: If he does not require us, why can he not do without us?

Criticus: In an obvious sense he *does* without us: that is, God is simply God and we 'make no difference' to him.

Scholasticus: Very well, then, if God had not created us it would have made no difference to him. Why should you hesitate to admit the hypothesis?

Criticus: To say that the *act* of creation makes no difference to him in that sense would be to say that there is something unnecessary in him, as I have said before. You seem to think that by asserting this power of God's to *abstain* from creating, you are maintaining one of his prerogatives. I am prepared to 'take refuge in a mystery' if I am bidden to do so by the Church. But I cannot pretend to attach any meaning to what you are talking about. The act of creation 'makes no difference' to God, so far as I can see, only in the sense that it is identical with his nature.

Scholasticus: But consider what consequences follow from your

[1] Denzinger, 1908.   [2] *ibid.*, 374.

position. Are you not in effect denying all meaning to 'possibility'? If there are no alternatives for the First Cause, are there any alternatives for anyone?

Criticus: To say that this is just *the* world is not to say that possibility is meaningless. It means that God has only one plan of creation. But it is a plan which involves human freedom—because it involves human blessedness; so *we can refuse* to accept God's actuations. But this 'can' is not itself a possibility for actuation by God. It is something *sui generis* to which we can refer only in negative terms.

Scholasticus: Do you really mean to say that this world could not be improved upon?

Criticus: St Thomas, as you know, says that God governs his chosen world with supreme wisdom and benevolence. But you refer, no doubt, to his doctrine that God could have chosen another and a better one. Does that doctrine satisfy you?

Scholasticus: It seems to me imposed upon us. Anything created could always be better than it is. There is no assignable limit to the power which God could confer upon a creature. And this applies to the created universe as a whole. It has always been the answer of the Thomist school to philosophical optimism that the 'best of all possible worlds' is a meaningless expression.

Criticus: I am suggesting that there are *no* 'possible' worlds. I should find it hard to believe that God could have a better purpose for his creation than the communication of himself in knowledge and love to his creatures, even if I could entertain the notion of God's having any plan different from that which in fact he has.

Scholasticus: Our knowledge and love of him are created qualities. They must always be capable of increase.

Criticus: Yours and mine considered in isolation—but in view of the knowledge and love of him enjoyed by Christ in his sacred humanity, in which we participate?

Scholasticus: It is all the same.

Criticus: I wonder. Are you not perhaps the victim here of your imagination? A maximum quantity is unthinkable in itself, but an optimum quality not necessarily, I suggest. Could there be anything created of higher value than Christ's human soul? And is not our world 'ordered' to Christ? Could God's purpose have been achieved with a more perfect adaptation of means to end?

Scholasticus: What, then, do we mean by speaking of God's generosity in redeeming us if there was no question of his not redeeming us, or of not redeeming us in the manner in which he has done?

Criticus: We mean, I suppose, that God's unchanging and supreme generosity is here most clearly indicated to us.

Scholasticus: That is true. But there is more behind it—a mystery of God's freedom which you are trying to evacuate. You seem to think that you can *explain* God's proceedings. You are claiming to see things from his side. You seem to think that God must have a reason, a reason perceptible to yourself, for what he does. But he is the reason for his act of creation and for the terms of this act.

Criticus: The real question seems to be this: what do we know about God? Do we or do we not know what we mean when we call him supreme wisdom and superlative generosity? Do we know him as creating out of that superlative generosity? And, if so, when we are asked to believe that he could create a better world and has not done so, how can we help saying 'why not'?

Scholasticus: God in creating has no end in view save his own glory. He cannot subordinate himself to our advantage.

Criticus: Gloria Dei vivens homo.[1] You cannot be suggesting that God gains anything by his creation. And, since *we* do, isn't it God's purpose in creating that we should?

Scholasticus: St Thomas says that God does not will anything for any reason (except himself), although he wills one thing to be on

---

[1] 'The glory of God is the living man'; and the passage in Irenaens continues: 'and the life of man is the vision of God' (*Adv. haer*, iv, 20, 7).

account of some other thing, as means to end. *Vult ergo hoc esse propter hoc: sed non propter hoc vult hoc.*[1]

Criticus: That is obvious enough if it means that God cannot be moved to will by anything outside himself. But if it is taken to mean that God has no concern with what he creates we are back at Aristotle's First Mover. Again I ask: are we, as theologians, really so ignorant of God's nature as your position would suggest? Is he so dark to us that we may as well give up trying to attach any meaning to liberty or necessity as applied to him and take refuge in the *indifferentia dominatrix* of the Thomist commentators?[2] Or do we in fact find in the Christian God the reconciliation of liberty and necessity? God is love—and Lover of us.

Scholasticus: I can think of one recent Thomist who uses, up to a point, the sort of language which you wish to use, and he—oddly, in view of what you have just been saying—was considered excessively 'agnostic' by some of his fellow-Thomists. Sertillanges says that it is only a way of saying that the creature could *not be* or be otherwise when we say that God could have *not produced* it or produced it otherwise—that the world has no necessity of itself.[3]

Criticus: Of course I agree that the world has no necessity of itself, and if that is all that I am called upon to say in this matter of God's freedom, then there is no difficulty. It does not surprise me that Sertillanges was considered 'agnostic'. It was his realization of who God is that made him reject so much which ordinarily passes for appropriate language about him.

There is no need, then, from the point of view of Catholic theology, to consider the activity of creation as an arbitrary business. We are entitled to consider the world not as one of many possible ones but just as *the* world, the world in which God has expressed himself 'externally'. Why it should possess just those features which it does possess and no others we do not know, but there is no reason why we should *have* to know. And we do not know what it would be like if the possibility of evil in it (a possi-

---

[1] *S. Th.* I, xix, Corp.   [2] Garrigou-Lagrange, *De Deo Uno*, 404.
[3] *St Thomas D'Aquin*, I, 249.

bility with which, not God, but God's creatures are necessarily faced) had not been realized. Professor Hick remarks in this connection that in fact many possible creatures do not exist.[1] But we have no right to say that, because we can conceive of an increase in the total number of gorillas throughout the course of time or of some species which has never existed and never will exist, these must be possibles offered to God's choice.[2] What God does is the 'best', not because it is at the top of a scale of 'possibles', whether in point of quality or in that of quantity, but because it is the 'reflection' or 'imitation' of him.

Something must here be said about the Encyclical *Humani Generis* of 1950 which emphasized that the language of necessity must be simply ruled out in regard to God's act of creation. P. de Lubac in his recent book *Le Mystère du Surnaturel* was nevertheless able to say, on the one hand, that we must not take up with any form of emanationism, which makes the world simply an overflow of God himself, but, on the other, that we must not think of God as faced by possible worlds offering themselves for his choice. So it is still presumably the danger of 'emanationism' and nothing else which the Encyclical was guarding against. We may reach a conclusion in accordance with its prescriptions by denying that either 'freedom' or 'necessity' can be attributed to God's act of creation in our ordinary understanding of those words. But we may suggest that our ordinary notions of freedom and necessity *coincide at infinity*. We shall see that this sort of coincidence is in fact the answer to other questions about the created world.

We now take up, then, the topic, touched on in the dialogue, that the created world proves to have a 'likeness' to God. We have called it a 'reflection' of him. Metaphorical expressions like 'reflection' will have no meaning in such a connection for those who can attach no meaning to talk about an apprehension of God, and they may be received with indifference or even with suspicion by those whose apprehension of God is not yet sufficiently explicit for them to recognize their own experience in these expressions. But it would not be difficult to show that this theme of God's 'manifestation' is a part, and indeed the keystone, of the classical

---

[1] *Evil and the God of Love*, 85-6.
[2] To imagine a 'possible' species could only be to hold together imaginarily the characteristics of several existing ones. We cannot step *outside* our own experience.

tradition of Christian metaphysics[1] (a tradition particularly clear in the patristic period). For those who accept it, it follows as an inevitable development (although not as a logically demonstrable consequence) of a recognition of the Infinite Other. That the source of being is apprehended as wholly other than the beings with which we are immediately acquainted is a statement which must be made in the first instance about the encounter of the human mind with God. But, if this apprehension is not in some way or other inhibited, then another statement, verbally in apparent contradiction with the first, must be made in conjunction with it: that created beings are not *alien* to their source, that they stand to it not only in a relation of total dependence but also in another relation, which, being from the nature of the case a unique one, can only be 'pointed to', just as the source itself can only be 'pointed to'.

Let us try to 'point to' this relation. It is easy to say what it is *not*. It is not the relation between cause and effect as we are accustomed to think of it in other contexts. Just as we cannot build up a knowledge of God by a merely logical operation with a notion of causality derived solely from the world of his creation, so we cannot find this relation in which his creatures stand to him by an application of that notion. It has been a fatal error of natural theologians in recent centuries to attempt such an application. They have imported into their premises what they wished to prove. It is notoriously difficult to say just what our 'ordinary' notion of causality in fact implies,[2] but it is certainly not part of it that the cause should be in some way superior to and 'contain' its effects. But it is that supposed principle which these natural theologians have employed in their attempt to establish this relationship.

The 'ordinary' notion of causality does not involve a source of being as a logical consequence. But to acknowledge the source of being is to acknowledge causality in the ultimate metaphysical sense. The relation in which creatures stand to God must be discovered, then, not by appealing to an abstract principle of causality, which proves to be an ill-defined notion only applicable to the commerce of created beings, but to the discovery of metaphysical causality, the discovery of God himself. The relationship

---

[1] Despite the fact that the world has been commonly envisaged as one of an infinite number of possible manifestations of God.
[2] As when we say that the match 'causes' the flame.

with which we are concerned cannot be discovered in the first instance between created things and then 'raised to the infinite'. What has to be discovered is a new and entirely different relationship. Creatures have no part in creation.

What, then, can we say? We can perhaps bring out more clearly what we are trying to say if we remember that we were led to discover the source of being through the awareness of *values*. We are concerned, then, with the relation of values to Value. What we are proposing is that infinite Value 'contains' all values, that this unique state of affairs can be *discovered* if we take the trouble. It is what we *find* if we are attentive to what we already know and to what we may be coming to know, if (to repeat) we allow the apprehension of God to become explicit. We are forced to use the word 'contain' or some word like it to refer to what we find. We find that in God there is not only the absence of any limiting complexity but also a fullness or richness. As always when we are speaking of God, words which have a positive sense will not of themselves convey the sense which we are here intending. It must be found in the light of the apprehension. It is not sufficient to say that God is a super-person, super-generous and so forth. But, although it is utterly inadequate, it is true.

So in discovering God as the indescribable we discover as well that the created values which we encounter are present in him in a way which is also strictly indescribable. As we saw earlier, our knowledge of God, although itself positive (indeed the very heart of our specifically human experience), cannot be described in any foolproof way except in negative terms, which plainly cannot of themselves convey what we mean. The 'pointing' words 'richness' and 'simplicity' announce that God is *not* just a blank, *not* a congeries of qualities, but an unbroken unity in which created values are, as it were, fused—but this must be *seen*.

This coincidence of created values at infinity is the charter of Christian humanism, and it is at least implicit in all Christian thought. But it has not been discussed, as a rule, in much detail. The notion of man as the 'image' of God is familiar enough, and it was once usual to call material objects 'vestiges' of him. The value of consciousness and of all that goes with it is found in God—all Christians, I suppose, would agree about that—but what of the values which, for example, we attach to the beauties of nature or to those of art? In an obvious sense, beauty does lie in the eye of the beholder, but there is nevertheless something 'out there' to be beheld. What happens, it may be suggested, when we encounter beauty, is that we find a unity, an intelligibility of parts which unite in an organic whole and which satisfy (for the moment) our desire for perfect unity. But we know the material world only in its interaction with ourselves. We know that it is *there*, that we have not invented it, and this is a genuine knowledge, for, as we saw, we do really know causes *in* their effects. But this is a very dim sort of knowledge. (And, as we have just seen, when we call creatures causes of one another, we do so in a very limited sense. In the ultimate metaphysical sense, causality works through them as its instruments.) We cannot talk about the value of the world 'in itself' and apart from its effects on us, although we know that it *is* in itself. And there can be no value except in relation to a mind—but perhaps there are other minds besides human ones. In any case we can find out a good deal *about* the world of nature. We can find out how it works—this is the way in which the scientist discovers its beauties. It is not simply an environment out of which we emerge, but it also speaks to us of God.

It is important at this point to appreciate a difference between our knowledge of God and our knowledge of material objects. We can know material objects only in their interaction with our bodies. A flash of lightning or a sonic boom is something very definite in our experience; that is, we are very clearly in contact with the effects of something, but we are not given much in the way of first-hand acquaintance with whatever it is. We think of these experiences as the most obviously 'real' ones, and so in a sense they are: that contact with the outside world has indeed occurred and that the sight or sound is unambiguously a fact is undeniable. But there is another way of being in touch with reality which is very much more interesting. We know God not through our senses but in his action on our minds. There is thus an objectivity about this knowledge, despite the obscurity of its early stages, which attaches to no other.[1] In our specifically human experience, our life of affirmations and aspirations, we are confronted with the power and the presence of God. That is what talk of a union of subject and object is driving at in the long run. It is *this* union, that of the mind with God, which is the paradigm of knowledge. Without it our knowledge of material things would not be *human* knowledge at all. When it is said that 'God is not an

[1] Von Hügel is among those who preserve this part of the Platonist tradition (*The Mystical Element of Religion*, Vol. II, 280-1).

object', one sees what is meant. But there is a sense in which he is more properly an 'object' than tables or chairs. As the medieval adage has it, '*Solus Deus illabitur animae*'. Unfortunately, however, as Eliot has observed, 'human kind cannot bear very much reality'.

We have been concerning ourselves in this chapter with the topic of 'analogy'. The word has not been used before not only because it is a technical one but also because some unfortunate associations have gathered round it. It may be useful to sum up what the doctrine of analogy ought and ought not to mean if it is to make sense. It has sometimes been represented as providing a sort of logical bridge between finite and infinite, which plainly will not do. The idea of 'being', it has been claimed, is an 'analogical' one, containing within its scope both finite and infinite. We can discover this by purifying such a notion of the limitations which are initially involved in it ('raising it to the infinite'). But as always with these attempts to find God in the world without *at the same time* finding him 'outside' it, the argument presupposes its conclusion. If we begin at the created end of the 'analogical' notion we shall not know that there is another end until we have *apprehended* it. Otherwise the purifying process will leave us with just a blank. Again, we cannot build up the infinite out of finite materials.

The doctrine of analogy has been often represented as a way of explaining how creatures can be 'like' God. Words are used of God and of creatures, it is said, not in the same sense, nor in a wholly different sense, but in a sense between the two, the 'analogical' sense, and attempts are made to find parallels to this in the relationships obtaining between created things. We need not investigate these supposed parallels. If the relationship obtains between created things, it cannot for that very reason obtain between them and God. All attempts to *explain* our relationship to our Creator are foredoomed to failure because explanation means appealing to some general principle which applies both to God and creatures. We have seen that the unique 'likeness' of creatures to God is a fact which we find when we have found God. This is what analogy means when it makes sense. It was once expressed by Penido, a Thomist who had perceived this point, in the lapidary sentence: 'Analogy begins where the Five Ways end.'

And this is perhaps the occasion for making a first reference to the proper function of St Thomas's 'Five Ways' of proving God's existence. They draw our attention to features of our experience which provoke or bring into focus an awareness of God.[1] If in fact the values of our world not only derive from absolute Value but are in this peculiar sense 'like' it, it is in contemplating them that we may be most naturally led to realize that such is the case. But they are no more than the natural occasions in which the awareness of God may arise or rather become more explicit. St Thomas's first three arguments from causality may help us to become aware of God's activity in the world (and especially upon ourselves). The 'argument from design' raises the question of the purpose, and so the value, of our world. There remains the Fourth Way, which is explicitly concerned with values. In effect it maintains that limited values imply (I should say, 'point to') an unlimited one. The Fourth Way has often been considered a sort of poor relation of the others. This discussion may perhaps suggest that it has its special usefulness. The notion of creation may always remain an obstacle until this relationship of 'likeness' between creature and creator has come to be accepted.[2]

Before I leave the notion of creation, there is one further difficulty which is often alleged against it, and, although it arises only on a superficial level of thought, something should be said about it. The difficulty, in its crudest form, is put as follows: 'What was God doing before creation happened?' Clearly anyone who asks this question is imagining God as living in a time-series and also failing to understand that God's activity cannot be distinguished from God himself. But behind the question is the difficulty of supposing either that the world came into existence at a particular time or that it has always been in existence. The answer to this must be that the world and time go together. Time is not a string on which events are hung; it is the order of events, and where there are no events there is no time. The question whether the world has always been in existence was discussed with great acumen by St Thomas Aquinas.[3] There is nothing in reason against it, he pointed out, because this is not to say that the number of events in the past is infinite (that would be a contradiction, because any number can be added to, and an

---

[1] On this subject Dr Austin Farrer's *Finite and Infinite*, supplemented by his recent *Faith and Speculation*, is of the first importance.

[2] What has been said in this and the earlier chapters might be usefully compared with what Professor Flew takes to be the evidence for God and the nature of God in his recent *God and Philosophy*.

[3] *Summa Theol.*, 1, q. 46.

infinite number of events would mean a number which cannot be added to); to say that the world has always been there is to say that if you started to count the events which have developed in it you would never come to an end. The events cannot be numbered in the sense of being all added up just because they go on endlessly into the past. St Thomas, however, thought that he had the authority of Genesis for saying that the world has in fact lasted for a finite time only. But the point that he was anxious to make about the whole business was that an 'eternal' world would be just as much dependent on God as a non-eternal one. When we are talking about creation, in other words, time need not come into the matter at all. The notion of creation in itself is not bound up with that of time. And if we call God's conservation of the world, as we naturally do, 'continuous creation', we have to remember that there is nothing properly 'continuous' on God's side but only on ours. His immutable creative act, which is himself, has as its term the whole created world in its whole duration.

9. THE CHRISTIAN METAPHYSIC

In giving notice that, before discussing the apprehension of God in any further detail, I should consider certain problems which seem to arise out of that apprehension, I remarked that this would involve some references to Christian doctrines, which may be regarded, for immediate purposes, simply an hypotheses. It is the problem of evil, in my opinion, which especially requires one to entertain these hypotheses if is is to be discussed in any thorough-going way. And so, by way of approach to that problem, I propose to devote this discussion to a Christian way of looking both at the relation in which we stand to God and at his purposes for us.

It appears that there is normally a feeling of 'coming home' about the apprehension of God, but especially when this apprehension becomes explicit in the context of a conversion to Christianity. God, who proves not to have been wholly unknown before (although it might have seemed so), is recognized in Christ. But, if I may repeat it, to recognize God is not necessarily the same as to accept him. We cannot, of course, acknowledge a truth and in the very act of doing so repudiate it, like the fabulous old lady who saw the giraffe at the zoo and said 'I don't believe it'. But we can realize that there is something which we ought to follow up and then fail to do so. We can sometimes dodge things before they have the chance to present themselves to us properly, and even when they have done so we can manage to forget about them. At some point in a man's career, or perhaps at the end of it, he comes across something which compels him to make a fundamental choice. It is not an arbitrary choice. It is a choice between moving forward in the direction of a light or retiring into the darkness. The philosopher who has analysed this situation most effectively for our time is, I think, Maurice Blondel.[1] If we take a brief look at his account of it, we shall find that it leads into a Christian view of God's purposes for us which he calls the Christian metaphysic.

Blondel recognized it as the mission of his life to show his contemporaries that the Christian fact is not an 'unrelated' one (that is, one which is irrelevant to the human situation), but the answer to the supreme human question and the centre of human history. His greatest achievement, or at any rate the achievement which will now concern us, was to make sense of the 'supernatural'. His use of the expression in *L'Action* can be easily misunderstood. When a Catholic theologian speaks of the 'supernatural' he is commonly understood to be referring to the Christian Revelation. When Blondel says in *L'Action* that an encounter with the supernatural is inevitable, sometime, for everyone, he does not mean that everyone is bound to come across the teaching of the Gospel. Obviously there have been many human beings who have not come across it. What he means is that everyone must come across God, who is our supernatural end. We cannot achieve our destiny, which is to be united with him indefectibly, by the employment of our native resources. We cannot enjoy the gift of himself until it has been both offered and accepted. Everything depends on what Blondel calls the 'great option'. It is the entrance to the life of faith and of grace. And all

[1] Blondel is still so little known in many quarters that a few facts about him must be mentioned. He was born in 1861 and died in 1949. His first book, *L'Action*, appeared in 1893. His influence, on French Catholic thinkers in particular, has been profound, and he has been called the philosopher of the Second Vatican Council. In what follows I shall be drawing sometimes on my contribution to *Maurice Blondel*, a book containing two of his shorter works presented and translated for the most part by Mr Alexander Dru (Harvill Press, 1964). I shall be drawing also extensively upon articles of mine published in *The Downside Review* and in particular that entitled 'Blondel's *Le Sens Chrétien*' (October 1967).

grace comes to men through Christ, whether the teaching of the Gospel is known or not and even when there is knowledge of this teaching and it has been rejected through prejudice or misunderstanding but with a good conscience.

In *L'Action* Blondel is conducting a purely philosophical or, as he calls it, 'scientific' enquiry. But this does not mean that the facts which he discloses are facts which will be inevitably accepted. It is possible to shut one's eyes to facts of this sort at any point. The 'great option' may be preceded by many minor options. Finding things out is not just something which happens to us. Sometimes it requires effort on our part. It is something which we *do*. It is an *action*. And it is not just a question of keeping our eyes open. A willingness to accept the truth is something which affects our whole being. It involves a commitment not only to whatever may prove to be the truth but also to whatever consequences for ourselves may prove to follow. 'True philosophy', Blondel wrote, 'is the sanctity of the reason.'[1]

L'Action is a phenomenology of human experience.[2] It shows on different levels and with increasing profundity a certain significant pattern in human experience rather as Teilhard de Chardin shows in *The Phenomenon of Man* a significant pattern in the evolutionary process. There is a 'logic of action'. We trace it at work from the level of mere sensation to the recognition of moral freedom and of the solidarity of the human race. No stage makes sense until we see what it is leading to, and so we are pressed onwards until we reach an ideal of human morality. And this is the stage at which so many people dig themselves in. They are not prepared to go beyond the human. They are trying to find absolute value in human activity alone (that is what Blondel calls 'superstition'). But this does not make sense either. The dialectic, the 'logic of action', demands that we should go further. Yet we are at the end of our resources. Something is necessary; yet it is inaccessible. We can *do* nothing about it, but we cannot get on without it. This is the point at which the *transcendent* makes its appearance, becoming immanent. It is 'the supernatural', but as yet anonymous, 'undetermined'. And so this is where the 'great option' takes place. We must simply hand ourselves over at this point, acknowledging our creatureliness. We must accept

---

[1] *L'Action*, 442.
[2] An analysis of it will be found in Fr J. M. Somerville's recent book, *Total Commitment: Blondel's 'L'Action'*.

AN OUTLINE OF THEISM

God's love. That is our great action, our total submission to the total truth, our passivity to the divine action. Only then can an awareness of God become a personal union with him. But that lies on the far side of mere philosophy.

It will perhaps bring out the force of this more effectively if I concentrate briefly on the final stage of this analysis, in which Blondel employs a distinction (already employed at each previous stage) between the willing which the will actually does in concrete fact and the will which does the willing, the distinction between the *volunté voulue* and the *volunté voulante*. The latter he calls 'the original essential aspiration' of the human will which is revealed by the analysis even in those cases when its existence is being denied. The former is the willing of this or that particular object which is never *adequate* to the *volunté voulante*. We find that our wills are in a sort of constraint or enslavement, and this means that we must be envisaging a state of perfect freedom. We are constrained to *seek* our freedom and constrained to accept the 'logic of action' in order to seek it. These constraints are senseless unless they bring us to our freedom. How do they do this? By bringing us to the source of our freedom so that we can accept it for what it is and make it our own at last.

So far this may seem to do little more than repeat St Augustine's famous words about the restlessness of the human heart. But Blondel puts a further twist on it. We are forced to be free, as Sartre has also said. But we cannot take refuge in Sartre's 'absurdity'. The will acts as a constraint upon itself. To be really free, it seems, it would have to choose *itself*, ratify itself, so to speak.[1] But this is just what it cannot do. It can only choose particular objects *for* itself. It cannot get rid of itself, but it cannot get at itself to make itself free by closing the gap between itself and its actual choosing. That is why something is necessary, but inaccessible. This is the point at which the *source* of the will makes its presence felt in our experience. The will is revealed as deriving from a source; because we *must* will ourselves *freely*, our freedom is to be found only beyond ourselves. It is only by uniting ourselves with the will's source that we can unite with it because it is only in its derivation from its source that it exists.

---

[1] In accepting itself as deriving from God and finding its destiny in him it frees itself from its state of enslavement and acquires a positive freedom. The exercise of *moral* freedom, the freedom to accept or reject, is the necessary precondition of this—we might call that a negative freedom.

Otherwise we have only a shadow of freedom, not the real thing. 'We attain the infinite', as Blondel puts it, 'only by *appropriating* nothing for ourselves.'[1] This is a *supernatural* relationship.

People tend to think of the supernatural (when it does not mean for them merely poltergeists and so forth) as a relationship with God in which we believe but of which we are in no way conscious, a realm of mystery of which we are assured by the Christian Revelation, a religious 'extra' which we take 'on faith'. For Blondel, and, as we shall see in some detail later, for the genuine theological tradition, the supernatural enters into our experience. But we have first to realize that we have need of it. Mere philosophy must first recognize its own incapacity to solve the problem which has arisen for it. This recognition is itself an awareness of God, because, as Pascal pointed out, we cannot seek for something unless we already have some knowledge of what it is. We recognize a *summons*. We are offered something. We cannot provide ourselves with what is offered—we can only prepare ourselves for receiving it. And if we are really prepared, really willing to face the consequences, we shall receive it. Philosophy can bring us to the point at which we know that we have a *duty* to hold ourselves ready for God's gift, the gift of grace. And although this knowledge is a knowledge of God, it is a knowledge in which we cannot rest. This 'natural' knowledge of God is not a state in which we can settle down but a stage on the journey to the supernatural. We are not compelled to pass beyond it. It is possible for us to move backwards, away from the supernatural. If we do move on, we enter into a personal relationship with God. We begin to see, in some sort explicitly, *who* God is.

So when earlier on I was making certain claims about who God is, I had already passed beyond the bounds of mere philosophy—but not beyond the bounds of our experience, for we all live under the Christian dispensation and the knowledge of God, supernatural as well as natural, is available for us all if we do not draw back from it. Nowadays one associates this theme of the pervasiveness of the supernatural with Karl Rahner's 'supernatural existential'. Rahner has acknowledged the kinship of Blondel's thought with his own in this matter, but the influence of Blondel's thought upon him has been indirect (if Blondel had been his philosophical prophet instead of Heidegger, there might

[1] *L'Action*, 339.

have been less occasion for the *bon mot* attributed to Hugo Rahner: that he was thinking of translating his brother's works into German). A contemporary theologian on whom Blondel's influence has been direct, and who has done more perhaps than anyone else to put his thought into currency,[1] is P. de Lubac and I must say something at this point about his own decisive contribution to the subject of the supernatural. We shall then be in a better position to evaluate Blondel's 'Christian Metaphysic'.

Surnaturel, de Lubac's most famous book, appeared in 1946 and was vigorously attacked on the ground that it confused the supernatural with the natural. We need not undertake a general defence of its orthodoxy. It is enough to say that the positions taken up in that book were reaffirmed twenty years later, with approval from the highest quarters, in a couple of volumes the second of which, *Le Mystère du Surnaturel*,[2] I have had occasion already to refer to in connection with the topic of God's freedom. The aspect of de Lubac's case which we need to notice here is that which establishes, or rather re-establishes, the doctrine that there is only one possible *end* for man, the supernatural one. It might indeed seem obvious that man would not be what he is if he were not, in fact, destined, as Christians believe, after death to the vision of God 'face to face'. But there had been an insistence on the fact that this destiny is not something which we can claim as of right (a reaction against talk which might suggest that we could), and it had led to the view that what is *natural* for man (and claimable as of right) is a knowledge of God which is something less than this vision. The vision itself was then thought of as a gratuitous 'extra', thrown in (so to speak) by God as a peculiar and unnecessary privilege, without which man would still be man. And anyone who attacked this view was thought to be attacking the rights of God by *claiming* the vision from him. De Lubac had to point out that this whole way of talking about God must be rejected. We cannot *claim* anything at all from him. Our very existence is his first gift to us. His second gift to us, the gift of grace, the gift of himself, is just as gratuitous as the first. But he makes us what we are in order that we may receive this

[1] But the most important book on Blondel will prove, I think, to be P. Henri Bouillard's *Blondel et le Christianisme* (1961). I have followed here his interpretation of Blondel's thesis about the supernatural. This has been contested in several works by Henry Duméry. If anyone wants to say that it is not Blondel's thesis, I need only remark that it is in any case mine.

[2] Now available in English from Chapman, *The Mystery of the Supernatural*.

second gift. The natural is *for* the supernatural and cannot be accounted for except in reference to it. Man is not a person who *can be given* a supplementary destiny. He is a person who *has* a supernatural one.

It is important to reject the theory of a 'natural end' because it makes the supernatural an intrusion upon man's nature. If we could get on perfectly well without the supernatural we might even resent its requirements. So we had better make sure that de Lubac's thesis does obviate such a theory in a satisfactory way. The Encyclical *Humani Generis* rejected the view that 'God could not create beings possessed of intelligence without ordering them and summoning them to the beatific vision.' De Lubac is not flying in the face of this. What he is saying is that such a created being would not be *man*. And it does not follow that a creature which has a supernatural end is itself supernatural. What follows is that, unlike 'natural objects', it has an end which cannot be attained by its native capacities, an end which is infinitely beyond the natural sphere from which it starts out. It also follows that, since it has this end, it has a 'natural desire' for it. Unless nature is conceived of not merely statically but also dynamically, as *ordered to* the supernatural, there can be no true Christian anthropology. It is fitting that the famous last chapter of *Surnaturel* should contain in its first paragraph a quotation from Blondel's *L'Action*. We may conclude this topic with a quotation from Professor Bernard Häring: 'Our nature as individuals and the place of each of us in creation rest on the fact that we are called by God in this way, can understand and answer him. So it is not the case that we exist first of all—that we are existent beings—and then, in addition to this, have been called by God. We are what we are because God has called us.'[1]

We have now to investigate more closely the implications of this 'call', and I propose to do so by considering certain passages from Blondel's *Le Sens Chrétien*.[2] His style is somewhat tortuous and in translation it will be, I fear, still less agreeable. But what he is saying is very much to the point. It is not enough, he says, just to speak of God's goodness in raising us to the supernatural level for 'what we have to make people understand is that this

---

[1] *The New Covenant* (Eng. trans. of *Gabe und Auftrag der Sakramente*), 22.
[2] Published in 1950 together with a companion piece, *De L'Assimilation*, by the Presses Universitaires de France, under the general title *Exigences Philosophiques du Christianisme*. It seems to be virtually unknown outside France.

very goodness imposes upon us a requirement which might seem at first paradoxical, tyrannical, even unjust and repellent. I have received a nature and I have not the right to remain simply faithful to this nature, disregarding a further offer which is described as gratuitous and which, moreover, cannot be accepted, utilized and justified except on condition of my transcending, rejecting and sacrificing this human nature . . . must we fall back, as people have so often done, upon the consideration that God is the absolute master of his creatures . . . and can impose upon them whatever he thinks good from his own sovereign point of view?' That, says Blondel, will not do. It is a question not of a 'jealous egoism which demands a blindly passive submission' but of 'a charity which, for our good, our dignity, our beatitude, is not content with a semi-elevation, a distant participation in the infinite beatitude'. For 'it is not in the last analysis a matter of depressing or curbing our natural being, but of employing the indispensable means for exalting, purifying and deifying man himself in the fullest measure without taking away his manhood. . . .'[1]

God's purpose in creating, Blondel continues later (here following St Thomas), is to multiply intelligent beings for eternal life, to produce other 'selves' like himself, but isn't this, he asks, metaphysically impossible? 'God remains indeed the incommunicable in himself, and yet he communicates something of this very incommunicability; there is no other God than God: there is no other beatitude, said St Thomas, than the divine beatitude; it is indeed that which is given to us, but it remains the property of God even though it is, by grace, our own fruition, in the technical language of theologians. Does this make clear the terms of the new problem which we are now called upon to resolve? God has found the means, not only of giving us what is other than himself but of giving us himself. . . .'[2] This 'new problem' is the problem of 'deification', and Blondel's first answer to it, I shall suggest, is not wholly satisfactory: 'In order to summon us to share his own felicity, God, Being-in-Itself, pure act and infinite charity, could not be content with creatures which should be mere passivity. If they were to be in his image and likeness, they must be able to produce and even, in a sense, to produce themselves so as to become like their author, *causa sui*. But how could such a creation take place? We can produce from our own resources only caricatures of being, and all our

[1] 124–7.   [2] 136–7.

aspirations to divinity lead, when they claim to satisfy themselves, only to idolatry. All that can liberate us is absolute detachment from our egoism, the substitution of the divine will in ourselves for our own ways, the renunciation of our purely human ambitions so as really to leave room for the divine action.'[1]

There are truths of great value in all this. It is no doubt true that the measure of our future beatitude is the degree of our courage in a trial which is only apparently a harsh one, but in reality the means of attaining the perfect joy. But the problem of 'deification' is stated rather than solved by the language which Blondel is using about it. In *what* sense can a creature become *causa sui*? Blondel speaks in this same place of 'restoring to God that empire over ourselves of which he had voluntarily deprived himself so that we may voluntarily restore it to him by our love'. We cannot take literally the suggestion that God could be *deprived* of anything. But a later passage, which involves some repetition but which cannot be conveniently condensed, Blondel offers us something more promising (he is concerned with the technical expression 'God's external glory'):

'It is a strange expression. . . . Glory is, first of all, in God himself, the plenitude which is concentrated in itself, which cannot be exhausted or increased or outwardly expressed. But there is also the external or, as theologians call it, "accidental" glory of God; and here we have to be on our guard against false analogies and unsatisfactory explanations. Too often people think to glorify God by representing him as a master who demands adulation and servility; and the rigorous requirements of his precepts and of our trials and mortifying transformations are interpreted along those lines. But the truth seems to be much greater and much finer. Let us dare to use the crudest and most childish words and say that the external glory of God is not an expansion of his divinity outside itself, as when a sphere expands with the excess of its own power and heat, but the production of other beings, real beings which as such have their own value, beings capable of knowing, loving and in some sense possessing God himself by sharing in his beatitude; so that, without going forth from himself, without creating other gods, God nevertheless lives himself in other "selves"; they are what they are, and so they remain eternally distinct from their author, and yet they are he in par-

[1] 137-8.

ticipating in his divine life. What could be more glorious than this expansion . . . ? This glory is indeed, in a sense, external to God; and yet again it is always the one same light or charity or beatitude which radiates in this celestial city. That is the vision which the Christian metaphysic presents to us. . . .'[1]

What Blondel is trying to say seems to emerge clearly enough in this passage, but he is not content to say it clearly. It is entirely obvious throughout his book that he is anxious to avoid any suggestion of a *confusion* between God and man, yet he often falls back into language which *of itself* does imply just this. The language which (I suggest) *says* what he wants to say, the language of possessing God by knowledge and love, he seems to regard as insufficient. It is because he has so keen an awareness of the difference between our knowledge and love of God and any other human condition that he is not content with this language, and the language which he uses instead belongs, in principle, to a Christian tradition. From St Peter onwards, Christians have talked about 'participating in the divinity', and 'deification' is an accepted expression in the West as well as in the East. But it has always been clear that it is a human condition, not the abolition of our creaturely status. In a philosophical context, where the language which we use should be as much 'disinfected' as possible, we do not expect the language of 'deification' to be the ultimate language of any theorizing which we may feel called upon to undertake. Blondel's language of 'other selves', which insists on some sort of reproduction of *himself* on God's part, seems to imply that in the last analysis it is the language of 'deification' which we must adopt. I want to say, on the other hand, that it is the language of knowledge and love which we must adopt.

It is true that we have to speak of an 'assimilation' of creatures to God in so far as they are found to be in some sense 'like' him. But 'likeness', as we have seen, is a word forced upon us here in our attempt to describe a unique relationship. We concluded that we should have to say that we are 'reflections' of God, a sort of distant echo of the perfections which are united, fused as it were, in his infinity. But we do not literally *share* anything with him even in the beatific vision. He is always the Other. We could not be united with him if he were not. Union, as everyone knows and as Blondel himself insists, is not unity, but the coming

[1] 145.

together of distinct elements, which remain distinct. And if we are speaking of the union of persons, a conscious union, must we not mean the union of knowledge and love? What other union is conceivable? To say that this is not enough, that there must be some closer union, although we cannot in any way conceive of it, is to make the same mistake as those who say that we know nothing about God although we must affirm that he exists. It is to say that we have no idea what heaven may be like—and in that case it is meaningless for us to talk about it. Eye has not seen, indeed, nor ear heard—but if we have no *inkling* of the truth we cannot know that it is there for us. Why is Blondel not satisfied with the account of union which I have been suggesting? One reason is clear: he thinks (mistakenly) that the Thomist account of the beatific vision is coldly intellectualist, and is anxious to dissociate himself from it. It must be allowed to his Thomist critics that he does sometimes caricature Thomism. It remains curious that his own doctrine of loving knowledge, of knowledge which is not fully itself without love, should not have been his guide at this point. No doubt he was impressed by the tendency of theologians to insist upon an 'ontological' change which is said to take place in the union of grace and still more in that of glory. It seems to me that there has been a great deal of unnecessary mystification in these connections. Certainly we cannot be too careful to avoid any rationalizing of the Christian mystery which would evacuate its transcendent uniqueness; but at the same time we must avoid expressions which are plainly contradictory or meaningless. No doubt the Christian is a 'new creature', radically transformed and raised to new powers. No doubt the consummate union of our spiritual faculties with the Three Persons of the Trinity is beyond our understanding—but, to repeat, we must have some clue to it. And there seems to be no other clue but the nature of those faculties themselves.

When St Thomas, following Aristotle, tells us that the mind is 'in some sort everything', he seems to be following the only clue to the meaning of such expressions as 'becoming God'. It is natural to say that we 'become' what we know and love, despite the objections of contemporary philosophers to this sort of language, because (if we are to this extent Platonists) there is a direct confrontation of the mind by its object. The prejudice against this account of knowledge is strong, as we have seen; I hope we have also seen that there is no ground for it. It is the fundamental characteristic of human awareness that it is united, in a way which we cannot describe, with its object. It cannot be described because it is fundamental. We cannot get outside our experience in order to talk about it. This seems to be the ultimate significance of union, and it does not seem to be meaningful to talk about human experience or awareness except in terms of it. If this is the basic law of human experience, then, since we remain human in heaven, even the beatific vision will not transgress it. Many theologians have taken up with theories of knowledge which reject this Platonist realism. As a result, what they say about our present knowledge of God is, to my mind, unsatisfactory, and when they speak of the beatific vision they acknowledge that their theory does not apply to it and in effect take refuge, illegitimately, in mystery. On the Platonist view, it is possible to give a fuller meaning to the thesis that grace is the seed of glory. Our present knowledge involves a genuine contact with God, however slight, and the beatific vision is its fulfilment.

It would be presumptuous to lay down the law on a matter of this kind, and I am really doing no more than raising a question. Can we conceive of a spiritual union which is not in fact an absorption or confusion except as the sort of union which is found in human *awareness*, 'intentional union' as the scholastics call it? Does it make sense to talk of a union which should be somehow between the two? There is high authority on the side of saying that there is such a half-way house. But, if the question is a legitimate one, it is important to ventilate it because so much that has been written about 'created grace' and 'uncreated grace' seems to depend on the answer. If there is no half-way house, the ecumenical dialogue might be, in these respects, considerably simplified.

If, with these possibilities in mind, we turn back to Blondel's answer to his questions, certain simplifications will perhaps suggest themselves. If we are to attain God, he has told us, we must act—we cannot be purely passive. We cannot attain him except freely.[1] That love must be free, that we cannot attain God simply by being caught up to him willy-nilly, is something, I suggest, which we can dimly understand because we have some dim awareness of who he is. He is not the sort of person who can be otherwise approached. Blondel explains our activity, in the

[1] That is, we must exercise moral freedom in order to attain the fulfilment of our natures, freedom from their deficiencies.

last analysis, in terms of our self-renunciation. And perhaps we can interpret that as follows. A creature has, *ex hypothesi*, its own finite nature. It must first know itself in its finite surroundings before God can approach it. His approach *is* its awareness of him. But this is not yet knowledge of God in the full sense. That knowledge is a possession—God's possession of us and so ours of him. And there is always the danger that we may use our power to refuse him. Because he is who he is, his creatures must have this negative power. Unless they evade this hazard, God's second gift of possession cannot be theirs. It is theirs not only because it is his gift to them but because they have evaded the hazard. They have renounced themselves—that is to say, God has taken them to himself and they have not refused him. They are in the end wholly his—and wholly themselves. Knowledge of the truth is itself a self-renunciation. Unless we are willing to expose ourselves wholly, as it were, to the object we shall not really know it. It then possesses us and makes us what we are. This is freedom in the positive sense. 'You will know the truth, and the truth will set you free.'[1]

More light will be shed on this 'Christian metaphysic' if we consider a passage in which Blondel applies his principles to the doctrine of original sin:

'It has been sometimes asked what would have been the condition of humanity if there had been no original Fall and how this single trial could have conditioned the whole of history. Our previous considerations will help us to elucidate a difficulty which has proved a stumbling block to certain minds, namely that the plan of providence seems to have been subject to a succession of afterthoughts or arbitrary interventions. . . . But there is in fact nothing more coherent than the biblical narrative if, while accepting certain data as historical but without being obliged to take the details literally, we examine the inner meaning of the facts. What we are taught is that in man's original state a certain prohibition restricted the range of human curiosity and human ambition. Of what nature could this prohibition be, addressed to a being in its native simplicity and, if one may say so, its simple-mindedness? Adapting itself to the infancy of that sentient and hungry being, the human *compositum*, the trial seems to have been concerned with that renunciation which God requires so as

[1] John 8: 32.

to obtain the sacrifice of natural aspirations both on the side of the flesh and on that of the intelligence. The fruit of the "tree of the knowledge of good and evil" was the spontaneous and, as it were, natural covetousness corresponding to the original gift of a rational nature. Yet that is what had to be forbidden if man was to remain in the right relationship to God; and such a renunciation, which seemed to frustrate his noblest ambition, could not fail to seem onerous and to provoke a temptation to an outraged pride and a redoubled covetousness: *non serviam*.'[1]

Taken by itself, this passage would not succeed in stopping the mouths of objectors. It still sounds like the description of a rather raw deal. But if Blondel's previous statements are kept in mind, it should appear, I think, despite its rhetorical form,[2] as a fruitful application of his principles. And the passage which follows will perhaps seem more satisfactory:

'This gives us some clue to the possibility of a fall which has often been judged implausible; for, it has been so often said, before ignorance and concupiscence, which appear only as consequences of the original revolt, how could a temptation find its way into the heart of man who was naturally sound and pure, and enlightened by God? The answer is that for Adam, as for the angels who were also, according to traditional teaching, subjected to the necessity of a decisive option, the trial to surmount is of such a nature that intellectual evidence and natural rectitude are not enough to ensure a triumph: there is also necessary a generosity which proceeds from the depths of one's being, which means facing an obscurity and a sort of immolation, a sort of death. In every case, indeed, the approach to supernatural life requires the sacrifice of the most fundamental and most legitimate of our natural endowments, even before we can see or taste the reward of such a holocaust.'[3]

Blondel may still seem to be laying it on rather thick. We may prefer to think that our first parents might have found the surrender of themselves to God a less frightening business if,

---

[1] 139–40.
[2] and despite a more literal interpretation of Genesis than we should make today.
[3] 140–1.

after all, nature is for the supernatural. But Blondel's general conception of the relation between the two, or rather the traditional conception rediscovered by him, does seem requisite for any tolerable solution. The reference to the fall of the angels is not to be considered as just a sort of polite gesture to traditional teaching. It is an all-important element in the traditional 'Christian metaphysic' which Blondel is restating for his time. The impossibility of attaining to God without choosing him finds its supreme instance in the trial of angels: and those who fall drag down with them in some sort the material world below them—for the created universe, according to this doctrine, is a whole of interrelated parts, and a failure on a higher level has repercussions on a lower one. The fundamental importance of this for the problem of evil as a whole will be immediately apparent.

I have been making a sort of advance raid on Christian theology, and it may perhaps help to make such a proceeding less objectionable if I end with a few remarks about the nature of this theology. It is an enquiry into that body of teaching which is handed down to us from the time of the Apostles. 'Handed down', however, is a phrase which can be misleading. It does not mean that certain propositions are simply passed on, guaranteed officially as true, from one generation of Christians to the next. Each generation has to *think* Christianity for itself, and in this process it may find more than had been found before (not merely by logical explicitation but by deeper penetration) or it may find less (as in an age when obscurantist tendencies exercise an inhibiting influence). The true notion of tradition, as implying development as well as stability, is another notion which has been restored to us more by Blondel than by anyone else, Newman not excepted. (Blondel was so far from being a 'Modernist' that his reply to Loisy, *Histoire et Dogme*, is the basic refutation of the Modernist position.)

Some Christian doctrines can be usefully envisaged merely as hypotheses, as I have been suggesting, but for a proper understanding of the Christian mysteries they must be considered in the light of faith, that is, in the light of that knowledge of God which is available to those who accept the gift of grace. It is this knowledge which gives a meaning to these mysteries, to the words in which they are declared, without which assent to them is only 'notional', not real. When, for example, we hear that in

God there are three Persons and one Nature, we cannot expect to make anything of it unless we bear in mind who God is. The knowledge of faith does provide us with a criterion for distinguishing, if once we realize that we *can* think about God, between the sense which we hear talked about him and the nonsense. (For example, a theologian once committed himself to the statement—in a dictionary of Catholic theology—that God, if he had loved us more, could have done without hell altogether; we may not have answers to all questions about hell, but we can realize that this statement is nonsense if we bring our minds to bear on it.) Belief in the Trinity should not mean just a passive acceptance of a statement that a certain collection of human concepts does apply, somehow or other, to God. Faith gives us a line on how they do apply. This is not to suggest that we have an insight into the life of the Trinity of such a kind that we intuit the three Persons as one Nature. But it means at least this: that we have some positive knowledge of God and that the concept of a plurality of persons in society is to be used in the light of it; in other words, that created value which we call a society, the sort of good which cannot be achieved by a single man but only by a community, proves to be found in an unlimited form (distinct human beings are always limits for one another) in the life of God.

St Paul in his letter to the Ephesians[1] speaks of 'the Father of our Lord Jesus Christ' as 'that Father from whom all fatherhood in heaven and earth takes its title'. The relation between a father and a son, that is to say, is a special sort of created value, a 'reflection' of a divine relationship. But it is not my purpose here to embark on a theology of the Trinity. I have wished only to suggest by means of this example that theologizing should not involve the abdication of intelligence.

10. EVIL

The problem of evil is a problem for a theist; it is the problem of God's governance of the world and therefore includes the problem of God's providence. And as soon as God's providence is mentioned, there is a tendency for people to throw up their hands in despair. This, they may say, is a completely insoluble problem and perhaps a mystery which we have no business to probe. I propose to say that we can think profitably about providence. The

[1] 3: 14

subject, I believe, has been approached in wrong ways with results which are certainly calculated to put people off the whole business. It has become bogged down in controversies between theological schools which have been so eager to refute one another's particular theses that certain general considerations which ought to control the discussion have been simply overlooked. I say this in advance, because anyone who supposed that I am going to discuss the matter in the old familiar way might very reasonably refuse to take an interest in it.

Let us go back for a start to the fact of our moral freedom and take up the topic, adumbrated earlier on, of our power to refuse God's offers. To say that we have the power to make moral *choices* (not just to decide things as our circumstances dictate to us) is to say that we have a power of initiative. And 'initiative' should be taken to imply a full responsibility. We are capable of something which has an absolute quality about it—our decision originates absolutely from ourselves. Now if we are going to acknowledge God as the source of being, the source of all positive increase in the sum of things, it follows that we cannot claim also for ourselves an initiative in the production of being. An initiative which is absolutely ours could be, therefore, only an initiative of a negative kind, an initiative in *refusing* God's offers of actuation. I realize that such a proposal is in the highest degree offensive to most modern ears. It seems to suggest that man is only a puppet in the hands of God, that he cannot co-operate with God in the world's development; it seems to degrade him and to involve a most depressing view of his status in the world. I hope to show that it means nothing of the sort—just the opposite in fact—but I know that this will seem paradoxical, at any rate when it is first suggested. For the moment I can do little except ask for patience. But I can perhaps make the point at once that for man to stand on his dignity before God, to make claims for himself against God's supposed encroachments on his own preserves, is to imply some notion of God which for me is wholly unacceptable. In the end it will come down to the question: 'What do we mean by "God" '? In what follows it will at least become clearer what I mean by 'God'. And I hope it may become clear eventually that if we do not mean this there is no point in talking about God at all. I should add that what I mean by God is not some merely personal theory of my own. Anyone who has some acquaintance with Christian thought down the ages will recognize that the

God of whom I speak is properly to be called the God of Christians. To say that he is the source of being is to say that he is the source of all good because it is fundamentally in terms of *value* (whether we realize this explicitly or not) that we discover him, so I have maintained. It follows, I repeat, that we exercise an absolute initiative only in *refusing* the good. And this is what 'spiritual writers', those whose experience of God is clearer than that of other people, have regularly said. When we face the problem of evil, it is this fact of our initiative in refusing which is all-important. If we accept it, we can develop a metaphysic which is free from contradiction, which is *thinkable*, although naturally not without obscurity because we, as creatures, cannot expect to find everything pellucid: our relation to God can be sufficiently understood, but we cannot see it as God sees it because we cannot know God as he knows himself. The important thing is to locate the obscurity correctly so that it becomes acceptable, a stimulus rather than a barrier to thought.

The best way to develop such a metaphysic will probably be to begin by considering a more familiar one which (I venture to think) is at fault only in complicating a truth which is profound indeed but yet essentially simple. So there is no question of producing a radically *new* metaphysic but only of returning to the familiar Thomist one viewed 'experientially'—that is, basing it on experience and removing from it unreal abstractions and systematizations. Sertillanges, then, in his *L'Idée de Création*, written more than twenty years ago and still probably the most valuable Thomist account on the more familiar lines, wrote the following passage about God's power to create beings which are autonomous in their activities:

'God is being, and by creation he communicates his being. He is activity, and by creation he communicates his activity. Those who admit an authentic communication in the first case must admit it also in the second, on pain of being led, by a process of reasoning a *contrario*, to contest the autonomy of created being and thus falling into pantheism. They have not realized that the transcendence of the creative activity allows an action of this kind to respect or rather to posit derived activities, which, despite this derivation, in virtue of it, have their own action, an action which belongs totally to them and totally to the first Cause, and that by reason of the difference between the levels [*plans*] in which they are situated, a difference between orders [of being], the created and the uncreated not entering into composition with one another, not adding to one another, which is the very mystery of creative communication.'[1]

The concluding phrases of this passage are perfectly satisfactory. It is necessary only to remember that the talk about 'levels' and 'orders' must not lead us to think of God as at the top of a *scale* with the created world lower down on it. We must simply affirm God as Other in affirming ourselves as mysteriously 'like' him. We cannot help *talking* about a scale of 'being', but we have to bear constantly in mind the experience which lies behind such talk and to which it must always be referred. We need not, then, be put off by the opening words of the passage; the great value of Sertillanges' book lies in his keen awareness of God's transcendence, and by the 'communication of being' he certainly does not mean that anything is literally *shared* by the Creator and his creatures. He constantly insists that God is the *source* of being and that, when we say this, we cannot use the word 'being' *of* him in the same breath. But he does not seem to realize that, just as 'communication of being' is an expression which requires careful analysis, so does 'communication of activity'. To be a creature is to receive the gift of oneself from God, to be wholly dependent on him for what one *is* and so wholly dependent upon him for what one positively *does*. Sertillanges, with this talk of a 'communicated activity' as an 'autonomy', seems to be saying that God grants us an initiative not only in the refusal but also in the production of 'being'. To deny this is not to deny that our actions are ours. It is only to insist that they are God's gifts to created persons and cannot cease to be such when they are 'taken over' by these persons.

The sort of language which Sertillanges has been using here about 'autonomy' has led to metaphysical obscurity of an unnecessary kind, to obscurity in the wrong place. It suggests that God gives us our moral freedom by a kind of abdication, that, although he has complete control over everybody and everything, he somehow resigns his rights where persons are concerned and allows them to function on their own. This, indeed, is the really splendid thing about God's creation, so we are told—that he should create persons who can be really originators like himself.

[1] 95.

But surely, if we are to think straight, we must regard such language as rhetorical. If we took it literally, should we not undermine the very basis of theism, the experience on which it rests?[1] It may sound all right at first; it may suggest some deeper understanding of God's generosity, but it is irreconcilable, I make bold to say, with what we know of God.

It will be objected, no doubt, that this is to return to the errors of Descartes and Malebranche for whom God's creatures had no 'natures' of their own but were mere automata in God's hands. But I am not a follower of Descartes or Malebranche in this matter, and I am not saying that we are automata. It is always possible for us to refuse God's gifts; to accept them is always to escape a hazard. But our willingness to accept is itself a gift of God, and this the Thomists have very clearly seen in their controversies with the Molinists. In that context they very properly insist that we cannot leave God out of things even when we are talking about our acceptances. Unfortunately they have so often failed to realize that, when it is a matter of *sin*, we *must* leave God out of it. An abstract notion of God's omnipotence has led them to suppose that, even in the matter of sin, God must be somehow in control of the situation. But *that* situation is the one for which we, and we alone, are responsible. It is this mysterious 'negative' power, bound up with the creaturely condition, which is the real obscurity.

It may seem strange that the Thomists should insist sometimes on our independence in a way which seems to give us a share in God's own creative activity and yet insist on God's omnicausality even in regard to our refusals. In the passage quoted from Sertillanges there is a formula which sums up this attempt to have things both ways: 'an action which belongs totally to them [derived activities] and totally to the first Cause, and that by reason of the difference between the levels on which they are situated'. There is insistence on the creature's independence, but an attempt at the same time to safeguard the rights of God, and this leads to such paradoxical assertions as that 'we are free, but God makes us free', of which all that can be said is that an appearance of profundity is given to what is (in this context) really meaningless. He makes us free to choose in that he creates us with that negative power which seems to be of necessity bound

---

[1] The experience of our value as deriving from, completely dependent upon, absolute value.

up with our nature, the nature of an intelligent creature summoned to know and love him. But he cannot *make* us love him, and that is what Thomists seem to be saying when they say 'he makes us free'. In another sense of freedom, in which it means the fulfilment of our capacities ('God's service is perfect freedom') God does make us free, for this is his gift to us. But the Thomists are talking about *choice*. And either we have independence, a power to refuse, or we have not. We cannot have it both ways. The difference between 'levels' is adduced in justification of this meaningless language, but the difference between 'levels' belongs, as we have seen, to a language of 'being' which requires interpretation in the light of our experience. And our experience does not force us to take up with paradoxical, mutually exclusive, notions. It tells us that we are wholly dependent upon God both for what we are now and for what we may grow to be—but that we can cut ourselves off from him if we decide independently to do so.

This approach to a subject which is usually thought of as indefinitely complex is certain to seem at first absurdly simple-minded. And it does seem at first to *deny* our moral freedom. To say that we can do nothing entirely of ourselves except to refuse God's gifts will seem to reduce us, not indeed to mere puppets, but to passive recipients who can be genuinely active only by rebellion. But it is in passivity to God's action upon us that our true activity consists, and sinfulness is not in a true sense activity at all. Sinfulness consists, by general admission, simply in the rejection of God. When we sin there is usually something which we want, a real something, a good therefore (the Thomists are quite clear about this): what is wrong about it is that it will lead, in the circumstances, to some kind of negation or destruction which we have no right to bring about. We go against our consciences, that is, against God. We reject the right alternative. Once we have done this, the attraction of the 'apparent' good, the good which leads to negation, operates upon us inevitably. God has so made us that we are moved towards good, the real good if we do not reject it, the 'apparent' good if we do. And this, as I have just been urging, is no arbitrary arrangement. It is what it means to be an intelligent creature. How can it be supposed that we should 'fall into pantheism' by an insistence that all good comes from God and is never exclusively ours if we add that all evil comes from us and in no way derives from him? How, indeed, could we be in danger of this when our very starting-point has been the joint affirmation of ourselves and of God as other?

The main issue, I want to emphasize, is capable of statement in straightforward terms. If we say (as we naturally tend to say at first) that God has provided us with the wherewithal for actions and left it to us to *produce* our own actions, then we are faced, not with a mystery, but with a contradiction for our thought. We cannot subtract anything *valuable* from the sphere of God's power because it is as the source of value that we come to know him; this, then, is what we must *mean* by God, and we cannot take this back without ceasing to be theists. Moral evil is a fact, a reality for which we must be responsible. But it is not a *valuable* reality—just the opposite. This does not, of course, mean that there is a sort of common stuff called 'reality', divided into two kinds. It means that we are aware of value and also of its opposite. What is common to these objects of our knowledge is simply that we are aware of them—we call 'reality' whatever we are aware of—but in themselves they are just different. We have to accept the fact of our responsibility for evil as an ultimate fact. Something has been said already about *how* it arises—it is the hazard which intelligent creatures necessarily face—but in itself it is ultimate and mysterious. It is a fact that we can see what is good and yet choose what is evil.

But we seem to have been saying that we are empowered by God to do acts which cause evil. How are we to make sense of this? It is all very well to make God responsible for the physicality of acts and to attribute a wrong intention, a rejection of him, to ourselves alone, but how can we say that pressing a trigger is *good* if it results in the blowing out of some innocent person's brains? What we must presumably say is that where physical acts are concerned there is always something positive which is aimed at. Anybody who blows out my brains will have a reason for it, however mad I might think it. The action will represent itself to him, perhaps, as the only means to a quiet life for himself. He is drawn to this good, and he refuses to consider the other factors in the situation. This may or may not be part and parcel of an all-out rebellion against God. (The ultimate moral situation—our moral relation to God—can so easily fail to be clear-cut that theist philosophers are coming more and more to take up with the notion that it becomes so for many people only in the separating of soul from body at the moment of death.) An internal act of rebellion against God must also have a motive—in this case it seems to be a bogus sort of self-preservation. Real self-preservation is the handing over of ourselves to God, which means the taking over of ourselves by God without interference on our part. It is this interference which is effected by the negative power, the power of refusal, but it represents itself to the sinner as the means to a positive advantage, the maintenance of his own independence. Moving out from oneself requires a kind of courage, and the sinner is not prepared to make the effort. He wants to remain as he is—and what he is in itself is good. Self-attachment is not evil in itself; the self is not destroyed but completed by moving outwards. It is the refusal to move outwards and nothing else in which moral evil consists, and it may result inevitably (as in the killing of the innocent) in physical evil.[1] God is responsible for the world-order which he creates, not for our refusals and their consequences.[2]

We must now consider more closely this world-order. If our previous conclusions have been sound, it is not just one of an infinite number of possible world-orders, but just *the* world-order. It does not make sense to suggest that it could be altered.[3] It is the 'moving image of eternity' and contains, as such, no evil—but it does contain, necessarily, the possibility of evil. In the Thomist account the necessary imperfection of creatures leads inevitably to collisions between them. Physical evil is therefore dismissed with a shrug of the shoulders as something which has to be accepted if there is to be creation at all. This robust treatment of the problem of evil seems to belong to a mentality which may justly be called out-of-date, like the attitude of mind which could regard the burning of heretics as in order—we may reasonably claim that there has been progress in such matters. We cannot

---

[1] I am considering moral evil here in its 'essence'. What we call moral evil in the minor affairs of life is commonly a distraction from the true, remoter, good by some immediate attraction and may be largely involuntary.

[2] On the whole subject of Providence, but especially on the aspect of it discussed in this paragraph, Dom Mark Pontifex's *Providence and Freedom* (Burns Oates, Faith and Fact Series) should be read.

[3] It is absurd to say that God has no business to create people who, he knows, will reject him. Their rejection of him presupposes their creation. God cannot know what does not exist—he could not be aware of a rejection which will take place without there being a created person to be the subject of it. (He knows the whole course of the world's duration, we must remember, *intemporally*, being 'outside' time.)

accept a God who is directly responsible for physical evil. We must therefore say that it results from moral evil, for which God's intelligent creatures are responsible.

Professor John Hick in *Evil and the God of Love* holds that God has arranged his world with its physical evils as the training-ground for our moral development—and it is inevitable, he tells us, that we should sin, for we can return to God only as his forgiven children. Everything comes right in the end, and there is no permanent separation from him. This sort of solution, although enjoying some popularity at present in certain quarters, will not long survive, I think, the modern challenge to theism. There is involved in it an anthropomorphic notion of God, and a failure to accept the absoluteness of moral responsibility.

It is, apparently, the doctrine of hell which Hick is most anxious to avoid, and one can indeed sympathize with him about this. But it will not do to talk about 'inevitable' sin, unless what is meant is 'material', not 'formal', sin. But 'material' as opposed to 'formal' sin means an *unintended* departure from the moral norm, and there can obviously be no question of repentance or forgiveness for what is, in effect, nothing more than a mistake. If all departures from the moral norm are just mistakes, we are not morally responsible for them—but God is; and Hick has to lay responsibility for all evil on God, for physical evil, since he arranges it for a purpose, and for 'inevitable' moral evil, since that is part of the purpose for which he has arranged it (it is necessary so that the world should be 'a vale of soul-making'). Hick cannot accept the fact that we start life morally innocent and yet have the power to lose this innocence by a deliberate failure. But this is essential to theism. Indeed the fundamental evidence for theism is bound up with this fact of responsibility.[1] Our commonplace moral failures are temporary distractions from God, not rejections of him. But even in these we are aware (or we can be aware) that as moral beings we have a total responsibility which must be exercised as such somehow and at some time. We cannot put off for ever an absolute unrestricted choice. It is possible for us to reject God absolutely. This is the meaning of hell. This state of ultimate failure has been described in lurid ways which we need not stop to criticize. It is enough to say that it is no act on God's part which produces it—it is the inevitable

---

[1] For value exercises a *claim* upon us.

consequence of a choice which it is itself inevitable. It is, perhaps we may say, a sub-human condition.[1]

We may now begin to consider what should be meant by Providence in more concrete terms. Blondel's *Le Sens Chrétien* has already suggested to us how we should regard not only the fall of man but also the fall of the angels as events in the world's history. We must now say something of their effects. But first certain prejudices in regard to these events must be touched on. There is a good deal of prejudice nowadays against the existence of angels at all. This seems to be partly because the theological (biblical) arguments in favour of it have been questioned and partly because philosophers have come to find something scandalous in the notion of a bodiless mind. But there is certainly nothing contradictory about such a notion, and the biblical evidence is not the ground on which I am asking anyone to entertain it. It does indeed seem too much bound up with traditional belief to be dismissed by a believing Christian. But the point for present purposes is that it seems a likely enough element in God's world; if that is God's manifestation of himself, we may reasonably suggest that there are other intelligences who, unlike ourselves, manifest him just as minds. And if this supposition makes it easier to understand the conditions on our planet previous to the emergence of the human race, that gives it added weight. Professor Eric Mascall has pointed out in his Bampton Lectures that the fall of the angels (and their control over the material world) was not thought up to explain those conditions; it was a belief of Christians long before it provided a possible answer to a question which arose in the last century.[2] The prejudice which I have in mind about the fall of man takes the form of objecting that the fall is not an historical event because Adam and Eve are not historical characters—to which it is a sufficient answer that sin must have started sometime.

The possible effects of the fall of the angels can be guessed at only vaguely, but they may be plausibly supposed to explain what seem to us disorders in the state of things in the earlier stages of the evolutionary process and indeed for many things which are or seem to be disorders at the present stage. If the material world was dependent on the angels (according to a law

[1] I have discussed Hick's book in an article published in *The Journal of Theological Studies*, October 1967.
[2] *Christian Theology and Natural Science*, 301–3.

of creaturely solidarity of which something more will be said in a moment), we are entitled to guess that it would have worked in ways very different from those in which in fact it works if there had been no angelic sin. It is *conceivable* that nature would not have been 'red in tooth and claw', that the behaviour of natural phenomena in general would have been in many ways more favourable to ourselves. This sort of thing has often been suggested. But it is a mistake to suppose that this settles all difficulties about the sufferings of the brutes. Our own sufferings have their compensations, sometimes in this world and always, according to Christians, in the next. But if it is said to be unjust that the brutes should suffer, it will not seem any less unjust because angels are to blame for it. The only solution available for us must lie in the difference between human awareness and the life of pure sensation —the brutes do not have what *we mean* by 'suffering'.

Here we may return to Blondel's *Le Sens Chrétien* to quote a paragraph which brings the present discussion to a point:

'In the perspective of the divine plan which is at the same time both a single plan and a plastic one, the same primordial condition imposed itself upon any being summoned to a supernatural vocation, before he could be raised to the *consortium divinum*. What varies [according to man's fidelity or infidelity in the event] is the modality of the elevation, logically contained within the Creator's prevision, so that his design, although gratuitous and imperative, is modified in fact in accordance with the use which man makes of his own free will.

'That answers an objection which has been so often made to the supposedly harsh and arbitrary consequences of the Fall. How, often, before or after Voltaire and Victor Hugo, have people attacked the apparent absurdity of dogmas which seem to present us with the following illogicality: man was blameworthy; to save him it was necessary for him to become more blameworthy still by crucifying Christ. But this is a purely superficial and entirely misconceived argument, which subordinates to the laws of temporal succession and of abstract deduction the eternal order and the implications of spiritual realities.'[1]

We shall be considering the connection between the Fall and the Redemption in another volume. What is to be noticed here is that the consequences of original sin involve no change in

[1] 142.

God's plan and are explained by Blondel in terms of human freedom—but only in the most general way, so that we still want to know why these consequences should be what they are. Why, in short, should they affect the whole race? There is, I suppose, only one acceptable answer: that God intends the best, that the solidarity of the human race, the interdependence of its members, is what is best for us, and that the law of hazard applies to the future of the race as it does to the future of the individual. There is inevitably the risk that men who were created to help one another may instead hinder one another, that the entrance of sin into the world may depress the status, so to say, of all members of the race. (And this principle of solidarity must be extended, as we have seen, to embrace the angelic world.) There is no need to discuss here the precise character of this depressed status. It is enough to observe that, whatever it implies, it cannot imply an unwillingness on God's part to bring men to him. There are difficulties to face which, but for sin, would not have to be faced. But there is still only one obstacle to grace: man's personal and deliberate unwillingness to receive it.

The importance of Blondel's conclusions in this passage lies in his insistence that God's plan is changed only in its working-out at our end. If we resist this plan, certain consequences occur, but God's purpose is always what it is. He wills, always, that all should be saved. What is best for us, at any moment, will depend on the circumstances which we ourselves have brought about; we are solely responsible for what goes wrong and so for the effects of God's unchanging plan upon the circumstances. He is ready to make the best of any situation if we are ready to take it. It seems to be only a matter of religious common sense. But we all know that theologians have quarrelled interminably on the issue of predestination. On the one hand, the Banezian Thomists have maintained that God must be ultimately responsible for everything, that, if grace is not received, it must be, in the last analysis, that God has decided, for his own inscrutable reasons, not to give it. On the other hand, the Molinists have seemed to give up the attempt to preserve God's transcendence by allowing that our free actions can determine the actions of God. One of the most hopeful signs about present-day theology is that theologians are more and more coming to see that this is an absurd *impasse*. That we should be able to add to the sum of things independently of God is metaphysically absurd. But that we should fail to accept

God's offers, obstructing the working-out of his plan and so controlling its effects, without affecting him in any way, is a conclusion which we may indeed find staggering but which we are perfectly entitled to accept. It would be possible to show in detail[1] that is is, in fact, increasingly accepted. I must be content to give a single example of this which is of peculiar significance.

We are accustomed to thinking of M. Maritain as a 'hard' Thomist (he has, in fact, referred to himself in these terms), and it was of particular interest to discover that he had abandoned the doctrine of predestination held by his associates. Twenty-five years ago he announced his agreement with the line of thought which I have been following, that man has a genuine initiative in respect of evil, a purely negative power of turning away from God, the exercise of which has nothing whatever to do with God.[2]

The doctrine can be found in St Thomas, and the question is whether it is to be applied to our present matter so as to rule out the doctrine of the Banezian Thomists, the doctrine that God's refusal to give grace to a sinner is logically anterior to his knowledge of the sinner's demerits. M. Maritain holds that it is to be so applied and in a recent book[3] controverts the views of a theological professor who continues to teach the Banezian doctrine (and who, incidentally, is one of the few contemporary theologians who continue to doubt the orthodoxy of Blondel's fundamental positions). M. Maritains's argument is just that which I have already adduced: that an initiative in respect of evil is an initiative which, so far from being necessarily attributed to God, is necessarily *not* to be attributed to him. It is only the initiative in respect of what is good that must be attributed to him. And it is perfectly obvious to everyone except the Banezian Thomists that God, in their view, is responsible for man's sin. For if he does not give grace, they say, we are bound to sin. And his decision not to give it is not caused by our sin. In fact, it need hardly be said, there is no question of causing God to decide at all. He is always ready to help us. It is we who decide that we are not going to accept his help.

It is amazing that the Banezian doctrine should have obtained so much currency, and it might be suspected that I am producing a caricature of it. But those who are acquainted with the theology

---

[1] For this v. *Novum Tentamen ad Solutionem de Gratia et Praedestinatione*, G. M. Most, Editiones Paulinae, Rome, 1963.
[2] *St Thomas and the Problem of Evil*, Milwaukee, 1942.
[3] *Dieu et la Permission du Mal*, Paris, 1963.

of the Reform will know that just such a doctrine has exercised and still exercises an enormous influence among theologians who are far from agreement with the Banezians in other respects, and indeed among Christians at large. It seems to me that one cannot take up an eirenic attitude in regard to it. At the risk of seeming to indulge in *odium theologicum* I shall state my opinion that this doctrine should be attacked with the utmost vigour, and it is my hope that it will disappear altogether in the more enlightened atmosphere of modern theological discussion. It can only appear tolerable when its implications are covered over by a mass of learned disputations on matters which are strictly irrelevant to the issue. The supreme importance of this question is, clearly enough, that it affects our conception of God in the most thorough-going way. The shadow which sin must cast over the Christian metaphysic, the obscurity which we must admit if we accept the fact of sin, would fall, in this view, upon God himself. We can make no accommodation with such suggestions. Christians can come to understand one another only if we all worship the God whom St John calls charity. We must hold with him that in God is only light and no darkness at all. For the darkness of which the mystics speak is not really darkness but the excess of light. We must hold that he is the Father of lights, with whom there is no vicissitude or shadow of turning.

Predestination, then, does not mean what it is commonly taken to mean: that our destiny is predetermined by God although (some would add absurdly) we are, nevertheless, responsible for our actions. We are destined to fulfil those capacities (different for each individual) which God has given us but only on condition of our accepting his offers. Predestination adds nothing to the meaning of providence. And providence means that God's generosity is absolute. He does not give the same capacities to all his creatures, but he is ready to provide each of them with all that is required for their fulfilment, to satisfy their desires completely. There is nothing capricious or arbitrary about his arrangements. But it follows from all this that we cannot claim to detect 'the hand of providence' in the particular events of the world-process. God is always pulling things into the straight so far as we co-operate with him.[1] But the events of the world-

---

[1] But could he not at least reduce the appalling extent of physical evil? We cannot claim that he should overturn the world-order, and miracles are of their nature exceptional. I am not suggesting, however, that no problems remain.

process are the joint products and the points of intersection of two forces—the positive force of God's offers when we accept them and the negative force of our refusals to accept them. Human history, if it makes sense, is real struggle between these forces, not the unrolling of pre-ordained decrees.

But the problem of evil is for most people the strongest inducement to concluding that the world does not make sense, or at any rate that, if in some mysterious way it does, we cannot be expected to see it. What is to be said to such people? Let it be admitted that what has been so far said can do no more than show that there is no contradiction between our awareness of God and the horrors of which we are perhaps more vividly aware. We may succeed in freeing God from any suspicion of willing them himself, of being directly responsible for them. But the fact is that (as we have to put it) he has taken the risk of them, and some of the results have been enormously disastrous. Can we accept such a God? The answer will surely depend on the degree of our interest in him. That is, if our awareness of him has developed to a certain extent, we shall find that the alternative to theism is unthinkable. We shall conclude with St Paul tht the sufferings of this present time are not worthy to be compared with the glory that shall be revealed in us. But if we have only a 'suspicion' of him, we shall be tempted to give up. What is to be said, then, in these circumstances is that, if it is allowed that there is no contradiction involved, if the *possibility* of theism has been satisfactorily established, this possibility must not be lost sight of. Anyone who is honestly convinced that there is a contradiction must acknowledge his atheism. And in following his conscience, acknowledging what he believes to be true, he will be (I have argued) in fact acknowledging God. But anyone who does not make this mistake, who follows up his suspicion that (in the words of Browning's rather poor poem) the All-Great is the All-Loving too, is unlikely to be disappointed. Those who search seriously for God may not find happiness in the vulgar sense of the word, but they will gain at least a sort of basic satisfaction which may be called peace, and perhaps there will be something more.

As an appendix to these very brief remarks on a vast subject, I offer the conclusions of Professor Cecil Gray on the sufferings of the brutes. In an article[1] on 'Pain, Consciousness and Death' he

[1] *The Downside Review*, Spring 1961.

tells us that 'some medical students were kind enough to volunteer for observations designed to elucidate the effects of "laughing gas" or nitrous oxide. They were submitted, under nitrous oxide anæsthesia, to a painful stimulus—intense and measurable pressure on the shin bone. They showed all the reflex effects of having received pain, and from this it might be deduced that they suffered. They withdrew the limb sharply. They shouted and struggled. In some cases they would even respond to such commands as "Raise your arm". Yet afterwards they emphatically stated that they had not been aware of any pain.' Professor Gray concludes: 'The simple and inevitable conclusion is that the presence of all the usual reactions to pain—screaming, shouting, movement and so forth—need not imply that suffering is present. Let us now draw some conclusions from this hypothesis. Theologically pain is neither good nor evil—in nature its purpose is good. It leads to the shunning of harm and injury; it is protective. It only becomes evil when "reflexion" is present, for then it becomes suffering. This concept has important implications. For example, if it is accepted, there is no evidence whatever that animals "suffer" pain. They receive painful stimuli and react to them in all the usual ways—but this reaction cannot be taken as evidence that they exercise that "reflexion" which is necessary for suffering.'

III

SOME MODERN THEISTS

II. DR EDWYN BEVAN, DR JOHN BAILLIE AND PROFESSOR H. D. LEWIS

In this chapter I shall be discussing the views of modern theists with whom I am broadly in agreement about the directness of our knowledge of God, its experiential character. And I hope that in the course of this it will become clearer what is meant by calling this knowledge 'direct'. I shall be offering certain criticisms of the writers in question, and this will bring out some aspects of the subject which have so far been glanced at only in a casual way.

The writer whom I shall take first, Dr Edwyn Bevan, was the Gifford lecturer thirty-five years ago, but *Symbolism and Belief* is still in some respects at least extremely relevant.[1] The first passage in it which I need to mention I find unsatisfactory. Bevan is critical of the doctrine, which he rightly calls that of the *philosophia perennis*, according to which 'all events are present to God in a *Nunc Stans* [a "timeless moment"], without any successiveness at all'.[2] He concludes[3] that this would seem an inappropriate conception for the eternal life of the blessed and an even less happy symbol for the unimaginable life of God than Royce's idea of a specious present (the specious present may be roughly described as the holding together in our consciousness of several successive events, that is, as a 'timeful' moment). As regards 'the eternal life of the blessed' I should readily agree that there must be, as Bevan puts it himself, 'something analogous to time' in the beatific vision.[4] Indeed I should go further and suggest that creatureliness is always bound up with successiveness, that the beatific vision is not a static affair but an indefinitely expanding awareness of the Infinite. But I should not agree that there must be something 'analogous to successiveness in God's apprehension of the universe'.[5] It seems to me that the symbol of the *Nunc Stans*

---

[1] It appeared as a paperback (Collins, Fontana) in 1962 and references are to this.
[2] 86.   [3] 90.   [4] 97.   [5] 99.

does help us, not indeed to imagine, but to *think of* an apprehension of successiveness which is not itself successive. Our evidence of God is evidence of 'otherness' or, as I have called it, 'beyondness'. We are aware of him, so it seems to me, as beyond time in the sense that the notion does not apply to him at all. We are aware of him, on the other hand, as beyond our consciousness in the sense that he has consciousness in an infinite form. We find consciousness as a value deriving from the infinite value which contains it in its own infinite richness and simplicity. Time goes with movement and development, and these do not possess value in their own right. It is the term of movement, what it is for, that is valuable in itself. The importance of that is that it draws our attention to the evidence of timelessness seen in and through timeful experience. The eleventh book of St Augustine's *Confessions* is perhaps the finest discussion of this theme.

Bevan then turns to the experience of beauty. After referring to Grant Allen's attempt at the end of the last century to find the origin of beauty in sexual attraction ('a ridiculous putting of the cart before the horse', Bevan calls it), he reaches the conclusion that our judgements of value can claim validity only if 'the spirit of man is a special representation of something which is, in its full being, the Whole enclosing man' and that 'such a view must be in some sense theist'.[1] This is his way of pointing to our 'likeness', our analogical relationship, to God. And he adds: 'An atheistic view of the universe can exalt human ideas of goodness and beauty to the rank of really valid ideas, of ideas which have a right to command or claim man's acknowledgement, only by a logical confusion.' This was my criticism of the claims of some secular humanists. But when he goes on to say that 'the beautiful is a revelation of the being of God', we may feel that some explanation of this should be forthcoming.

The account which I should offer begins by proposing that a beautiful object is one which constitutes a permanent possibility for certain of our experiences. It is beautiful in the sense that the post-box is red—it causes certain effects in our awareness. There is a subjective element in our aesthetic judgements in that our grading of things as more or less beautiful is in terms of our capacities for enjoying them. But they do cause our enjoyment. And when we are able to grasp them with some measure of

[1] 130.

completeness the effect upon our minds is of peculiar significance. As Mr Harold Osborne put it in his *Aesthetics and Criticism*, 'It makes us more vividly alive than we otherwise know how to be'.[1]

In the case of a work of art we can explain this up to a point by saying that we are put in touch with the artist's mind; we are enabled to see or hear something to some extent at least as he saw or heard it. But it is, I think, the value which we recognize in the activities *of our own minds* which is the peculiarly significant thing about these situations. We recognize that the mind has a capacity for indefinite expansion. No doubt the 'overtones' of aesthetic experience, the sense of the 'numinous' which so often accompanies it, can be accounted for with some sort of plausibility in naturalistic terms. But if it is true that we become aware of God in his action on our own minds, it will follow that we should be aware of him in a special way when we are 'more vividly alive that we otherwise know how to be'. The experience of beauty helps us to realize what is meant by saying that God is 'Pure Act', infinite activity. It is perhaps a particularly effective safeguard against anthropomorphism in our thinking about God.

That is the next topic which arises for discussion in Bevan's lectures for my present purposes. In discussing 'the wrath of God' he asks us to 'consider the reasons . . . for regarding the retributory view of punishment as valid'[2] and concludes that 'by the principle of justice, God wills that the doing of evil should issue in pain for the doer'.[3] But there is no principle of justice, any more than there is a principle of causality, which can be invoked as distinct from God himself. God does not give any man his due, to speak strictly, because we have no dues where he is concerned. God simply gives, and we accept or refuse. A final refusal of God means the loss of God, not because of a principle of justice but because there is nothing left for God to work on—the spiritual capital, so to say, which had once been given, has now been completely exhausted. Bevan supposes that, according to Catholic doctrine, the fact that God's grace is never given in hell is a result of a divine *fiat*. He is also under the impression that this doctrine 'comes in the end to very much the same as the Calvinist doctrine of predestination'.[4] His treatment of this subject does seem to be a lapse into anthropomorphism.

The root of this trouble is perhaps a certain tendency to anti-

[1] 229.   [2] 196.   [3] 215.   [4] 209 n.

intellectualism in regard to our knowledge of God. In a particularly interesting discussion of Dean Mansel's famous Bampton Lectures, Bevan defends Mansel against charges of pragmatism. Mansel, he tells us, is not just saying, as he is often supposed to have said, 'Act as if there were a God who is a Loving Father, and you will find certain desirable results follow'.[1] He is saying that although 'our best conceptions of God remain symbols of a Reality we cannot imagine, it is because these conceptions, when acted upon, produce a life of a certain quality, as compared with other conceptions of the universe, that the man who believes in God gains assurance that he does right in believing'.[2] This, Bevan claims, presupposes that God exists in independent reality. No doubt the defence is sound, so far as it goes. But I should want to say that our knowledge of God tells us more than that there is an 'unimaginable reality'. There is a certain agnosticism about Mansel's account which leaves the door open for speculations about God of an anthropomorphic character, and Bevan's sympathy with Mansel is perhaps a clue to his own occasional moves in that direction. I should want to say that, although our positive knowledge of God is a knowledge of the indescribable, it does enable us to make negative statements about him which are to be taken in a perfectly literal straightforward way; thus we can say, for example, that God does *not* punish as that is understood in the retributory theory of punishment.

So far I have been more critical than appreciative of Bevan's Gifford Lectures. There are in fact many excellent things in them, and especially in what he says at the end about the grounds for belief in God. Like so many Gifford Lecturers before his time and after it, he considers it 'highly improbable that anyone who had no belief in God was ever led to believe in God by any of the standard "proofs" of God's existence. . . . What actually causes anyone to believe is direct experience of the Divine.[3] The ultimate ground of belief', he also writes, 'is not so much the perception of God but the perception of the Divine', which is explained to mean 'the perception of a peculiar kind of value, belonging to existing things and existing men'.[4] If we are to make sense of this, we must surely say that God is apprehended in this value as its source. Finally I must comment on Bevan's statement that it is 'a dogma of the Roman Church that the existence of God can be demonstrated by rational inference from visible phe-

[1] 298-9.   [2] 298.   [3] 344-5.   [4] 316.

nomena'[1]. In fact there is no mention of inference in any authoratitive statement on this subject.

I now turn to a recent set of Gifford Lectures, those of Dr John Baillie, published in 1962 under the title *The Sense of the Presence of God*. The appearance of these lectures cleared up for me a difficulty which I had felt about his book *Our Knowledge of God*, published more than twenty-five years earlier. It seemed to me that it left no room for a distinction between natural and supernatural knowledge of God, by which I mean (to repeat) the distinction between an awareness of God's summons and that loving awareness of him which follows upon acceptance of the summons and which constitutes baptism by desire, the beginning of faith and of the life of grace. It now appears that Baillie, although his vocabulary differs from mine, does not disagree with this. On the subject of baptism by desire he quotes with approval Cardinal Gasparri's Catholic Catechism and Maritain's *True Humanism*, pointing out that his own Church of Scotland has reached substantially the same conclusion in two of its Declaratory Acts.[2] What he is unwilling to accept is what he calls 'the traditional distinction between natural and revealed knowledge', because he sees in this a claim to a natural knowledge of God which relies wholly on logical processes and does not require a self-presentation of God to the human mind. It should be clear that I am not proposing that sort of natural knowledge of God. He must always take the initiative (that is, act upon us) whenever we have knowledge of him.

That Baillie admits a distinction between a natural knowledge of God and God's *revelation* in Christ becomes clear when he speaks of 'natural religion'. He is even willing, he tells us, to speak himself of such a natural knowledge if this means, as he puts it, 'what men already believe' and 'not what has been offered to men by the philosophic theologian', that being 'what is properly called natural theology'.[3] I should want to say that there can be a philosophical account of 'what men already believe' which consists in showing that a knowledge of God is implicit in human experience. That is what I should mean by 'natural theology'. So it seems that the difference between Baillie and myself in this matter reduces, in principle, to a difference about the use of words. We agree that a knowledge of God is available for all men, whether they accept it or not. Baillie, like Gabriel Marcel, calls

[1] 345. [2] 193–4. [3] 174.

all knowledge of God 'faith'. It seems to me desirable to reserve the word 'faith' for the state of affairs constituted by the acceptance of God's summons.[1]

It follows from all this that Baillie, like Blondel, for example, holds that there are, strictly speaking, no atheists but only people who do not recognize (and may be unwilling to recognize) God, and that they must have, as I should put it, a 'cognitive contact' with God at some time (Baillie tends to say 'at all times', which seems to me going too far). Other theists have vigorously attacked this view on the ground that we must accept what a professing atheist says about his own state of mind and that we have no right to accuse such persons of self-deception. But there is no need to talk of self-deception. All that needs to be said is that, in encountering what he calls the 'moral order', an atheist encounters the transcendent Other without realizing that this is what genuinely philosophical theists are talking about when they talk about our basic awareness of God. But I think we have to admit that some people do not encounter this 'moral order' in the course of their everyday lives: it is conceivable, as I have suggested before, that this may not take place, in any definitive fashion at any rate, until a choice is required of them in the parting of soul and body. Baillie has exaggerated his case in affirming on several occasions that professing atheists always believe 'at the bottom of their hearts' what they deny 'at the top of their minds'. And although, as I have tried to show, it is not unreasonable to call some of them theists in disguise (and with no suggestion that they are self-deceivers), it would be misleading to call them, as Baillie has sometimes done, Christians in disguise. What he is entitled to say is that, if they have in fact accepted God's summons, the grace of Christ is at work in them. What they are aware of is, in fact, God; there is a genuine cognitive contact with him. But they have not recognized him as the God of religion and they have not recognized him in Christ.

But Baillie's fundamental position I find wholly satisfactory except that he calls our knowledge of God not only direct but 'immediate'. This is again hardly more than a difference about language. This knowledge is a product, he tells us, of the intuitive, not of the discursive, reason.[2] It is an 'apprehension' not of 'a

---

[1] In what I have said so far about Baillie's Lectures I have been drawing on an article published in *The Downside Review* for 1962 but with certain modifications. In what follows I shall be simply repeating some of it. [2] 51.

SOME MODERN THEISTS

truth or proposition' but of an 'aspect of reality'.[1] And such an apprehension is verifiable 'only by appeal to the region of experience out of which it arose'.[2] Faith (that is, in his language, any knowledge of God) is a mode of 'primary apprehension'. And on the last page of the book we read that 'we have to do, not with an absent God about whom we have a certain amount of information, but with a God whose living and active presence among us can be perceived ... this is the true burden of Kierkegaard's—the only original—existentialism'.[3]

But I am not altogether happy about the way in which Baillie treats the important topic of certainty and its scope; it may be worth while to spend some more time on it here. He writes:

'... while all authentic experience has some certitude in it and is, as it were, transfused with certitude, it is never possible to distil this certitude in its complete purity into the particular theoretical affirmations we make. We are convinced we are in touch with reality, we do know something assuredly, but when we try to express in theoretical terms what we know and are sure of, we never have the same assurance that we have got our answer quite right. We know we are thinking something that is certainly true, but there is always the risk of error in our way of thinking it.'[4]

To say that there is always a risk of error does not mean that we cannot guard against error, that we do not successfully guard against it on certain occasions, even in the expression of our knowledge. If all that Baillie wishes to say here is that conceptualizations are never *adequate* to the reality which they express, then there is no need to disagree with him. On occasion he does say something like this: the Christian's thinking, we are told, 'has been invaded, and continues to be pervaded, by an infallibility, an absoluteness, and therefore a certainty, which he nevertheless remains unable to hold securely in his own very human grasp, or, to vary the figure, to domesticate in the household of his own very human mind'.[5] But in the passages which immediately follow (and in others later) he seems to accept the view that the human mind inevitably distorts, all along the line, and does not merely reduce, the reality which it encounters. He quotes to this effect from Tillich and from Barth and observes: 'It is for such reasons that, instead of claiming certainty or finality for our particular

[1] 54. [2] 64. [3] 261. [4] 8. [5] 10.

thoughts about God and the unseen world, I must content myself with claiming that certainty "pulsates through all our thinking" and that our experience in this realm is everywhere "transfused with certainty".'[1]

But, he continues, 'the difference between these two claims calls for further elucidation, and I should wish to elucidate it by distinguishing between two kinds of knowledge—knowledge of truth and knowledge of reality'. This leads him to consider 'whether it is really true that there are no objects (within which category we can for our purpose include other subjects) whose existence is indubitable'.[2] He refers to G. E. Moore's contention that the meaning of certain affirmations is quite clear and that it is possible to be quite certain of their truth, and he sums up his account as follows: 'If I say that I know John Smith and also the village in which he lives, these statements, unless I am lying, are certainly true in the sense in which I mean them.'[3] He acknowledges that he finds it difficult to 'escape from these conclusions', but passes on at once, without considering the possible implications of this admission, to speak of the knowledge of reality— primarily the knowledge of persons, which is 'the very type and pattern of what we mean by knowledge'[4]—as opposed to knowledge of truths, knowledge of propositions. He concludes as follows:

'The point, then, that I am most concerned to make is that, however difficult we may find it to ascribe certainty to these truths, we may nevertheless enjoy the certitude of having authentic acquaintance with the realities they fallibly seek to describe. It is in this way that our experience is everywhere transfused with a certitude which pulsates through all our thinking, and whose pervading presence can on occasion make even of our most speculative theorizings something better than mere fantasy and baseless fabric.'[5]

It seems to me that, in his desire to emphasize the more-than-propositional character of faith and to refute the theory that all knowledge is knowledge of propositions, Baillie has treated propositions in an off-hand and rather inconsistent fashion. If it is 'difficult to escape' the conclusion that some propositions can refer to persons in a way which, as far as it goes, is correct and

[1] 12.   [2] 13.   [3] 15.   [4] 17.   [5] 18.

informative, then we cannot feel happy about a general principle according to which our human expressions distort the realities which they attempt to express. Or are we to say that this is true, not of our statements about human persons, but only of statements about God? We must indeed say, if I may repeat it once more, that the words which we use about God will have a merely human reference for those who do not see them in a certain light. But we can hope that by considering them attentively they may come to see them in that light. And one of the most remarkable and valuable strands in Baillie's writings is, in my opinion, his insistence on this very point, although he approaches it in a rather different way. Taking the line that the knowledge of God is never wholly lacking to anyone and rejecting the view that it 'is reached by analogy from our experience of the finite or created world', he writes later as follows

'To say that we gain the conception of perfect being by arranging our feeble human approaches towards perfection in an ascending series, and then imagining the indefinite prolongation of this series, is to forget that such an arrangement could not have been made by us save by the aid of a standard of perfection already present to our minds.'[1]

And again in a valuable criticism of Barth:

'I believe that the word "father" applies in the first place, and quite non-figuratively, to the fact of natural human procreation; so that when I say, "The man who has just entered the room is my father", I am in no sense using transferred or improper language. But some have unfortunately been heard to say, "Yes, he is my father, but he has been no real father to me". Clearly, then, the word is employed by us both in a factual and in an ideal sense. Not all who are in the bare factual sense fathers display the character of fatherliness even in a minimal degree. Only God possesses it and displays it in perfection; and it is only by the standard of his perfect fatherliness that we can measure the appropriateness or inappropriateness of the attribution of fatherliness to any man.'[2]

So our human words are capable of a true divine sense.

[1] 116.   [2] 120-1.

It is worth noting, too, in this connection, that Gilbert Murray was criticized in the second chapter[1] for asserting in *Literature as Revelation* that 'of all the famous sayings that have come as a revelation to human beings, not one is strictly true'. 'Is he saying', Baillie asks, 'only what we ourselves have been insisting upon, that not one of the concepts in which we seek to imprison the realities of which we are aware is every fully adequate to the realities themselves?', and he concludes with regret that Murray did not mean only this. Yet he repeats in his concluding chapter 'Retrospect' (and other such passages are found throughout the book) that 'it seems impossible to enunciate any theoretical propositions concerning God and the unseen world about which we could be certain that they were true just as we enunciated them. . . .'[2] One may suspect that the clue lies in the word 'theoretical'. And this suspicion is increased by the passage which follows in Baillie's summing up:

'I contended that the affirmations of faith are always practically orientated, providing us with a frame of reference within which our lives are to be lived rather than as adding to the sum of our theoretic, speculative, not to say scientific, knowledge . . . elsewhere I remarked that there is nothing of which I am more firmly persuaded than that the right attitude of life is that of the man whose whole comportment and activity have their root in the sentiment of gratitude, and I added that "it is precisely in regard to such a conviction as this that I feel able to speak of certitude, and to do so without the least scruple or diffidence".'[3]

But the affirmations of faith, I want to say, *are* 'practically orientated'. If, as certain other passages might suggest, Baillie is only tilting at the ramifications of scholastic theology, mere opinions of theologians, then there is no difficulty. He would have been surprised, no doubt, to hear how many Catholic theologians have complained about the abuse of metaphysics in theology. Theologians have so often indulged in metaphysical speculations which have lost touch with the object of faith, and this is notoriously one of the great obstacles to ecumenical understanding. It has led, by reaction, to a disastrous distrust of the intelligence in theological matters, which I have been in the habit of calling 'antimetaphysical theology'.

Yet Baillie's final remark about certitude suggests once more

[1] 23. [2] 256. [3] 256-7.

that its only object is, if I may so put it, God *tout court*. We do indeed find God, I would say, in the fact of certainty, especially in the certainty of moral obligation, but the light of certainty falls also on the world of our immediate experience, on the world in which God acts—and on the Church in which he acts and speaks, and which assures us that certain statements about him are indeed genuine 'pointers'.

I now turn to Professor H. D. Lewis's book *Philosophy of Religion* (1965)[1] in order to consider in some detail the chapter called 'God and Mystery'. It begins by distinguishing between 'explanation in the normal sense and the curious sense of explanation or of "ground" or "cause" which is relevant to the questions "Why is there a world?" or "Why is there anything at all?" '[2] Lewis goes on to say that 'whatever "explains" the whole system of things within which other explanations are possible must fall outside that system, and nothing can be explicitly known about it except that it must *be* to account, in this special sense, for the way things are as a whole—or for there being anything at all'.[3] He also writes that 'God is everywhere and in all things, not, in the first instance, as some recognizable formative influence, but as a reality wholly unseen and unknown which is involved in all things and is beyond all things.... We cannot prove that our very radical or ultimate question is significant, we cannot lead to it directly from other questions. But there are devices by which we can awaken in others the sense we have of there being something to account for the whole world in some way which involves being itself ultimate and perfect as nothing within the world can be.... We seem to see that in the last resort the world just could not exist by some extraordinary chance or just happen....'[4]

A difficulty in Lewis's account may be already apparent: how can it be legitimate to talk at all about a reality if it is, as he says, wholly unseen and unknown? But let us continue with it for the

---

[1] It develops the views expressed in his book *Our Experience of God* (1959) and his contribution to *Prospect for Metaphysics* entitled 'God and Mystery'. I should like to express the opinion that this book contains some very valuable comments on contemporary empiricist philosophers and on secularizing tendencies among theologians, and that Lewis's remarks on the study of comparative religion should be read by anyone who supposes that what we know of primitive societies tells against theism. I ought to add that Lewis, like some other Protestant philosophers of religion, is under certain misapprehensions about Catholic dogmas, especially that of original sin, which has not been so clearly defined as he supposes.

[2] 142. [3] 143. [4] 143–4.

present. 'This sense of the Unconditioned', he writes, 'has sometimes been described as a "feeling of dependence". But if this phrase is used, we have to be very careful. For it is not just a feeling we have, but a conviction or insight . . . a cognition in more technical terms. It is not easy to find an adequate name for this particular cognition or awareness.' The word for it which he eventually selects is 'intuition' on the ground that we use it of seeing something directly, like a step in an argument. He then rejects the idea that we can have 'direct confrontation with God or know him as he is in his own nature or essence'[1]—we must not claim an intuition of him in that sense. It seems to me that 'intuition' is not the right word, because it suggests a knowledge which is not only direct but immediate, and I have argued that our knowledge of God, though direct, is mediated, in particular by our knowledge of ourselves. So I prefer to speak of an 'apprehension'. Nor do I feel happy about denying that we know God in his own nature or essence. If all it means is that our knowledge of God is a limited one, of course I accept it. But it can easily suggest that we do not know God at all as he really is—that we know him as he is not, which makes no sense. Nor can we say that we know only his existence if this means that we know nothing whatever *about* him, for that too would make no sense. Thomist metaphysicians make great play with a distinction between essence and existence, but even Maritain in *The Degrees of Knowledge* has admitted that we cannot claim to know of God's existence without knowing anything of his essence. We must suppose Lewis to mean that we cannot know God comprehensively as he knows himself.

He maintains, however, that God is 'a Being who exists by necessity, but what it must be like to be that sort of Being we cannot from the nature of the case ever know'. It is true that we do not know what it is like to be God in the sense that we do not *share* his nature in the literal sense of that word. But, again, either we have some knowledge of it or we do not know him at all. Lewis considers that 'if we knew that God existed by inference from the way the world goes or what we find in it . . . we would have to postulate a certain kind of Being to account for this or that'. He seems to be arguing that, since we do not know him by means of such an inference, we have no knowledge of his 'essence'. But it does not follow from the fact that our knowledge of him is not

[1] 145.

inferential that it must be knowledge only of his existence. What Lewis is pointing to in all this is the mysteriousness or 'beyondness' of God, and in that lies the great value of his account. And that what he is saying is *fundamentally* what I have been saying is brought out a little later in the following passage: 'He [God] is closer to all things than distinct finite things ever are to one another, and also remote beyond conception. This we see, not as inference, but in one insight or leap of thought.'[1]

Lewis's chapter now takes a fresh turn. He points out that 'to see that there must be God is not a matter of ordinary understanding. It requires a certain attitude of mind. . . . There must also be conditions which conduce to the sort of contemplation which can lead our thoughts beyond the here and now.'[2] This is finely developed in considerable detail. Lewis also points out that 'the sense of a Reality altogether beyond the world as we know it is not the result of elaborate ratiocination. It comes directly in the impact of certain experiences upon us, and simple-minded folk are in some ways more open than others to the thrust of the Beyond into their lives in this way. . . . The sense of there being this Beyond is at the heart of all religion'.[3] It is hardly necessary to remark that this all-important fact is the only answer in the end to attempts to secularize theology. That is not in the least to deny that we need nevertheless a theology of the secular, as Professor Mascall has more than once observed.

These experiences of which Lewis speaks are always bound up, so it seems to me, with our knowledge of ourselves, but he does not himself make this emphasis here. As we shall see, when we turn to some recent discussions about the relationship between ethics and religion, Lewis does not see moral obligation as evidence of God in any special sense. This is perhaps one reason why he seems to be leaving us sometimes with a knowledge that there must be God but not a knowledge *of* God, a knowledge of who he is.

At the end of the chapter he may seem to be moving from side to side on this issue, but as always his purpose is to emphasize the transcendence of God. He thinks that Tillich sometimes seems to be supposing or vaguely suggesting that 'as God is not a subject of predicates in the normal sense, he is nothing at all in himself and must be thought of as some fundamental aspect of our own existence and not as such any reality on its own account'.[4]

---

[1] 146. [2] 147-9. [3] 150. [4] 153.

He is also suspicious of the language of 'encounter' because this may lead to the *reduction* of God to an aspect of human experience. But it is not necessary, in order to avoid that pitfall, to say, as Lewis does, that we know him 'only in the inevitability of his being as the transcendent ground or condition of the limited conditioned existences which we can understand and discuss in the ordinary way'. He does, indeed, continue: 'It is not that our thought here is empty or without content, it is the richest of all, but from the nature of the case we cannot make it more explicit than the affirmation of there having to be Supreme or Ultimate Being. That is all we know directly of God.' But that language about the content of our thought must surely imply a contact with this Being in himself, and Lewis admits the difficulty that he may seem to have 'made God so unlike everything else, so "wholly other", that he does not seem to be anything at all'.[1]

What we have to say, I have urged, is that in coming to know God as the 'wholly other' we come to realize also that we nevertheless stand to him in a unique relationship which we can only call 'likeness'. Our awareness of God is itself non-conceptual, but it leads us to see that our concepts of what is positively valuable do apply to him in his own way. This leads me to a final criticism of this chapter. Lewis, when treating of concepts in the course of it, writes that 'in the case of God, to understand the concept is to see, in the very same thought, that there must be one instance of it and that there cannot be more than one'.[2] I agree that we do construct a concept of God, but I think that this is a secondary operation. In our original non-conceptual apprehension of him, I would say, we are already aware, however dimly and inarticulately, of his oneness and indeed of all that we mean by his 'perfections'.

There is a later chapter in which Lewis returns to this topic of analogy and refers to Rudolf Otto's famous book *The Idea of the Holy*.[3] As he says, in Otto's work 'particular importance attaches to the sense of transcendent worth in our experience of the holy, for this provides a link at the very centre with moral ideas as we find them in normal experience'.[4] Lewis does not pursue this line

[1] 154. Lewis, of course, does not really deny that we know something of God's 'perfections' any more than he denies that we have some 'experience' of him. I am venturing to criticize certain passages not only to emphasize my own position but also to obviate a possible misunderstanding of Lewis's.
[2] 147.   [3] Available as a Penguin paperback.   [4] 219.

of thought, but continues: 'Otto is fully convinced of the very close link between the sense of God's mystery and the attributes which enlightened religion ascribes to God and which determine the place which religion should have in our lives as a whole.'[1] Still expounding Otto, he goes on: 'We have still to talk about God in highly symbolic ways. . . . God, as Eternal Being, is not "spirit" or "power" in the way in which we manifest or exercise these, but we have none the less a justification for speaking of God in these terms and ascribing to that the utmost importance. Religion is not left without content or discipline.'

That is the position which I have been adopting. Let us now see what Lewis's own attitude to it is. He continues: 'I think Otto is quite correct in holding that when we use particular terms of God, or ascribe attributes to him, we do so in a symbolic way. . . . But I am not happy about the way he establishes the link between the transcendent and the particular terms in which we refer to it.' What worries Lewis is that Otto has based his account on the experience of fear and awe which the numinous evokes ('numinous' has come into our vocabulary from Otto's book). He has claimed that this fear and awe have a special character, only analogous to that of fear and awe in the ordinary sense of the words. These are 'felt analogues' and lead us to discover God as Spirit, Will and so forth. Lewis writes of these 'felt analogues' that they 'should prove a very helpful guide to the sense of the numinous and a way of evoking it'. 'But', he goes on, 'I wonder just how far they take us. Do they help to give us more than a firm grasp of what the consciousness of God as ultimate and transcendent Being involves? Must we not go deeper into what religious experience as a whole is like to understand what justifies the more specific ways in which we speak of God?' And he concludes that we are still 'far removed from specific affirmations like those of the Christian faith. . . .' That may be, but I would say that the answer to Lewis's difficulty about the 'otherness' of God and the content which our knowledge of him nevertheless possesses has been supplied in principle by Otto. Our original knowledge of God has describable repercussions which are revelatory of him. In itself it is strictly ineffable, but it does reveal the analogies to us. In knowing God we know him as the source in which all value is contained in a way which is not only profoundly mysterious but also profoundly illuminating.

[1] 220.

12. PROFESSOR JOHN MACQUARRIE AND PROFESSOR H. H. PRICE

It will have emerged that by 'metaphysics' I mean natural theology. A metaphysic which is a 'science of being' and not a natural theology seems to me in the precise sense an abortion. It is disastrously incomplete. But surely, it will be said, even if natural theology were the complete form which metaphysics ought to take, there would still be topics, that of the nature of mind, for example, which can be discussed by the metaphysician without its being necessary to drag God in. But what I have been trying to show or rather to suggest (for these things can be seen only if people are prepared to look for them) is that our knowledge will not be recognized as the metaphysical experience which I believe it to be unless we realize that it is, in so far as metaphysical, a knowledge of God. We do not reach definitive conclusions about the nature and workings of the mind until we discover its source and its ground. I am not saying that we must first be certain of God *before* we can become certain of anything else. I am saying that *in* becoming certain of anything else, in recognizing truth as such, we are in touch—in cognitive contact—with God, and that if we were not we should not be thus certain. So in the end it is a question of all or nothing. Either metaphysics *is* meaningless or it must be a theistic metaphysics. Talk about 'being' can always be put on one side by a modern philosopher as not really referring to anything if it is talk about 'being' in the abstract. It seemed desirable to put my cards down on the table—even at the risk of sounding intolerably dogmatic—before returning for a moment to Professor John Macquarrie's book *God-Talk* and then examining in some detail his approach to natural theology in his earlier book *Principles of Christian Theology*. I am in agreement with this approach in so far as it starts from a concrete situation; what I shall be questioning is the desirability of describing this situation as an encounter with 'being'.

In *God-Talk* Macquarrie writes: 'We may say that theological language communicates by awakening the person to whom it is addressed to the encounter with holy Being.'[1] He goes on to say that we must not expect from this language the sort of precision which we may expect from other languages but that this 'does not mean that it is to be denied genuine cognitive insights'.[2] I agree,

[1] 83. [2] 89.

of course, with his general position that 'the whole theological vocabulary is tied in with the word "God" '[1] and that 'if Christianity rests solely on an alleged once-for-all revelation and has no support in reason and common sense, it is doubtful whether it can survive or whether it deserves to survive'.[2] But when he tells us that ' "God" is the religious name for Being as experienced in a faith-awakening revelation'[3] I feel that this language has an imprecision about it which is unnecessary. It is not that I object to his use of the word 'revelation' in connection with natural theology. It is the identification of God with 'Being' which seems to me unfortunate. In the Preface to *Principles of Christian Theology* Macquarrie tells us that he is indebted to Martin Heidegger for many of the philosophical categories which he uses. Heidegger's thought, he continues, can be of service for 'the articulation and elucidation of the whole body of Christian truth in a contemporary way'. He then makes a reference to Karl Rahner in a passage which is worth quoting: 'Among contemporary theologians, I have found Karl Rahner the most helpful. In saying this, I am acknowledging that the leadership in theology, which even ten years ago lay with such Protestant giants as Barth, Brunner and Tillich has now passed to Roman Catholic thinkers. Among them Karl Rahner (himself a penetrating student of Heidegger) is outstanding.' I have quoted this passage because it indicates that Heidegger's language about 'being' has been taken over not only by Protestant theologians but also by many Catholic ones; for, since it is used by Rahner, it is, of course, also used by his disciples. But the point which I want to make here about this language of Heidegger's is that it is an obscure one.

It is well known that Heidegger does not himself identify 'Being' with God. There is a certain danger that anyone who proposes to use his language to mean something which he does not mean by it may find himself in difficulties. I shall suggest that this is the case with Macquarrie. But first I ought to say that I do not profess to know what Heidegger does mean by 'Being'. His thought is for me too opaque to be useful. I am concerned with him only in so far as Macquarrie uses what he acknowledges as Heidegger's concepts. And it will be convenient, in view of what will follow, to repeat an earlier remark: that Macquarrie regularly uses the word 'metaphysics' in a pejorative sense because he regards metaphysics as being necessarily a

[1] 99.   [2] 121.   [3] 100.

system of abstract ideas and nothing more. It is surely very odd, however, to deny that 'Being' is a metaphysical term, as he appears to do in the following passage from the fifth chapter of *Principles of Christian Theology*:

'What is the meaning of "being"? We must first recall the manner in which the question has arisen for us. It is not the metaphysical question of being—if there is such a question—that is to say, a detached, speculative question which one can take up or lay aside at pleasure. Our question is rather one that has arisen in an existential context. For we began by asking about ourselves, and it was the confrontation with *nothingness* in our existence that opened our eyes to the *being* which contrasts with nothing. So our question about being is not a theoretical question, in the sense of one that is asked by someone who merely beholds; it is an existential question in the sense that it is asked by someone who is involved in the question of being—someone for whom being, as Heidegger is so fond of saying, is an issue. Man has to decide about his own being, in so far as he must choose among his possibilities. But he cannot properly understand his own being unless he has some understanding of being as such. Thus the existential question leads into the ontological question: this does not mean that it becomes a metaphysical or speculative question, but that the so-called "ontological" question is itself existentially oriented.'[1]

I am in sympathy with the general spirit of that passage. What I question, apart from the somewhat arbitrary definition of metaphysics, is the usefulness of this talk about 'being' and 'nothingness' for those whose minds are not already attuned to certain specifically German ways of thinking and feeling. But let us see whether Macquarrie succeeds in recommending that language by the explanation of what is to be understood by 'being' on which he now embarks. He tells us that it must not be taken to mean *a* being, and that in some way it is common to all things.[2] Strictly speaking, he goes on, one should not say that 'being is'; the exigencies of language sometimes compel us to say so, but then we must remember that we are not using language strictly. Nor is 'being' a property; we cannot predicate it of things as we can predicate properties of things. Nor is it a class,

[1] 97.   [2] 98.

for we construct classes on the basis of properties.[1] So far this is in line, it may be remembered, with the analysis of 'being' which I offered in an earlier connection. Macquarrie further maintains that 'being' cannot be equated with 'substance' because that suggests what is static and 'being' has also a dynamic significance. It refers not only to the existent entity but to the whole act or energy of existing. Finally, it is not 'what philosophers have sometimes called the "absolute" ', and by the 'absolute' Macquarrie means either 'an all-inclusive being' or 'the sum of beings'.[2] This is a restrictive use of the term: it is not at all unusual to speak of God as the Absolute.

Macquarrie now attempts a more positive characterization of 'being' by presenting us with a series of contrasts. First he contrasts 'being' with becoming. And this is where the real difficulties begin. 'Whatever becomes,' Macquarrie writes, 'must, in some sense, *already be*; yet the fact that it is becoming implies that it *is not yet* what it is on the way to becoming. . . . The fact that whatever becomes both is and is not shows that the distinction between them is of a peculiar kind.'[3] 'Very peculiar', some of our philosophical friends would say in dismissive tones, and they might also ask why 'becoming' should not be regarded simply as a succession of states of existence, one state of activity followed by another (there are difficulties about that suggestion too, but this is not the place for discussing them). The point is that we are faced here with a highly controversial doctrine (and one which most people would certainly call 'metaphysical'), not with an analysis of concrete experience. And Macquarrie goes on at once to say that 'in so far as what becomes is, then becoming must be included in being as well as distinct from it'. This seems to me very confusing. Since being is not a class, becoming cannot be a *kind* of being. Presumably, then, it is a part of being, and so being is a whole of parts—but that is what Macquarrie called 'the absolute', which is different. His own conclusion now follows that 'the fundamental contrast between being and nothing would seem to be made possible only in so far as being includes becoming and gets differentiated, otherwise being and nothing would be indistinguishable'. I have to confess that I can make nothing of that at all. In the first place to say that being is distinguished from becoming because it includes it is hardly a way of making clear what being itself means. In the second place, if it 'gets differ-

[1] 99. [2] 100. [3] 101.

entiated', it must (I suppose) have been undifferentiated once when it did not include becoming. Macquarrie, however, thinks that this peculiar distinction and connection between being and becoming is an answer to those who complain that 'being' is a static notion. If we hold that it includes becoming, we can, he adds, 'do justice to concrete dynamic experience'. I should have thought that it would be wiser to hold on to the 'concrete dynamic experience' of becoming as an established fact without thinking that becoming must necessarily be also found in any less immediately obvious metaphysical regions into which we may succeed in penetrating. Macquarrie seems to be saying that there must be change going on everywhere, even in 'being'. Now I am not at all clear what he means by 'being' at this stage of his discussion, but I would remark that it is, in my opinion, a mere prejudice to hold that whatever we come across must be necessarily in process of changing.

Macquarrie next distinguishes, or rather purports to distinguish, being from appearance. He tells us that, since nothing can appear unless in some sense it is, 'appearing too belongs within being as well as being distinguished from being'. Curiouser and curiouser. The problems which broke out about being and becoming break out again here in just the same way. And finally Macquarrie draws the same sort of distinction (which seems not to be really a distinction at all) between being and the ideal. Here, he says, 'the distinction seems to call attention to different levels, or, perhaps one should say, to different degrees of plenitude, not so much in being itself as in the manner in which being is present in the beings, or in the states of affairs which these beings constitute'. But to say that being can be found on different levels or in different degrees of fullness does not make any *clearer*, so it seems to me, what is *meant* by 'being'. Indeed it may suggest that being is literally *shared* by all the levels to a greater or less extent, which would turn it back into a class-concept with fatal results for the whole theory.

However, Macquarrie is still only making approach-shots at 'being'. He now proposes to 'make a third attack on our problem and . . . try to fill out, in the clearest and most affirmative terms that we can find, what we mean by "being" '.[1] There are three stages in this process. The first adds to what we have been told already only that 'being "is" . . . more beingful than anything

[1] 102.

that is, for it is the prior condition that anything may be'.[1] That is a statement which many of our contemporaries would regard as 'metaphysical' in a wholly pejorative sense. As I suggested before, we can write off 'being' without contradiction or manifest absurdity as just a word which refers to all objects of our thought simply in so far as objects of our thought. The second stage in this account begins with the tentative question: 'Would these paradoxes be sorted out somewhat if we thought of being as a kind of energy that permits things to be?' The formula which is eventually adopted is: 'Being, strictly speaking, "is" not, but "lets be".'[2] And by 'letting-be', Macquarrie goes on to say, he means 'bringing into being'. By 'being' must therefore be meant the source of being. And one might be inclined at this point to ask in an exasperated tone why he did not say so at once instead of leading us such a dance. But when we reach the third and final stage of this account we find that we are not, after all, out of the wood. For we read that Being 'is nothing apart from its appearance, in and through and with particular beings', although it is 'transcendent of every particular being'.[3] And so confusion seems to be even worse confounded. Apparently God both is and is not bound up with, dependent upon, the created universe. But soon after this Macquarrie points out that the 'words "God" and "Being" are not synonyms'.[4] One is left wondering what he means by either of them. The last section of his fifth chapter, however, is headed 'God and Being', and so we may hope to discover in it the answers to our questions.

Our first discovery is that the words 'God' and 'being', which were said not to be synonymous, are now said not to be synonymous only for people who do not take up what Macquarrie calls 'a certain attitude toward being, namely, the attitude of faith'. I suppose we must take this to mean that they do not recognize God in 'being'. Macquarrie goes on to say that ' "God" is not a neutral designation, as "being" is, but one that carries important existential connotations of valuation, commitment, worship and so on'.[5] He does not mean that we import these connotations into being, for he adds at this point: 'We could, however, say that "God" is synonymous with "holy being" . . . it makes sense to recognize the holiness of being, and to take up before it the faith-attitude of acceptance and commitment.' 'Being', then, is holy, though some people do not see it. And so it proves that we

[1] 103.   [2] 103.   [3] 104.   [4] 105.   [5] 105.

were right the first time in concluding that, for Macquarrie himself, 'being' and 'God' are synonymous. He puts this beyond all further doubt by a formal announcement at the end of this chapter that 'Being' with a capital letter will indicate henceforth that the word is being used as an alternative for 'God'.[1] The trouble about this is that 'Being' does not seem to be, in his account, genuinely transcendent of the created universe despite his assertions about transcendence, for we have seen that it *includes* becoming and appearances and becomes differentiated into degrees or levels of plenitude. It does not transcend change.

Macquarrie defends the position which he has adopted by saying that 'contemporary theology is beginning to move out of the phase in which "God" meant an exalted being beyond the world'. 'The next phase', he goes on, 'would seem to be the identification of God with what I have called "holy being", and we may think of this as the phase of *existential-ontological theism*. So far is it from volatilizing or eliminating the idea of God that it makes it possible for the idea to have an ultimacy which it did not have in traditional theism.'[2] What Macquarrie has in mind here in speaking of 'traditional theism' is far from clear, for he goes on to refer to the 'association of God with being' in patristic and mediaeval thought, based on the Bible. He seems to think that the idea of God as transcendent and immanent being had disappeared from theological thought until quite recently and that it is only now appearing in a really satisfactory form. It hardly needs to be said that both the immanence and the absolute transcendence of God were taught quite unambiguously by St Thomas Aquinas, to take only the most famous example. In so far as Macquarrie introduces change into God his view coincides with pantheist theories. But he is not in fact a pantheist. He insists that God has 'a "wholly other" character as over against whatever is within the world'.[3] But he also continues to insist that 'Being always includes becoming.'[4] I must characterize this as a confusion. Macquarrie tells us that he has 'abandoned the traditional "substantial" reified conceptuality in favour of one that takes time and becoming seriously'.[5] I do not know what the tradition is to which he here alludes. But the alternative to regarding God as a 'thing' (if that is what this tradition is supposed to have done) is not to introduce time and becoming into him. And to take them with proper seriousness is to take them as

[1] 110.   [2] 106.   [3] 109.   [4] 110.   [5] 110.

leading us, beyond themselves, to him. Macquarrie has succumbed to a tendency in modern (and especially American) thought, to attempt a divinization of time and becoming. In consequence we are told in the ninth chapter on 'The Triune God' that 'Being . . . expands and realizes itself in history.'[1] This is 'Being' with a capital letter which has been formally identified with God. I must take leave to say that this is not the way to talk of God.[2] (I should add that I have no objection to talking about him as 'pure being' if that is properly explained, as it has been sometimes in the Thomist tradition.)

By way of contrast to Macquarrie's Heideggerian approach I shall now turn to Professor H. H. Price's contribution to *Faith and the Philosophers*, the record of a symposium held at Princeton in 1962 and edited by Professor John Hick. This is Price's first piece of writing about the philosophy of religion.[3] But in his Presidential Address to the Aristotelian Society in 1945 he had made significant criticisms of the anti-metaphysical movement. In it he asks whether we can properly dismiss 'the long line of speculative metaphysicians from Plato to Whitehead' and points out how often metaphysics has been thought to be finally extinct but has revived with more vigour than ever.[4] I must quote here one passage from the final paragraph: 'Has it not happened sometimes that an important question was first asked by poets and religious teachers and other unphilosophical persons, who were blissfully ignorant of the terminological rules which the philosophers of their day had laid down? "Nonsense! Nonsense!", says the professional philosopher, when he is told of the question these people had asked. But his successors a generation or two later may call it unconscious wisdom or untutored insight. . . .'[5]

Price's paper, with which *Faith and the Philosophers* begins, makes no use of any special metaphysical language. He does

---

[1] p. 191.
[2] But Macquarrie's formal theory of 'being' has surprisingly little effect on the value of his book as a whole. What he has to say about Bultmann's disciples, about neo-Calvinism and about the secular humanism of the 'new theologians' seems to me most valuable. His book is in many other ways richly rewarding, and his attitude is admirably 'ecumenical'. I hope that my strictures on an issue of such importance will not have seemed harsh or captious. It is because the issue is so important that I have pressed these points with such vigour. If I have misconstrued Macquarrie in any way, I hope to discover it and to find an opportunity of acknowledging my error.
[3] His Gifford Lectures of 1960 were published in 1969 (*Belief*, Allen & Unwin). I find myself in agreement with his main conclusions.
[4] *Clarity is not Enough*, ed. H. D. Lewis, 34.   [5] 41.

indeed refer to God as the 'Supreme Being', because this is the way in which ordinary religious people would speak of him in certain conjunctions. But he advances no theory of 'being' and constructs no metaphysical system. He makes a straightforward appeal to experience, and considers the difficulties which the fact of his experience may present to a believer who happens to be also a professional philosopher. I quote some sentences from the first pages of the paper, written with consummate tact and skill, as an illustration of how this sort of undertaking should be, in my opinion, begun:

'It may happen to a person that he realizes, with surprise perhaps, that he cannot help believing in God. . . . He would not wish to give up his belief, even if he thought it psychologically possible to do so. It is the most precious possession that he has, and, far from wishing to give it up, he would wish anyone else to be in a similar condition. . . . A clergyman, we think, ought to give up his job if he does not believe in God. It almost seems that a philosopher ought to give up his if he does.[1] . . . What is called wishful thinking, believing something merely because one wishes it to be true, is a weakness in anyone. But surely in a philosopher it is . . . a plain breach of professional duty. . . . One of the misfortunes of the theist is that the state of affairs which he believes to exist would indeed be the best conceivable if it did exist. At any rate this is so if he believes not only that there is a Supreme Being who created the Universe, but also that the Supreme Being loves every single one of the persons he has created and loves each of them for his or her sake, with an unconditional love. This same version of theism also maintains that God invites each one of us to love him . . . and finally that loving him is our highest good. Indeed, this version of theism might almost be described as the metaphysics of love.[2] . . . Such a doctrine will always appear to outsiders "too good to be true". . . . But a theist philosopher is faced with other difficulties. . . . The first is that there is something inappropriate, something almost blasphemous and impious, in talking *about* God at all. The proper thing is not to speak about him, but to address him. . . . There is another difficulty. . . . Love is an embarrassing subject to all of us, and especially to a philosopher. A philosopher (at least in Anglo-Saxon countries) is not supposed to mention it, still less to discuss it.[3] Moreover, if we

[1] 3.   [2] 4.   [3] 5–6.

are to discuss religion at all. . . . we have to assume that each of us has an inner life, and lives through experiences which only he can describe at first-hand. Moreover we have to assume that what goes on in this inner life is of great or even supreme importance to each of us, far more important than what we do or say overtly or publicly in the market-place.'[1]

Price now returns to the original problem. What reasons can there be for the philosopher's belief in God? If it seems to him that he has no reason for holding this belief, then it is his duty 'at least to try his best to give it up'.[2] But at this point Price introduces the distinction between 'believing *in*' and 'believing *that*'. The philosopher would rightly feel that he had to look for evidence if believing in God were just a case of believing 'that'. But it is not just a matter of justifying hypotheses.[3] 'Surely', Price goes on, 'when a person is actually in the faith attitude, he would never say that he believes that God loves him. It is rather that he *feels* God's love for him or feels the loving welcome he receives. . . .'[4] It is good to hear such things from a one-time occupant of the Wykeham Chair of Logic at Oxford. Price's essential point is clearly that the evidence of faith lies in faith itself.

He adds something of great importance:

'There is something in us (perhaps in everyone) which makes us wish to love God. But perhaps there is also something in us which makes us wish *not* to love him, nor to have anything to do with him, and even to wish that he did not exist. It is worth while to bear this possibility in mind when theism is described as "wishful thinking". There may be some wishful thinking in atheism too, and in agnosticism. Denial, or doubt, or even suspense of judgement *can* be "wishful", as much as affirmation.'[5]

Price then points out that 'beliefs that' are not unconnected with faith. They are usually 'precursors' of it. He gives as the commonest instance of this in our society 'the acceptance of human testimony, the testimony of religious people'. A personal relationship leads us to seek for 'another personal relationship—for that is what faith in God is',[6] which is testified to by the qualities which we detect in some religious person. And here

[1] 7.   [2] 8.   [3] 9.   [4] 11.   [5] 12.   [6] 13.

Price begins an account of what 'seeking God' is which is perhaps the most valuable part of the whole paper. 'All that is required of us', he says, 'is the suspension of disbelief; or, if any more is required, it amounts only to "suspecting that". . . . What matters is that we should be *interested* in these theistic propositions and willing to take them seriously. . . . If they are ruminated upon, they have power to change a man's whole life.'[1] And further, Price suggests, we can try out prayer, for 'it is quite possible to act on a hypothesis, to do voluntarily things which we should have done if we believed or knew it to be true. . . . Sometimes we have to act in this way to find out whether a hypothesis *is* true'.[2] But so far we have only the evidence of testimony and a suspicion, although perhaps a growing suspicion. We may say, Price continues, that when people persist in this search they are 'already being moved by a kind of incipient love. . . . This perhaps is the interpretation of Pascal's paradox: "Thou couldst not seek me unless thou hadst already found me".'[3] I have no doubt that Price is right about that.

When he turns to the topic of 'finding God' in the last part of the paper, although, he says, 'it might be more appropriate to say that he has found us . . . there is still some cognitive factor on our side. If he has found us, still, in some way or other, we are conscious that he has.'[4] There is 'a new personal relationship', and 'the new awareness of him which we seem to have is just the cognitive aspect of this. . . .'[5] At this point Price makes some comments which I should like to make my own: 'The claim to *know* the One and Only Lord of All is so enormous that one shudders at it. . . . We might perhaps say that we have come to be acquainted with God—just a very, very little. . . . The finding which we are trying to describe is more like the removal of an illusion, the illusion of an absence.' We have something like a 'negative hallucination', Price suggests, but one which is 'self-induced', and 'the hypnotist's part is played by our own lack of love for someone who is with us always'. This is, I believe, the sort of way in which the business of 'encounter' is more profitably discussed than it can be in the language of academic phenomenology or of scholastic metaphysics. But it is not what is commonly thought of as philosophy, and some participants in the Princeton conference were naturally disconcerted by it. I shall conclude with a few references to their reactions.

[1] 16–17.   [2] 18.   [3] 20.   [4] 21.   [5] 22.

Professor Charles Hartshorne objected to all talk about 'wishful thinking' in the present connection because in his view 'the question about God has an impersonal aspect'. There is, in addition to the religious question, a 'purely intellectual question' presupposed by it. 'The necessary Principle of all existence cannot be simply absent, even from a single experience.'[1] The non-theist has simply failed 'to think things through'. Price in his reply points out that, even if the atheist or agnostic is in a state of intellectual confusion, it 'makes sense to say that he wishes to remain in that state and not to take steps to remove it'.[2] Hartshorne seems committed to saying that the denial of God's existence is simply unintelligible, not even false, and I agree with Price that this is not the case. I mention Hartshorne's view because I want to make clear that I do not hold it.[3]

But the most important objection came from Mr Keith Gunderson. It is that 'in virtually all of our personal relationships with other *people* there seem to be many sets of criteria one could resort to in order to justify our "belief in" this or that person' whereas 'it's not at all clear that we could make available various sets of criteria for determining whether one has had or does have a well-grounded belief in God'. Gunderson adds: 'No one, so far as I know, has been able to make much sense out of "self-authenticating" or "self-verifying" experiences of God.'[4] The importance of this familiar objection, thus rather tendentiously expressed, is that it drew a reply from Fr Norris Clarke of which I wish to avail myself for the building up of my own case.

Clarke agreed that the question does need an answer. He then referred to Price's description of the move from praying to God

---

[1] 31.   [2] 35.
[3] A note on Hartshorne's Introduction to *Philosophers Speak of God* (1953) will be in place since his doctrine of God, as there expressed, has a bearing on Macquarrie's views on the subject. Hartshorne complains (p. 3) of classical theism that it considers God more simple than the One but not more complex than the Many, although all conceptions of God are declared insufficient. I would answer that God has 'richness' but *not* complexity. To deny 'process' in God is not to deny 'activity' in him, as Hartshorne supposes. He goes on (p. 4) to advocate 'panentheism': there are two main aspects in the essence of the Supreme Being—we must affirm both poles of each pair of ultimate contraries. God includes all things, but in his accidents, not in his essence. This complexity, I hold, introduces into God an opposition, a negation, which is refuted by our experience of him. It may be added that Hartshorne presses the difficulty about 'possible worlds' in a very useful way.
[4] 57-8.

as if he were there to conviction that he *is* there. 'What kind of evidence', Clarke asks, 'can I find within this experience which gives it intellectual respectability, the sense of being objectively grounded and not merely arbitrarily projected?'

The answer which he offers is as follows:

'It seems to me that the crucial new element is a certain awareness, elusive and intangible though it may be, that I am no longer experiencing merely my own *activity* of pondering and reaching out for God, but also a new sort of *passivity* . . . as though I am being *acted* upon, *being* stirred to my depths and changed, *being* awakened and drawn by some hidden Presence not out in front of me but somehow deep "within", or just "beyond", my own profoundest centre (the directional images can vary). The conviction grows upon me that such a profound stirring, awakening, bringing to light and drawing (sometimes even imperious summoning) of what I now recognize as my deepest, most authentic and most "full" or total self cannot be merely the effect of my own effort, but exhibits rather the tidal pull on my soul from some greater force beyond. This is not an abstract deduction but a responsible intellectual (though not necessarily conceptual or self-consciously analytic) weighing or estimation of an experience and its implications.'[1]

One comment on this is perhaps necessary. When Clarke speaks of estimating an experience and its implications he might be taken as meaning that a subsequent judgement is passed upon it or an inference drawn from it. But his claim to an objective certainty must be based, if I am right, on the awareness itself; a judgement passed upon it or an inference drawn from it will be in order only before it has declared itself as fully objective and will lead back to it so that it will so declare itself. Thus we might call such processes of thought 'pointers' to the awareness in its fully developed form. But they cannot produce it of themselves or substitute for it. The demand for a *criterion*, in fact, must be rejected here as out of place. What can be done is to attempt some *description* of objectivity in an awareness of God.[2]

---

[1] 59.
[2] It seems to have been partly Professor Flew's failure to realize that Fr Clarke was really doing this which led him to attack his remarks with such violence in *God and Philosophy* (131).

13. A CONTINENTAL SYMPOSIUM

In a symposium called *L'Existence de Dieu* (1961) several writers express views about theism very closely related to those which I have been advocating. In an article about the so-called 'proofs' of God's existence based on the moral consciousness and the perception of value, Père J.-H. Walgrave, basing himself largely on Newman,[1] concludes that the best starting-point is the reality of which we have the most intimate knowledge, namely the human person. 'We may ask ourselves', he writes, 'whether a translation of the metaphysical ways [that is, the Thomist "proofs"] into personalist terms would not show more plainly the metaphysical character of these proofs themselves and the personal character of the Supreme Being whose necessary existence they reveal to us.'

Walgrave goes on to claim that, unless the appearance of the human person is only a passing phenomenon in the evolution of nature, we must conclude that it explains the existence of nature. This sums up what I have been trying to say about the insufficiencies of secular humanism. If the human person is only the product of a blind evolutionary process, there is no particular reason for supposing that it has any splendid future in store for it in the long run. It would be most natural to conclude that it will eventually disappear into the darkness from which it emerged. If on the other hand we are going to attribute some purpose to the evolutionary process, then we shall have to describe it in a metaphysical way. That is, we shall be forced to look behind it so as to account for its having a purpose. The person must have been *planned* all along, and obviously it could not have planned itself. So Walgrave writes: 'On this supposition the person is at the origin of nature, it is the beginning and the end.... And since the person [the original person] cannot be the human person, we must conclude that at the origin of the world of nature and of the finite person there is the infinite Person.'[2] It is always open to anyone

---

[1] Walgrave's writings are, I think, of great importance as showing the value of Newman's general approach to philosophical questions. Newman was not a professional philosopher, and there is a certain lack of rigour about his treatment of philosophical questions, for example in what he says about certainty in the *Essay in Aid of a Grammar of Assent*. But his insistence on the philosophical significance of personality, obvious as it seems to us today, is an instance of his power to seize upon essentials and especially those which his contemporaries were overlooking. The modern 'personalists' in philosophy rightly look back to him as one of the great founders of this movement of thought.   [2] 130–1.

to deny purpose in the world of nature and of the finite person, but, if anyone is not prepared to deny it, then, I think, Walgrave's argument cannot easily be set aside.

Another contributor to this symposium, Père Dominique de Petter, to whom I have referred earlier, considers that the radical contingency or, as he calls it, the 'gratuitousness'[1] of the beings of this world as beings is the all-important consideration. This suggests one of those metaphysics of 'being' which I have ventured to criticize as likely to cut no ice in our time, in some places at any rate. But de Petter does not first develop a metaphysic of being and then base a natural theology on it. For him the approach to metaphysics and the approach to natural theology are one and the same. So, although the language of 'being' may be off-putting, it is only a matter of language. It is our relation to God that de Petter is talking about. 'We just have to see', he writes, 'the gratuitousness of the world around us, and this metaphysical discovery is itself the introduction to natural theology.'[2] He also writes: 'The proof of God's existence is so completely metaphysical that metaphysics might be said to be wholly contained in it. . . . The distinction between ontology and theodicy or natural theology introduced by Leibnitz and accepted by so many others has no meaning at all.'[3] How do we *see* this gratuitousness? De Petter speaks of 'a sort of sliding movement (*glissement*) which passes from the existence of the beings of this world, which is a problematic, gratuitous and derived being, to the essential Being (*l'Etre par essence*) who is God'.[4] Whatever we may think of this, the movement of thought which is being described is clearly not that of syllogistic inference or of any process known to the logic books. This 'sliding movement' does not work in definite stages which can be set forth and, as it were, tapped over. The meaning must be that God is *seen through* the beings of this world, and that must mean that God himself is in some sort descried.

What the 'personalist' approach always amounts to, in the end, is that the finite person, starting (I should say) with the recognition of value at least in some implicit form, becomes aware of his own entire *dependence* upon the infinite Person. And we find de Petter, like other contributors to this symposium, pointing out that this is most obviously the case in the experience of moral freedom. It would appear, in fact, that without this experience the 'gratuitousness' of the world at large would not be sufficiently

[1] '*gratuité*'.   [2] 168.   [3] 167.   [4] 168.

recognized. And there is a further indication that de Petter's position is not really different from my own in his remark that we could not recognize 'signs' of God in the world unless there were already a certainty, 'at least implicit', as he puts it, of Gods' existence. But God is not *immediately* experienced. That is what the requirement of a 'sliding movement' recognizes. St Thomas, indeed, does say that there is an 'implicit' awareness of God in all human knowledge. But his official interpreters have been commonly content to see in this contention a reference to an action of God upon the mind of which we are in no way conscious until it is brought to light by a process of logical argument. Some Thomists have allowed that there can be a previous 'suspicion' of God, but have still maintained that logical argument is necessary before this 'suspicion' can receive confirmation. But if in fact a 'suspicion' is formed by non-logical methods it does not appear how it can be confirmed by a logical one. And, if there were a convincing logical process for proving God's existence, there would be no need to insist upon a previous non-logical 'suspicion'. Such a process added to the 'suspicion' would be more naturally described as replacing it than as confirming it. If the logical argument is not supposed to be convincing but merely persuading, then it will not successfully combine with a mere 'suspicion' to produce a certainty.

At the end of his article de Petter rejects the suggestion that he is appealing to 'religious experience'. 'The affirmation of God', he writes, 'is the rational justification of the religious life and the prerequisite of religious experience.' It is rational, I agree, in that it is the work of the human reason or mind, but it is not, as de Petter himself has made very clear, what is usually meant by a matter of rational *argument*. Since de Petter also calls it 'the entrance to the religious life' and since it arises in experience, his objection to calling it 'religious experience' must be that he understands this expression in some rather narrow sense. I think he would have to agree that a 'suspicion' of God can be turned into a certainty only by concentrating upon the 'sliding movement' or rather upon the term to which the 'sliding movement' brings us. And this, I have suggested, is the beginning of prayer. Our experience, if we fully attend to it, is itself the *reason* why we become believers.

De Petter observes that 'if the religious life rests upon God, it is necessary nevertheless to enter upon it, and that, in fact, we never cease to enter upon it'.[1] This seems to be his way of pointing

[1] 177.

to the fundamental importance of our original contact with God and to the importance of re-establishing this contact when it proves to be necessary. We must not, that is, forget *who is* the God of whom we have come to know something. This is again the thesis that the supernatural life does not cancel out its natural beginnings, and it prompts the reflection that, if this natural 'point of insertion' of the supernatural life is not recognized for what it is, one may wonder whether that life is in a healthy state. It seems cut off from its roots.

There is one more remark of de Petter's which I must not fail to mention. He writes that 'the metaphysical affirmation of God is the sole source of all our natural knowledge of God's attributes... the birth of this idea in human consciousness'. This is important, if I understand it rightly, as confirming my contention that we discover what we know *about* God (apart from the fuller knowledge revealed by Christianity) not by processes of reasoning based on an *idea* of infinite perfection but from our own experience of him. We do not *work out* that he is super-generous and so forth—we discover him as such. I have already discussed, so far as I can, the apparent absence of such knowledge outside Christianity.

Another contributor, Père C.-F. Geffré, writes in a somewhat similar sense. After warning us against 'those who insist upon the historicity of Christianity to the extent of passing over in silence the structures presupposed by this history' (that is, the metaphysical presuppositions of Christianity), he tells us that 'the God attainable by reason is already the one true God'.[1] In other words, Pascal's famous contrast between 'the God of the philosophers' and 'the God of Abraham, Isaac and Jacob' must not mislead us into supposing that the philosopher as such cannot encounter the one true God of Christianity.

The last of the contributors to this symposium whose work I propose to discuss is Père J.-D. Robert. But his contribution was rendered out of date, as he remarked of it himself, by the appearance in the following year, 1962, of his book *Approche Contemporaine d'une Affirmation de Dieu*, to which I shall therefore turn at once. It takes a very long time to come to the point, but it is an important book, extremely illuminating about the condition of metaphysics, in France especially, in recent times. The first chapter lays down the conditions which must be fulfilled by any 'proof'

[1] 298.

of God's existence. Robert puts the word 'proof' in inverted commas and constantly emphasizes that there can be no coercive demonstration of God's existence.[1] Whether we see the point depends on whether we *want* to see it. And that depends on what we have made of ourselves. A dialogue with the Transcendent cannot be entered upon except freely. Robert makes the point that the discovery of God is not just the answer to a problem for our thought because in making it we discover ourselves as standing in a personal relationship to him. As he himself puts it, God is not just 'the ultimate principle of intelligibility' but proves at the same time to be 'the Absolute End of humanity'.[2] The second chapter describes the present state of affairs in the philosophy of the sciences and concludes that in the end one must choose between a materialistic view of things and a 'metaphysic of the mind' on pain of lapsing into a 'lazy agnosticism'.[3]

The third chapter contains a valuable critique of attempts to avoid the objectivity of mathematical truth and raises the question of the necessity for internal coherence which controls the procedures of both mathematicians and scientists. That is to say, there are certain rules of thinking to which they must submit. They cannot have invented these themselves, therefore. Robert admits that the question about the origin or 'foundation' of these rules of thought can be and is simply rejected by many people who call themselves 'empiricists' and that, if they are unwilling to face the question, there is no way of making them do so. But he argues effectively that the 'veto of empiricism' goes, so to speak, against the grain of human thought, as is evidenced by its history as a whole. That was the point made by Price (and by so many others) that the abolition of metaphysics always proves to be a temporary phenomenon. In this connection Robert refers more than once to 'the metaphysical revival of the last fifty years', a phrase which illustrates in a striking way the difference between an impression of the philosophical scene received on the continent of Europe and that received in the English-speaking countries. At the end of this chapter Robert refers to the confirmation of his views in Blondel's book *La Pensée*, which he had only recently discovered. He is anxious to make clear that his original debt is to St Thomas, although what he has to say is in fact more characteristically Augustinian and Blondelian. This emphasis on Thomism gives the book a certain 'party-line' flavour, but that

[1] e.g. 47.   [2] 48.   [3] 89.

should not prevent anyone's recognizing that it is an up-to-date version of an ancient thesis which stands firmly on its own feet. It is one to which I have already referred, and Robert's account of it may help to make it seem more convincing. This account occupies the last four chapters of the book; fortunately it is possible to present an outline of it in a modest compass by summarizing Robert's own summaries.

The scientist, this account begins by saying, is persuaded of the validity of scientific thought. He is striving after a system of truth which transcends his individual personality and is essentially communicable. He does not, indeed, expect to achieve a system of truth to which nothing needs to be added; there will be fresh formulations and fresh hypotheses; but there must be a certain stability about his undertakings, certain accepted procedures without which there could be no continuity and no progress in the sciences and no means of communication between scientists themselves. They must have some sort of common logic, some agreement on the reasoning processes which are implied by the very existence of scientific thought. There are 'intelligible necessities', as Robert puts it, which the scientist must recognize. But this is something which cannot be just written off as a brute fact. It raises inevitably certain questions. These necessities do not depend upon any particular subject or object existing in the concrete and considered precisely as such. That is, they have a validity in themselves. To realize the significance of this conclusion, we may ask ourselves, Robert says, whether there would be no truth in a state of affairs in which all human minds had been abolished. We have encountered this question before. Truth, I suggested, as Robert now suggests, does not depend upon its appearance to our minds, although we know it only when it does so appear. Our thoughts are contingent—they happen to us and pass away; the truths which our thoughts present to us do not. They exist in their right, therefore, in some mysterious way. What sort of existence can truths have *in themselves*? How can there be truth without thought?[1]

Could we perhaps say that, although truth cannot exist without thought, this thought is not our thought, but Thought with a capital 'T'? Unless we are to take up with some kind of pantheism, we shall have to conclude to 'an absolute Thought, which is really distinct, though not separated, from the individual

[1] 183.

thoughts which depend upon it'.[1] A pantheistic solution, an appeal to an all-inclusive Absolute Thought, would be the denial of personal experience, its reduction to the status of a sheer illusion. The only possible conclusion, Robert tells us, is that our minds must find their origin in a divine act of creative freedom; the intelligible necessities of truth must find their ultimate foundation in an absolute which is the necessary Primal Truth. He significantly refers to our experience of moral responsibility as the final answer to pantheism. He points out that in a pantheistic system we should be obliged to *merge* ourselves in the One Spirit. 'How could such an obligation arise in a mere phantom of a personality, something which only seems to have an existence of its own as the result of some strange illusion for which no plausible explanation has ever been offered?'[2] Only theism can account for the way in which the contingent and the necessary are found together in human thought.

'Theism', Robert goes on, 'adds that it is God's thought, the first Truth which is the foundation of all truth, which illumines minds from within . . . but it must be understood that each created mind is left with the obligation of *making its truth itself*, whether in the sciences, in philosophy, in morality or in art. For all genuine participation in the divine Thought must be itself a constructive vital force (although wholly dependent upon God) and not an amorphous passivity merely reflecting scientific, philosophic, moral or aesthetic truth already constructed by the Supreme Artificer.'[3] Robert adds that 'this human "creation" of truth and value . . . is certainly profoundly mysterious', and he refers in this connection to the mystery of the performance of free human acts under the so-called 'premotion' of God. We have already met the Thomist attempt to assign responsibility for human actions both to God and ourselves on different levels, and I have claimed that we have a responsibility, a power of refusal, which in its exercise is ours alone and not also God's. It would be a pity to confuse the present issue by introducing the Thomist thesis about freedom of choice. It is, I would say, fundamentally the mystery of human awareness that presents itself to us in this business of making truth and value our own. Knowledge is certainly not just a passivity —it is an active grasping of the truth, a vital union. But God makes us active when we accept the truth because he is the source of all existence, of all *growth*. When we reject the truth, on the other

[1] 184. [2] 185. [3] 186.

hand, we diminish ourselves, and God has nothing to do with it. He does not make us *sin*. He makes his world develop through us and makes us, if we will, develop in it—that is what it is for. Everything is his gift to us. We are not strictly creators. But we are strictly distinct agents, seeing things for ourselves and also genuinely productive—the more productive, the more completely we are God's instruments.

The formal statement of Robert's thesis is now presented as follows. There is, he says, 'an evident antinomy between the contingent and multiple characters of truth in so far as possessed by knowing subjects and as realized by objects on the one hand, and, on the other hand, the undeniable properties of unity and necessity possessed by the truth *as such*'.[1] The tension between these two aspects of the situation is something for which a metaphysician has to find an explanation. 'For', Robert goes on, 'what has no necessity in itself—the thought which registers the necessary truths—actually *exists*; whereas it seems impossible to find an *existential* foundation for the intelligible necessities of the truth ... Unless we have recourse to a sort of Platonist notion of truth existing in itself [that is, in a kind of vacuum], we can only suggest that the existential foundation of the multiple and contingent truth which appears in our minds is a necessary existence which is at the same time pure thought and subsistent truth. In this case what is necessary is not just thought up as an idea by a contingent thought which is incapable of providing a true foundation for it; and thought, in its turn, is no longer contingent but takes on the very conditions of an existence which is necessary in itself and is identical with the truth.'[2] This, I believe, is a genuine insight. Truth is not the exclusive property of any one of us, but common property, as St Augustine, among others, pointed out. It stands over against all of us. It is the supreme value of which we are in search. It must be borne in mind that this 'necessary existence' is ontologically, as opposed to logically, necessary. This necessity we do not create but encounter.

Robert tries to maintain the regular Thomist position according to which we do not actually 'have *experience* of'[3] or encounter this metaphysical foundation of our thought which is God himself. His position is that we discover God as the necessary condition for human thinking,[4] something which follows as a necessary consequence from the facts at our disposal—in fact, it would seem,

[1] 187. [2] 188. [3] *'Expérimenter'*, 188. [4] 187.

by an inference. It is difficult to see how this can be reconciled with his insistence that his chain of reasoning can be broken off at any point by a refusal to continue with it. That must surely mean that there is a 'suspicion' of God which someone is unwilling to follow up. And this 'suspicion' cannot itself arise, so far as I can see, as the result of an inference (that is a topic to which I shall return). I regard Robert's essential thesis as the gradual penetration of an original *datum*—namely, the fact that we can *know the truth*. The real character of this *datum* reveals itself to us through a concentration of thought the result of which we must call, I think, a 'metaphysical experience'. This would seem to be the true setting for those 'options' which Robert, unconsciously echoing Blondel, finds constantly presenting themselves along the way. And this would seem to be the true explanation of the state of affairs described in Père Dubarle's preface to Robert's book: 'Everything seems to suggest', he there writes, 'that the love of the primal truth takes its rise, beginning from its joy in human truth, and leads the mind up to the supreme degree of recognition (*reconnaissance*) and affirmation.'

There seems in fact to be a certain incompatibility between the Thomist and the Augustinian elements in Robert's account. He considers himself immune from the charges levelled by Gabriel Marcel against those who 'make God part of the series of causes which explain the created order' instead of finding him *beyond* such a series.[1] But this is what any appeal to 'implication' as opposed to 'experience' involves, and it is not possible, I hold, to avoid this pitfall unless one maintains, with Marcel, that God is *experienced as* transcendent, which is what Robert seems unwilling to allow. He seems to be advocating, at times, a knowledge *that* God exists which involves no direct acquaintance with him at all, and this has seemed to make no sense. He accepts Marcel's dictum that 'the metaphysical requirement of God is indissolubly accompanied by the "invocation" of God,' for his primacy must be recognized in love and adoration. 'We cannot have recourse to him', Robert goes on, 'as to a mere abstract principle of explanation, but as to a Person with whom a dialogue is necessarily engaged. It is no longer simply a question of devotion to an impersonal Truth, such as a man of science simply as such might envisage, so long as he is still ignorant of the final end of the

[1] 196.

human intelligence in its quest for truth. . . . The authentic truth which a valid proof must reach is that which St Augustine regretted to have found and loved so late and which once found could never be forgotten'.[1] The fact that we know the truth does indeed raise the great question, and Robert has done a very valuable job in stressing it. But he is still hankering after a valid proof which, although not coercive, has the impersonal quality of a piece of abstract reasoning. This is a halfway house where one cannot settle down. The conclusion which he ought to reach, so it seems to me, is that God is present to us under the form of truth, the supreme value for the human mind, from the very beginning. We have only to recognize him.

That may be underlined by referring to a long footnote in which Robert refers to the way in which existence, truth and necessity have been linked together by so many great philosophers, Kant, Hegel and Kierkegaard in particular. And he then quotes several passages from Blondel's *La Pensée*, discovered only after he had finished his own book.[2] I quote them in my turn to show that their emphasis is not the Thomist emphasis which we find in Robert's book. 'Between the empirical and the intelligible', Blondel wrote, 'between the real and the rational, there appears a sort of incompatibility . . . But does that mean that this conflict is insoluble and that the agelong effort of thought to appease it must be finally condemned to an avowal of incompetence?'[3] Blondel concludes that we find in this a *sign*, that of a reality in which the conflict disappears to make room for the identity of the real with the rational (he is using 'rational' in the broad sense in which it means 'thought' in general). 'For', he goes on, 'our thought in its full reach even in what it has of limitation . . . bears witness not only to immortality but also to eternity in the measure in which it participates in a truth which is independent of time and space and their limitations. . . . There is no truth . . . except in function of an absolutely subsistent and intelligible reality.'[4] 'The human reason', he writes in the same book, 'is led to affirm what is beyond the reason in its reasoning . . . a unitive principle which appears to it, in the fundamental activity of the intelligence, as a concrete absolute.'[5] This 'concrete absolute' does not follow as a necessary consequence from the facts at our disposal but, as Blondel puts it, *appears*, is *manifested* to us, however obscurely, in a *sign*. The

---

[1] 197 (referring to *Confessions*, X, 24).   [2] 190.   [3] *La Pensée*, 160.
[4] 172-3.   [5] 320-1.

reality which *signs* to us is present in the sign. It is the same to say that the cause is present *in* the effect.

Before leaving Robert's book I should like to draw attention to certain passages[1] in which he shows very usefully how the rejection of metaphysics is based on a refusal which proves on examination to be an arbitrary one, the result of a negative 'option'. In these passages he is discussing the work of Merleau-Ponty, a thinker whose influence is at present widespread. Merleau-Ponty was convinced that to acknowledge the existence of an absolute self-subsistent divine mind would have the effect of paralysing the philosopher's endeavours. Robert quotes from *Phénoménologie de la perception*:

'If the unity of the world is not founded on that of consciousness, if the world is not the result of a labour which constitutes it, it may be asked how it comes about that the appearances presented to us are concordant with one another and gather themselves together into things and ideas and truths? . . . Why does my life succeed in concentrating itself so as to be projected in words, in intentions and in acts? This is the problem of rationality . . . classical thought as we know, seeks, in effect, to explain their concordance by a world which exists in itself or by an absolute mind. Such explanations borrow from the phenomena of rationality all the convincingness which they seem to have; they do not explain it and they are never more clear than it is itself. . . There is nothing to be done save to acknowledge these phenomena which are the basis of all our certainties. Belief in an absolute mind or in a world separated from us is only a rationalization of this primordial faith.'[2]

Robert remarks justly that Merleau-Ponty is committed to a general agnosticism, and he quotes in evidence of this another passage from the same book:

'Words in ordinary speech and in particular scientific expressions are cultural existents which claim to translate truths about nature in itself. We realize that this is not really the case at all; the modern critique of the sciences has revealed the constructive element in all this. "Real" triangles, that is to say perceived triangles, have not necessarily, from all eternity, the sum of the angles equal to two right angles.'[3]

[1] 148 f.   [2] 467–8.   [3] 448.

Robert very properly replies that the relativity (or, as some people like to call it, the 'historicity') of scientific knowledge and the element of construction which is found in it do not justify one in concluding that scientific research is not presided over by objective norms, that is, by principles of thought which the scientist must accept if he is to make any progress. He quotes two more sentences from Merleau-Ponty's book: 'The eternity of the truth is only the sublimation of the present.... We have experience not of eternal truth or of participation in a One but of concrete acts of thought by which, in the midst of time's hazards, we experience participation in the world, and being with the truth is not distinct from being with the world.'[1] The last remark, as Robert points out, is capable of a satisfactory interpretation. But nothing in all this justifies the rejection of the metaphysical problem, that of the one system of necessary truth which is available for the multiplicity of contingent minds. Merleau-Ponty simply refuses to accept this as a problem, and, as Robert says, the dialogue which goes on between the real and human thought becomes incomprehensible if there is no ultimate foundation for it.

The conclusions to which Robert comes deserve quotation at length:

'Merleau-Ponty always produces a caricature of the problem of the foundation of truth in order the more easily to reject it... his options are made on the basis of... a notion of the divinity which is much like that of Sartre, that of a God who possesses a sum of knowledge which man has only to rediscover by using the book of nature in which it is set down and, as it were, preformed. ... I reject both the tendentious way in which the results of the sciences are here made use of and the solution of the problem of truth in terms of a "world in itself" or of an "absolute mind" in the sense in which those expressions are being used. ... We are rejecting a notion of truth in itself of which our human knowledge would be only a passive and dead replica. For we hold that human knowledge builds itself up and grows gradually by means of language which is affected by "historicity" and by judgments which are in certain respects always relative ones. ... But, with all this admitted, it is still necessary to maintain in all scientific or philosophical knowledge two elements which are essential for its equi-

[1] 451–2.

librium: necessity and unity on the one hand, contingence and multiplicity on the other.... One has the definite impression that it is the fear of the Absolute which places Merleau-Ponty in his ambiguous position. What else can be said of one who has written the characteristic sentence "metaphysical and moral consciousness dies at the touch of the absolute" and who asks "whether the natural and rational concept of God as necessary being is not inevitably that of the Emperor of the world..."?[1]

This makes it clear, Robert here comments, that 'Merleau-Ponty conceives of God only as a supreme Artificer.... That is to introduce sheer absurdity into the notion of the divine'.[2]

14. ENGLISH THOMISTS AND THE TRADITIONAL ARGUMENTS

When people talk of the traditional arguments for God's existence they usually mean St Thomas's 'Five Ways' and often some degenerate version of these. They are thought to work out on the basis of generally accepted facts by a simple process of inference. In fact they presuppose a certain background of thought, and it is not established that St Thomas, when he puts forward these 'ways' in the second question of his *Summa Theologica*, really regarded them as coercive just as they stood. But they have been so regarded by many of his followers, and it is regularly pointed out in answer that God cannot be produced as the result of any deductive process for the simple reason that he cannot 'follow' from anything more fundamental than himself. He cannot, for example, be an instance of some general law or principle which would have to be the case if he emerged as the conclusion of a categorical syllogism. But all this must be looked into more closely. I shall thus be enabled, I hope, to add certain precisions to what has been so far said and to guard against certain misconstructions.

Two English philosophers of our time have made persistent claims for the syllogism in this connection, Dr D. J. B. Hawkins, to whom I have been so much indebted in considering our basic awareness, and a distinguished Thomist scholar, Fr Edward Sillem. They were convinced that any directness in our knowledge of God is ruled out as both contrary to the facts and as

[1] 151-2.   [2] 153.

unorthodox. In *The Basis of Belief* I summed up a series of arguments with these two men which had appeared for the most part in English periodicals, starting, in Hawkins's case, more than twenty years ago. I think it fair to say that their fears about unorthodoxy are now recognized on all hands as unfounded. Here I shall add some further details about this series of arguments, leaving aside the discussions about orthodoxy, which should suffice to make it clear what is at stake. After that I shall turn to Professor Mascall's work on the Five Ways. I have explained in *The Basis of Belief* how his view about the apprehension of God has become fundamentally the same as my own, although he does not put the emphasis, as I do, on the moral aspect of the evidence, that is, on the fact of moral obligation.

In the *Church Quarterly Review* of 1950,[1] Hawkins, reviewing Mascall's book *Existence and Analogy*, remarked that the author 'follows a contemporary fashion in hesitating to describe our apprehension of God as an inference' and went on to say that certain writers 'have put forward theories which are really inferential, but have been deterred from calling them so by an unduly restricted conception of what inference means'. The writers whom he mentioned were Dr Austin Farrer, Dom Mark Pontifex, Dr Langmead Casserley and myself. In using the word 'fashion' Hawkins was not, I am sure, intending to suggest that the writers to whom he refers were copying one another. In fact articles had been appearing in *The Downside Review* since 1941 by a number of writers working independently and reaching substantially the same results on the issue in question—to say nothing of books appearing in France like P. de Lubac's *De La Connaissance de Dieu*. Hawkins and I had been engaged in an amicable contest on the subject since 1946. In October of that year, writing in *The Downside Review*, he had maintained that God's existence is discovered by the use of a hypothetical syllogism having as its first premiss: 'If there is contingent being, there is necessary being.' In his review of Mascall's book he repeated this as follows: 'The general process of thought may be represented in abbreviated fashion thus: if finite being exists, infinite being exists; but finite being exists, therefore infinite being exists.' In reply I pointed out that no one could accept the first premiss that, if finite being exists, infinite being exists, unless he had *already apprehended* infinite being through

---

[1] January–March. I replied to Hawkins in an article published in the next issue, and in what follows I draw upon it.

finite being, which is what this syllogism is supposed to be enabling him to do. Unless the relation between finite being and infinite being had been discovered (which means that infinite being itself would have been discovered) this first premiss would not be allowed. You cannot know that a relation obtains between two terms without acquaintance with both of them. What is said to be the first premiss of a syllogism is itself a claim to acquaintance with God. This seems to be unanswerable, and in fact there has been no attempt to answer it.

It may perhaps help to drive the point home if I refer to another round in this debate. Reviewing my book *Certainty*, Hawkins wrote in *The Month*:[1] 'We can only repeat that, if the existence of God were part of the datum when we apprehend the existence of creatures, the knowledge of God would not be inferential at all; if it is inferential, it can be appropriately expressed in syllogistic form. Fr Trethowan says that this movement of thought is unique, but even a unique process of thought must either be an analysis of the given or an inference from the given; it cannot be both.' The suggestions might seem to be that the total datum, in my view, is the existence of creatures which is then held (absurdly) to include that of God, and that God can be kept distinct from creatures only by keeping him at arm's length, so to speak, at the end of a syllogism. What I am saying, of course, is that God is 'given', in a way which is necessarily unique, as well as creatures. The movement of thought *is* an analysis of the given. The only reason offered by Hawkins for alleging it to be a syllogism is that he cannot admit it to be an analysis. He went on to suggest in the course of the review that my rejection of the syllogism might be due to my supposing that inference can never produce results which are more than probable. In reviewing Casserley's admirable book, *The Christian in Philosophy*, I took the opportunity of rejecting this suggestion.[2] It is perfectly possible, I hold, for syllogistic reasoning to provide results which are certain, not merely probable; the point is that this process of thought has no application when we are talking about the discovery of *God*. This may partly explain what Hawkins had in mind when he referred to 'an unduly restricted conception of what inference means'. If so, then he was under a misapprehension so far as I am concerned, and, I believe, so far as the other writers in question are concerned.

For example, the nature of Dr Farrer's objection to a syllogistic

[1] May 1949. [2] *The Downside Review*, October 1949.

proof of God is made clear in the following passage from *Finite and Infinite*: 'We make a formal false syllogism . . . if, for example, we treat divine causality as an instance of a universal "causality" and as logically required by the application of the universal causal rule to the case of the world as such. . . . But we avoid the charge of paralogism, if we abandon the pretension of syllogizing at all and allow that the "syllogism" is not the simple application of a rule to an instance, but a challenge to us to recognize a genuine analogy. . . . '[1] (The passage conveniently shows how the 'traditional' arguments can be useful provided that we do not suppose that they 'work' syllogistically.) Oddly enough, Hawkins remarks (in his review of Mascall's book) that 'it is not clear what sort of argument Dr Farrer had in mind' when he rejected syllogistic inference in the matter of God.

I may now venture on a further possible explanation of Hawkins's attitude. It may be remembered that what are normally called perceptual judgements are held by him (and, it seemed, rightly) to be inferences. We do not directly experience the bookcase over there, but we are sure that it is there because we have been in actual contact with it on several occasions. Our knowledge of it at present, however, is indirect. Did Hawkins think that our knowledge of God is thus firmly grounded but indirect? It is clear, however, that the parallel does not hold. For such knowledge must be based on a previous direct contact, and that is what Hawkins is not willing to admit in the present case. Nor can our knowledge of God be indirect in the way in which our knowledge of a fact can be indirect. We can obtain reliable information about the existence of black swans without having seen one because we know what swans are and we know what blackness is. What we did not know was that they were found together, and we can understand that this is the case without being eyewitnesses of it. We cannot acquire knowledge of God in that sort of way. In this case it is not just a question of putting together pieces of information already acquired, but of moving out into a fresh dimension. Unless we make direct contact with it, unless it enters into our experience, we cannot become aware of it. This seems so very obvious, and it rules out of itself any 'proof of God' which is supposed to work in virtue of an inference.

It seems to me very strange that people should be satisfied that the bookcase is there because they touch it with their fingers but

[1] 263.

unhappy about the proposal that our minds make contact with God in his action upon them, For if we take our own experience as the basis for discussion (and what else can we take?) it is the contact of our minds with objects which we are talking about. Touching the bookcase just physically is neither here nor there, so far as we are concerned, if we never become *aware* of it. Why should cognitive union, a contact with what is other than ourselves, have to be only with bodily things if physical union, apart from the *experience* of it, is in fact no good to us? The point of our whole business is experienced union, spiritual union (even when we are talking about bookcases), and to suppose that it can come about only in our tenuous relations with extended objects seems most unreasonable. It must make life very dull to suppose that the mind has no other concern than to register the presence of our material environment and to organize it for further registration.

I proceed to discuss the position taken up by Fr Sillem. In his book *George Berkeley and the Proofs of the Existence of God* he had claimed that God can be proved by reasoned arguments in terms of cause and effect. I pointed out that he had not explained how this could be done. He replied that he would do so in his next book and remarked: 'When D-Day dawns, I presume this will start a regular turmoil in the ranks of the opposition.' In this second book, *Ways of Thinking about God: Thomas Aquinas and some Recent Problems* (1961), it was announced in the second sentence that it did not 'even attempt any proof of the existence of God'. That was disconcerting, but the next sentence reads: 'It is rather a book on what St Thomas considered an argument for the existence of God ought to be', and it transpires, as one reads on, that Sillem did himself accept and was here recommending what he explains to us as being St Thomas's position—at any rate in so far as this involves a demonstration of God's existence by an appeal to causality and a process of inference, which, so far as I can see, must be a process of syllogistic inference if it is to have even an appearance of relevance to the matter in hand. If inference were used in any other sense it would have to refer to that movement of thought in which we discover God as acting on our minds (mediately, though directly) and that, as we shall see, is just what Sillem was rejecting. (I may remark at this point that I was at one time willing to use the language of 'inference' and 'entailment' to describe this mediate knowledge, but I came to see that it was most misleading—we must choose, in the last analysis, between appealing to experience and appealing to processes of abstract reasoning which are what is regularly understood by 'inference'.)

Towards the end of my review of Sillem's second book in *The Journal of Theological Studies*[1] I described its conclusion as follows:

'In the last chapter . . . we are startled to meet "an imaginary group of philosophers", assembled to welcome Kant and St Thomas, who have returned to life for the occasion. Nearly all the talking is done by St Thomas. . . . He scores some points against Kant, but gives us no satisfactory account of the way in which, according to himself, the human mind makes the passage from finite to infinite. He tells us that his idea of God "expresses not what I have experienced of God, but what I have come to think of him while thinking of the transcendental ideas I have derived not from God but from the world of experience. . . . "[2] . . . "I reject", he continues later, "the theory that we have any intuitive perception of God's Being of any kind, even in the mitigated sense that we perceive Him indirectly as the background on which we somehow realize the contingency of the universe."[3] It is asserted that we are "logically compelled to ask what is the cause of the universe, and of its being limited as we know it to be".'[4]

What does Sillem offer in justification of these statements? It seems to be simply the following: 'We have argued that a universe made up solely of contingent things must itself be contingent; because it is contingent, we conclude that it is an effect; as it is an effect, it must have a cause of some kind.'[5] This is begging the whole question. The world can be described as 'contingent' in a sense which entails a cause for it only if this cause has been already apprehended as at work in the world. It is precisely this apprehension which the agnostic does not allow and it is impossible to persuade him to do so by purely logical means. Causality *in* the world is commonly acknowledged in some sense, but a cause *of* the world is disallowed by innumerable writers who cannot be accused of overlooking a merely logical nexus, for this would be mere stupidity. As for acquiring a knowledge of God 'while thinking in terms of the transcendental ideas [that is, "being", "goodness" and so forth] I have derived not from God but from the world of experience', it is surely obvious that a 'world of experience' in which God is not found cannot provide the materials out of which we can build up knowledge of him.

[1] 1962, 228.   [2] 122.   [3] 124.   [4] 137.   [5] 165.

Turning now from Roman Catholic supporters of the 'traditional' arguments to the work done by Professor Mascall on the Five Ways, I shall consider the comments on them made by him in an early book, *He Who Is* (1943), which has been described by Professor H. D. Lewis[1] as a 'minor classic' and is closely followed by him in his own recent book *Philosophy of Religion*. I shall draw on Lewis's book for its summarization of the first three ways. The first way, the argument from movement, begins by pointing out that certain things are in motion and others at rest. Something must have started this movement. But this must have been set in motion by something else, and we cannot go on like that indefinitely. The series of 'moved movers' implies that there is an 'unmoved Mover'. This must be God. Mascall points out that St Thomas's thought is based here on the Aristotelian distinction between potentiality and the act. He himself accepts this distinction on the ground that it is necessary to account for change. If X changes into Y, it must have had the potentiality for change all along; otherwise it will be simply annihilated and give place to Y, which contradicts the notion of change. And a being cannot possess the power to actualize its own potentiality because in that case, Mascall says, 'it would have done so from the start'.[2] I am not convinced by this and have offered another analysis of change in my contribution to Dom Mark Pontifex's book *The Meaning of Existence*[3] which explains it in the terms of God's creative power. I should agree that a being cannot in fact give itself what it has not got, but this has to be *seen*; there is no way of proving it if it is rejected.

Mascall admits that the second stage in the argument, that we cannot go on indefinitely with the series of movers, gives us in any case only 'a first mover which is itself a member of the series, and therefore is nothing like the Christian idea of God'. 'Its status', he continues, 'is essentially the same as theirs, except that it happens to have no predecessor. It would appear that here St Thomas has followed Aristotle in the wording of the argument in a way which does not really express his own convictions, for the whole essence of his position is that God is of an entirely different nature from all other beings, that he belongs to an infinitely higher order of reality.'[4] All that I accept.

---

[1] In his contribution to the symposium *We Believe in God* (Allen & Unwin), 133.
[2] *He Who Is*, 41.   [3] 118 f.   [4] 43-4.

The second way is the argument from efficient causality. An 'efficient cause' means here not just something which invariably precedes some occurrence, but something which actively produces it and is, as we might say, wholly responsible for it. Everything that happens, the argument runs, must have an efficient cause, and, as in the first way, it is impossible to postulate a sequence of causes causing one another without end. There must be a first Uncaused Cause. To this, says St Thomas, 'everyone gives the name of God'. Mascall remarks excellently: 'Efficient causality is not a physical concept but a metaphysical one, and it is only because the physical scientists of the eighteenth and nineteenth centuries insisted on illicitly talking physics in terms of efficient causality that their successors, having discovered that efficient causality is not what physics is as a matter of fact concerned with, have only too often assumed that it is non-existent.'[1] Mascall denies that the objection applies to which the first argument *seemed* liable —that it seems to give us 'only the first member of a series having the same status as all succeeding members except for the fact of being the first'. He points out that we are here concerned not just with causes which bring things into being but with those which keep them in being, and that the eighteenth-century deists, who failed to realize this, took up with the idea of a God who created the world and then left it to its own devices. The argument, then, is not just about 'a chain of causes stretching back into the past', but about 'a chain of causes existing in the present and each depending on the one beyond'.[2]

Here I may return to a point which is well brought out in Lewis's discussion in his *Philosophy of Religion*. He remarks that the notion of a cause which accounts for everything in its effect is one which is not in fact verified in our experience of the world around us. Effects in the world around us are the result of a multiplicity of previous happenings. It seems that we have in this notion 'an importation into a principle of the natural world of something that has its proper significance in a relation of the finite world to its transcendent source'.[3]

The third way starts from the fact that some things certainly exist. It then claims that there is nothing in the nature of the entities which we find in the world to make them exist, or require that they must exist. In fact they come into being and pass away. But it cannot be true of the totality of things that they just happen

---

[1] 45.   [2] 46.   [3] *Philosophy of Religion*, 177.

to be. For in that case there would have been a time when there was nothing at all. But then nothing could ever have come into being. Nothing will come of nothing. So these contingent beings require necessary being to account for them. And if we suppose that such a being gains its necessity from another, again we are faced with a regress which cannot go on indefinitely—there must be a being whose existence is necessitated by its own nature. (Here I have to point out that a question arises about the wording of the text in St Thomas; Mascall accepts the only reading which can be reasonably supposed to make sense.) He remarks that the introduction of the time element into the argument adds an unnecessary complication. What the argument amounts to is that any existing being which can cease to exist does not contain in itself the reason for its existence.[1] So we must admit a being which exists of itself, even if we postulate an eternal series of contingent beings. Mascall reserves judgment on this argument for the time being.

The fourth way is set out by him in the following terms: 'Among beings some are more and some are less good, noble and so on. But more and less have a meaning only in so far as things approximate, in regard to the quality under consideration, to that which possesses the quality in the supreme degree, which "has all that there is of it", as we might say. And this being . . . must be the cause of its occurrence in other beings in lesser degrees; as, for instance, fire, which is the supreme degree of heat, causes all other heat. Therefore, concludes St Thomas, "There must be something which is to all beings the cause of their being, goodness and every other perfection: and this we call God".'[2] Mascall points out that we cannot take the reference to heat as more than a remote parallel, for St Thomas cannot be saying that God is perfectly hot. It is only to qualities like goodness, he says, 'which of their nature demand something directly akin to them as their cause' that the argument applies. The question is, he continues, 'whether the concrete existence of finite good necessarily implies the concrete existence of an absolute maximum good' and so on with the other types of perfection.[3] He adds that beauty must be one of these perfections, since St Thomas regards it as the good known and loved.[4] And he reserves judgement for the present on this argument also.

The fifth way is the argument from design, often called the

[1] *He Who Is*, 48.   [2] 52.   [3] 53.   [4] 54.

teleological argument. Mascall points out that St Thomas is not arguing from the appearance of design in living organisms or from the course of actual processes in the history of the world; he is making the quite general assertion that the question 'what is the purpose of it?' arises in regard to any being at all just as necessarily as the questions 'what began it?' and 'why does it go on?'. A final cause, a cause which draws things to their end, is just as necessary, he maintains, as an efficient cause. It may not be so obvious that intelligent creatures are not final causes for themselves but, says St Thomas, 'we see that things which lack intelligence, such as natural bodies, act for an end, and this is evident from their acting always, or nearly always, in the same way, so as to obtain the best result. Hence it is plain that, not fortuitously, but designedly, do they achieve their end. Now whatever lacks intelligence cannot move towards an end, unless it be directed by some being endowed with knowledge and intelligence: as the arrow is shot to its mark by the archer. Therefore some intelligent being exists by whom all natural things are directed to their end; and this being we call God.' There is no need to examine this argument in detail. 'Design' in the world may indeed prove a 'pointer' to God, but we cannot 'prove God' in this sort of way. A single comment of Mascall's must suffice about this: 'The teleological nature of beings in their separate particularity ... might conceivably be accounted for by supposing that each of them was provided with a spiritual guardian or angel to direct its operations'.[1] That is to say, whatever the argument may be supposed to prove, it cannot prove the Infinite.

Mascall has seemed to accept the argument that there must be an uncaused Cause, but when he makes his final judgement on the evidential value of the Five Ways[2] he concludes that 'what is necessary ... if we are to pass from a belief in the existence of finite beings to a belief in the existence of God is not so much that we should thoroughly instruct ourselves in the laws and procedures of formal logic as that we should thoroughly acquaint ourselves with finite beings and learn to know them as they really are'.[3] 'Since ... the human mind,' he continues later, 'just because it *is* a mind, is essentially adapted for the understanding of being as such ... the mind is not only able to apprehend the mere existence of finite beings

---

[1] 55.
[2] It will be remembered that he suspended judgement on the third and fourth.
[3] 73.

and their existent properties, but is also capable in some degree of comprehending them, of entering into their inner essence and making them its own, of recognizing not only their finitude but that on which their finitude rests.'[1] What Mascall says about 'being as such' I find unconvincing, but it will be clear that, even in this early book, he regards syllogistic reasoning as at any rate insufficient as a means of discovering God.

But he was not yet in substantial agreement with me, as he would seem to be today,[2] about the content of our apprehension of God. Here he still supposed, apparently, that it makes sense to say that it is 'not God himself that is perceived, but the fact of his existence'.[3] That this difference of view was more apparent than real may be indicated, perhaps, if I quote what he then goes on to say: 'Provided that we put ourselves in the right frame of mind for seeing things as they really are—and this, of course, in practice involves a real effort of moral and intellectual integrity—we can grasp the fact of God's existence . . . with just as much certainty as we perceive the beings themselves.'[4] (I cannot too strongly urge anyone to read the whole of the sixth chapter from which these words are taken.)

In the course of his exposition St Thomas refers to the famous ontological argument attributed to St Anselm (it is arguable that Anselm did not intend it as proof of God's existence at all). Mascall remarks that St Thomas's statement of the argument, though succinct, makes no change in its substance.[5] The statement reads as follows: 'By this word [God] is signified that thing than which nothing greater can be conceived. But that which exists actually and mentally is greater than that which exists only mentally. Therefore, since as soon as the word "God" is understood it exists mentally, it also follows that it exists actually. Therefore the proposition "God exists" is self-evident.' In other words, if the idea were only an idea and did not also stand for a reality, it would not be the idea of that than which nothing greater can be conceived. But it is rather obvious that we cannot inject reality by any mere process of reasoning into what is offered to us only as an *idea*. And so St Thomas's objection to this argument is, again in Mascall's words, that it proves only 'that, if you define God as

---

[1] 73–4.
[2] In *Words and Images*, in particular, where he takes a firmer line about the syllogism.
[3] 74–5.   [4] 75.   [5] 31.

St Anselm does, you are bound to think of him as existing. But that does not prove that he exists. That is to say, the idea of a necessarily existent being does not necessitate its existence.'[1]

To this I would add that if 'to have an idea of' means 'to have knowledge of' then St Anselm is simply making a *claim* to have knowledge of God, and I need hardly say that I have no objection to that. But if it means something else, it will be of no service for purposes of logical argument. And that, I venture to suggest, is really the long and the short of this matter in spite of ingenious attempts which have continued to this day (and are, indeed, being made with particular earnestness just now) to rehabilitate the argument as an argument. It was in connection with it that Kant made his celebrated point, so often referred to by later thinkers, that existence is not a predicate—obviously it is not an ordinary predicate, because it is a presupposition of anything which you may say about anything, but this does not prove that our use of the word can have no significance. It is now generally accepted that Kant did not state Anselm's argument correctly, but he did point to the flaw in it all the same. My chief reason for mentioning him here, however, is that it is still so often alleged, as it was by Kant, that all arguments for God are reducible to the ontological argument. And I want to point out that this cannot be said about my defence of theism, whether or not we think that St Thomas, in spite of his rejection of Anselm's argument, is really committed to it. For this defence is ultimately *not* a logical argument at all—it is not about abstract ideas—but a reflective analysis of our actual condition.

[1] 34.

IV

THEISM AND ETHICS

15. THE AUTONOMY OF ETHICS

Any view that there is an acceptable foundation for ethics which has only an indirect connection with God or none at all contradicts the view which I have been putting forward that the evidence for God is, ultimately, moral evidence. I must therefore consider at some length the claim that ethics is autonomous in regard to religion.

People who maintain the autonomy of ethics will commonly hold that moral obligation cannot be reduced to the effects upon us of our heredity and our environment or to mere long-sighted selfishness. They will reject all reductive accounts of it and insist that the claims of morality impose themselves absolutely—they just have to be recognized, and there is no justifiable appeal against them. And they consider that, if any explanation of this state of affairs is offered in terms of religion, there will be a dependence of ethics upon religion which will detract from the absoluteness of moral obligation and put our moral intuitions (as they sometimes call the deliverances of conscience) under the control of religious dogmas—with the probable result that our ethical standards will be lowered. It is contended that religion cannot judge our moral intuitions; indeed it must itself be judged by them, so that the autonomy of ethics proves to involve the subordination of religion to ethics.

My answer to this, in general terms, is that it is a mistake to suppose that ethics must be in control of religion on pain of being itself controlled by religion, that they are not rival claimants for a position of supremacy but two interpretations of the human condition, one adequate and the other inadequate but, so far as it goes, true and therefore inviolable. Moral obligation, that is, is the ground floor of religion, which is very much more than ethics but cannot interfere with moral obligation because that is its own basis in human experience. Moral obligation *is* religion at that point where it arises for us; it is the awareness of God who acts in us and draws us to him. If conflicts arise between moral intuitions and religious dogmas, the intuitions or the dogmas, or both, will be pseudo-intuitions or pseudo-dogmas. I cannot pursue the intricacies of the enormous subject opened up by that last remark. It must suffice to discuss the question about the origin and significance of the fundamental concept of obligation.

It should be helpful for a start, I think, to consider how this notion of the autonomy of ethics has established itself in modern philosophy. Its great prophet is Kant. The practical upshot of Kant's revolution in philosophy, which like other such revolutions before and since proved to be less revolutionary than it claimed to be, was that metaphysics was thought to be an exploded science and that ethics was substituted for it as the proper study for a philosopher who was still interested in the life of the spirit, who was not prepared to go along with Hume and his successors in the reduction of our experience to sense-experience and not prepared either to merge the human spirit into the One Spirit (whatever that would mean) with the abolition of ethics following from such a merger as its logical consequence. And in the nineteenth century a widespread turning away from Christian belief was accompanied by an increasing development and refinement of the moral consciousness which we must stop to consider for a moment.

In that century there was an attachment to the Christian way of life—or rather to certain aspects of it, for there was also a good deal of blindness to certain other aspects of it (the full meaning of the Christian way of life is something which we come to grasp only gradually as time goes on, and there have been, moreover, many setbacks in this process). This attachment to Christian moral values, or rather to some of them, was the more intense because there was nothing else to live for—Christianity itself, with its promise of union with the transcendent Absolute not only in the next life but also here and now in a preliminary way, was no longer animating Western culture. And there was often the reasonable suspicion that Christian moral values would not long survive the eclipse of Christian doctrine, so that they were clung to with a sort of desperate fervour. For example, there was that incident in the Fellows' Garden at Trinity College, Cambridge, when George Eliot, after some dismissive remarks about religion, breathed out the word 'duty' in a tone of almost ecstatic awe and wonder. Such a person, I contend, is religious without realizing it. And I think we should see in this development and refinement of the moral consciousness a notable outpouring of the Holy Spirit. Christians have often much to learn from professed unbelievers who are, without realizing it, bringing back into currency, or giving fresh development to, Christian attitudes of mind and principles of conduct. Conversely, these people may owe more to historical Christianity than they realize.

The autonomy of ethics in its contemporary forms is in direct succession, I think, from the nineteenth-century moralists. The first exponent of it on whose work I shall touch is Professor H. D. Lewis, in whose book *Philosophy of Religion* I have pointed out so much which seems to me of great value. In that book he is rightly anxious to counteract the current tendency to reduce religion to morality. But this leads him to insist on a sort of divorce between them. Ethics, he holds, depends on God like everything else in the created universe, but it is not necessarily bound up with God in our consciousness—that is to say, we can grasp ethical principles without knowing anything about him. Lewis regards it as obvious that agnostics, in acknowledging moral obligations, must be acknowledging something which is distinct from God.[1] He does not consider the possibility that their interpretation of moral obligation in non-theistic terms may be due to a misunderstanding of what is meant—or ought to be meant—by a belief in God. I shall not here repeat the details of my own analysis of this situation which was sufficiently discussed (I hope) in connection with Dr Baillie and which will emerge again to some extent as we proceed.

Lewis argues that we must first 'have some understanding of goodness as a finite concept' if we are to talk of God as supremely good.[2] My answer to this, it should be clear by now, is that if we recognize 'goodness' as a *value*, we are at the same time recognizing God as the source of value. Of course we can use 'good' in a positivistic way to mean what we happen to like or what the society which we live in happens to approve. But if we are going to use the word with a specifically moral sense, in a sense in which we are asserting *value*, then we must be using it at the same time in a metaphysical sense. God is involved in this meaning of the word as the absolute standard of reference. Our goodness derives from him; so does our idea of goodness. We do not first find a purely human meaning in moral goodness and then attach it to him; still less do we judge him by a standard which is not his own. And I must say that it does seem to me in the highest degree

[1] 262.   [2] 263.

unlikely that a 'reductionist'[1] would be much impressed by talk about an absolute moral value existing in a sort of metaphysical vacuum; he will naturally regard it as a hangover from an outworn cultural heritage and will invoke the names of Marx and Freud.

Just as moral goodness is something separable from God and religion, in Lewis's view, so naturally is conscience. He holds that the voice of God is heard in our conscience, but that our conscience has first to be something on its own if he is to speak to it. He argues that otherwise it could not be 'a medium for divine disclosure to *us*'. He does not mean by this merely that we need to have minds in order to be aware of God's voice. Conscience is, he says, 'operative, as a human endowment, on its own account', and God's voice is a 'refinement of the working of conscience'.[2] What is 'the working of conscience'? When it is a matter of acknowledging obligation, then the working of conscience is, I should say, simply the recognition of God's voice. When we are working out where our obligation lies at particular moments, we use our powers of reason and we may make mistakes. But, although we may be mistaken in thinking that *this* is what we ought to do, we are always right in thinking that we ought to do *something*—it is the existence of obligation as such which establishes our contact with God. And of course if we do what we think right, even if we are wrong about the facts or their implications, we are still acknowledging God in acknowledging obligation. We are intending to do the right thing, and this means that *so far as our relation to God is concerned* we *are* doing the right thing. To do what we think is wrong, even if we are mistaken about our facts, is to *move away* from God. To say that we must always follow our consciences is to say that in doing what we think right we are *aiming at* God. Catholics are sometimes heard to say that conscience is not the only guide in moral matters, for there is also authority to be reckoned with. This can be misleading if it is not properly explained. Anyone who accepts an authority must listen to what it says in order to work out what he ought to do in particular circumstances. If he has decided that he ought always to obey this authority, that it is always reliable, then *that* was what his conscience told him to do, what he thought was right. If the authority then tells him to do something which is in his eyes *certainly* immoral, then he will decide that it is, after all, no reliable authority. But in all cases it must be what he thinks

---

[1] A positivist who reduces obligation to social pressures.   [2] 265.

right—his conscience, as we say—which must be the final arbiter, whether or not it leads him to accept an authority and whether or not he, so to speak, gets his sums right. (Obviously we make mistakes not only about facts but also about priorities, failing, culpably or inculpably, to appreciate the relative *values* of things.)

What, then, in view of all this, is Lewis talking about when he distinguishes God's voice from the workings of conscience? There seems to be here a presupposition that we must be able to make moral judgements without involving God in any way. It is possible to *think* about moral questions without involving him, but not, I would say, to make moral *decisions*. But Lewis has something further in mind, for in the same place he says that conscience 'is not absorbed into religion, and we fall into grievous eror if we suppose that it is—as many theologians have unfortunately done'.[1] What this means, I suppose, is that conscience can never be cancelled out by theological decisions, and I hope now to have made it plain that this is the case and how it is the case. It should be added that, although we ought always to do what we believe to be right (that is, indeed, a tautology), we can confuse believing something to be right with a mere *feeling* that it is right. Believing that something is right in this context means that we have satisfied ourselves, satisfied our *minds*, in regard to it, that we have taken all the necessary steps for reaching an intelligent conclusion. A man who thinks that he has no duty to face all the relevant facts—which may include, for him, the statements of an authority—may indeed be still aiming at God in a muddled way, but it is surely a very muddled way.

At this point it seems desirable to observe that Christian moral theology follows from what Christ has taught us about his Father and our relation to him and to one another; it clarifies and adds other dimensions to the often very vague and confused outlook which follows from the acknowledgement of God without benefit of Revelation. But Christian moral theology cannot interfere with what we can know of God as philosophers, that he is perfectly loving and generous, that we are all his creatures and have in consequence certain duties, not indeed all clearly defined, to one another. I agree with Lewis that ethics must not be absorbed into religion if that means only that genuine moral principles must not be traversed (or simply invented) by theologians. But

[1] 265.

what I mean by religion begins as an acknowledgement of moral obligation.

There seems to me a further difficulty about Lewis's position. It may be remembered that he is not all disposed to accept the view that there are no genuine atheists in the sense of people with whom God does not make at any time any sort of contact. But one might have supposed that he would accept the view, nowadays a commonplace among Christian theologians, that a man who calls himself an atheist will be judged by God, that is, will succeed or fail in attaining to him in the end, according to whether or not he follows his conscience. It would seem a logical consequence of this that, in following or not following one's conscience, one is accepting or rejecting God, and surely one cannot accept or reject God without being in conscious contact with God himself, even if this contact occurs in a form which does not reveal him to the person in question as in fact the God of religion.[1] Lewis is not prepared to accept this conclusion. According to him, it is possible for a man to live a morally good life or a morally bad one without accepting or rejecting God. But if we are all destined to attain to God (unless we deliberately reject him), how is this destiny to be accomplished for vast numbers of people who appear to have no means of contact with him except through their consciences?[2]

Let us now consider the autonomy of ethics as maintained in a book which has already engaged us in an earlier connection, Professor Hepburn's *Christianity and Paradox*. He begins his eighth chapter, 'Secular Ethics and Moral Seriousness', with a quotation from the first page of Paul Ramsey's *Basic Christian Ethics:* 'God has something to do with the very meaning of obligation', and he alludes to the view that a man who recognizes moral obligation is 'already a theist—even if unknown to himself'. It seems that he is unable to take the suggestion seriously because the God of whom he writes is anthropomorphic, lacking in perfection, or just a metaphysical muddle. His main purpose in

---

[1] An answer to this might be found in the theory, which I shall discuss later, that a definitive choice of God is made at the moment of death, when there is an awareness of him which is not possible before. But, according to this theory, the definitive choice is preceded by non-definitive ones which are highly relevant to it.

[2] In the last few paragraphs I repeat some sentences from an article in *Religious Studies*, Vol. 2, No. 1, 1966, 'In Defence of Theism—a Reply to Professor Kai Nielsen'.

this part of the book is to argue that a morality without God is not condemned to meaninglessness and disintegration. I shall be chiefly concerned with what he has to say in the course of it about God's goodness.

According to Hepburn, there can be no question of discovering that God is good through an acquaintance with him. He writes: 'It is only by having direct moral insight into *some* at least of God's commands, by being able to judge these as being morally worthy, that we could be justified in *occasionally* arguing, that although we have no such insight in a particular case, we may be sure that God's will still ought to be done.'[1] The assumption is that we could not know God's beneficence, the nature of his will, in virtue of a knowledge which we have of God himself. I agree with Hepburn that an appeal to an authority, even a supreme authority, considered in the abstract, does not of itself entail the goodness of this authority (a rather obvious point which is constantly stressed by secularist moral philosophers, by Professor Nowell-Smith, for example, in his well-known book *Ethics*). But Hepburn supposes that God's goodness could be established only by a moral judgement passed upon his commands and upon particular activities of his in governing the world.

A little later he considers the question of a Christian's reasons for obeying God. If the Christian, he writes, 'is to continue *praising* God for being good, he must believe that God *might* (without logical contradiction) have been bad, *might* have issued commands which ought not to be obeyed (if not, there would be nothing to be thankful about)'.[2] And he adds: 'Further, if he is to call God good, it can be only by experience of his consistently good acts. One cannot go on *indefinitely* saying: this looks like cruelty, or callousness or indifference on God's part, but it *can't* be, since he is good; for we cannot know his goodness save through these and the like acts.'[3] To offer a full reply to the final words of that passage it would be necessary to rehearse one's theory of God's providence. All that I am concerned with at the moment is Hepburn's failure to realize what sort of knowledge of God a Christian has and how he reacts to that knowledge. A Christian knows God as the source of being and the meaning of goodness. He praises him for his goodness, not by way of congratulating him for avoiding moral failure, but because the question of moral failure cannot arise in his case. To praise God, that is to say, is

[1] 130.   [2] 131-2.   [3] 132-3.

to adore him in all his works. The suggestion that *God* could do evil is, for a Christian, meaningless.

I now quote from Hepburn's account of his own position as a moralist: 'Lying, stealing, or murdering', he says, 'is no whit more or less reprehensible if men are mortals or immortals, whether their way of life is to last a generation or all eternity.'[1] Certainly, I agree, these things do seem reprehensible to the secular humanist. But his recognition of the rights of others does not make sense unless it satisfies some requirement, some want of his own—Nowell-Smith and other analysts of a positivist sort are surely right about this, although their views about human requirements seem to me very narrow ones. To say that we can do no other, faced by some need to help a fellow-creature in distress, implies that we need to satisfy our own consciences, and to do that, I have urged, is to initiate our union with God. We see value in our fellow-creatures because they derive from God, and this makes an absolute demand upon us. 'Ought' does not, indeed, follow logically from 'is', as Hume pointed out (and as positivists gleefully repeat), but it is found along with it: reality makes a claim on us. It sounds very fine to say, as Hepburn says in effect on various occasions, that we should fulfil our obligations just because they are obligations and even without hope of reward, or ideally without hope of reward. This is Kant's position—we ought because we ought, and moral obligation is contaminated by any element of self-regard. It sounds very fine, but it proves, when it is taken absolutely, to be unthinkable. It is true that what we want is something not ourselves, the relief of human distress in the case which we were considering, but it remains that *we want* it. Our own need goes along with the needs of others, and our action would not make sense if it did not fulfil such a need, although that is not what we advert to in the ordinary way when we set our hands to the task.

It might be asked whether we should not be obliged to suffer in this life for justice' sake even if God did not destine us for happiness with him hereafter. This is not a hypothesis which I should be able to entertain. But to anyone who thinks otherwise I should suggest that the defence of justice is not just an obligation but something which satisfies our deepest desires. Hepburn would no doubt allow that in the last chapter of his book his defence of secular humanism does make claims for the satisfactions which it

---

[1] 134.

is thought capable of affording us. He cannot, then, cast a stone at Christians for the hope which they have in them of the satisfaction of all conceivable desires in the vision of God.

It may be noted in passing that a good deal of Hepburn's book is devoted to criticisms of theological theories to which a Christian need not feel himself committed. In the eighth chapter (and earlier in the book) he might seem to be supposing that in refuting Brunner he has somehow undermined the Christian faith. Brunner, like so many Protestant theologians (it is these theologians with whom our academic philosophers are chiefly acquainted), has a view of original sin according to which it would seem (on occasion, at least) that man's will has become totally corrupt and his intelligence inextricably confused as a result of the Fall. Hepburn has no difficulty in showing that on such a view moral philosophy is no longer viable nor indeed is any form of rational discourse. It may be noted too that his method on a number of occasions is to select a particular line of thought from a writer's work and argue against it, often to considerable effect, without attempting any assessment of the writer's overall position. His only reference to Marcel,[1] for example, is a criticism of the remark that 'to love someone is to say "Thou shalt not die" '. This claim of Marcel's, taken in isolation, may well seem arbitrary.

More important, however, for our present purposes is Hepburn's treatment of some remarks of T. S. Eliot's about human *value*. 'People like Eliot', he writes, '... feel that ... the denial of Christian doctrine alters, in some objective sense, the *value* of humanity.' 'The moralist has to protest here', he goes on, 'that this language very easily warps and distorts our understanding of the concept of "value". It suggests that values are price-tags, affixed authoritatively on the objects evaluated. The Great Evaluator may, at his pleasure, remove such price-tags, or down-value them as at sale-time, and so on.'[2] Here I must protest. 'People like Eliot' should not be interpreted in such a way. What they are saying is that God, by creating man and destining him for himself, confers upon him, by so doing, the highest value possible for a creature. For those who do not accept these truths, the importance or value of man in the scheme of things must plainly be less than it is for those who accept them. The picture of God affixing price-tags is a grotesque caricature of the anthropology professed by thinking Christians.

[1] 145.   [2] 148–9.

One more passage in Hepburn's book requires comment here (I alluded to it in the earlier discussion of his book, but it seemed better to reserve comment until now). In his criticism of Professor H. H. Farmer's book *The World and God* he quotes the remark: 'It is in the unique experience of recognizing absolute value that I say our awareness of God as personal will is given.' 'Farmer wants to say', Hepburn comments, 'that the unconditional judgements, those which have priority over all rivals, can be satisfactorily accounted for only by seeing in them the will of God.'[1] His criticism is that Farmer must be here 'assuming as an indispensable premiss that God's will is itself unconditionally good—otherwise the fact that he backed up some moral judgement of ours would do nothing to settle the question of its absoluteness or even its rightness'.[2] Hepburn continues: 'Now here is a judgement to the effect that something is unconditionally, absolutely good, namely God's will. It is (necessarily) we ourselves who are making this judgement. But on Farmer's view absoluteness is given only by adding to a judgement about morals the further judgment that "This is willed by God". But when it is that very will which is being evaluated . . . then obviously *that* judgement cannot be given its authority in the same way as other judgements.' Whatever we may think of this as a criticism of Farmer's position, it has no force whatever against what I have proposed as the explanation of unconditional moral obligation. This is not based on a distinction of particular obligations into conditional and unconditional; it does not determine unconditional ones by adding to the conditional ones the further judgement that 'this is willed by God'. We find that we have an all-over obligation to make something of ourselves, and this, I have proposed, is itself an awareness of God, an awareness which contains within it the judgement, the truth, that God's will is unconditionally good.

Before leaving Hepburn's book I ought to say that he does try to be fair and open-minded. At one point he goes so far as to say: 'I *do* seem able to attach something rather *like* good sense to the notion of a Ground for the world's existence . . . especially when the vision of such a being is expressed through the medium of great poetry'[3]—a very clear case of a 'suspicion' of God.

In a recent book, *Deity and Morality*, Mr Burton P. Porter concludes, rather with the air of one announcing an important discovery, that the concept of God embraces the notion of absolute

---

[1] 42.   [2] 42-3.   [3] 178.

goodness. Since, as we have seen, it is a discovery which so many modern philosophers have failed to make, the conclusion is very welcome. A review of the book in *Theology*[1] by Mr H. P. Owen questioned it. Owen's difficulty about it is that the proposition 'God is good' seems to him not to be an analytic one. 'It is', he says, 'a sheer fact that "God" has often been taken to signify a being that is supramoral or even immoral.'

I do not, of course, deny that the word has been used in that way. But when it is used in English, it will not be taken in that way unless there is a special prescription to that effect. And there is nothing arbitrary about the standard use. Christians have put it into currency and established it because the identification of God with absolute goodness is something which their awareness of him has taught them. The identification is logically self-evident in the sense that the logic of the English language insists upon it. Owen would perhaps reply that our knowledge of God's love for men is not a matter of normal experience, even for Christians, but a matter of revelation, and he might say that the philosophies and religions of the East sometimes claim a knowledge of a God who has no such love. There is a sort of pantheism, I should then say, which carries with it adoration, which acknowledges God's benefits, even though by a confusion of thought it may not properly distinguish him from the created world and fears to anthropomorphize him by using the language of love as Christians do. And there is a form of monism which is not religious at all but simply a philosophical theory about the unity of the universe or the unity of all minds. There are also beliefs about some superhuman but finite power or powers. We cannot stop people talking about God or about gods in such connections; a Christian can only say that what he is talking about when he talks about God has nothing to do with such fancies, and a correct English-speaker will be following his usage unless he gives notice to the contrary.

But whatever we are to say about other usages of 'God', a Christian is perfectly entitled to claim that he does not need to *argue* from the notion of infinity to the notion of goodness. This is a scholastic procedure which seems to have no place in real life. The claim must be made that to be in contact with God is to be aware of him as good. Nor can it be shown that a natural knowledge of God cannot be the basis of such a claim. I quote

[1] September 1968.

from Canon Maurice Nédoncelle's *Conscience et Logos*: 'Despite the degradations and perversions of our epoch, there remains happily in every man who comes into the world a minimum of the perception of God's attributes which is indestructible.'[1] I doubt whether this minimum is indestructible, but I have no doubt that it must exist, somehow and sometime, in every man.

Owen, in his book *The Moral Argument for Christian Theism*[2] does not accept the view that 'the moral sense is itself an awareness of God'. God, he says, is himself in contact with atheists, but 'to say that he is the origin of moral concepts is not to say that he is known as such'.[3] Owen is an exponent of the autonomy of ethics in so far as he believes the acknowledgement of absolute obligation to be possible without its having any religious significance, in the sense that the subject of it has himself no cognitive contact with God.[4] As we shall soon see, he nevertheless regards it as irrational to acknowledge such an obligation and at the same time not to acknowledge God, and we shall find that he has something to say on that topic which was well worth saying.

16. THEOLOGICAL ETHICS

Mr H. P. Owen accepts an autonomy of ethics in that he does not identify, as I do, an awareness of an absolute moral claim as an awareness which bears on God. He does hold, nevertheless, that the absolute claim of the moral order does not make sense unless there is a judgement, over and above the acknowledgement of this claim, that this order derives from God. Owen does not claim that the facts of the moral life provide the premises of a cast-iron argument for God but does claim that they cannot be satisfactorily explained without him, and for this, I think, he makes out a very good case. It is one which may make a secular moralist realize more clearly the difficulties of his own position. If we were to grant him, for the sake of argument, that the moral claim *can* be acknowledged without an awareness which bears on God, it will then be useful to show him, using Owen's method, that, even so, unless a theistic *explanation* of the facts is going to be admitted, he is in a very odd position. Owen is saying that

---

[1] 122. [2] Allen & Unwin, 1965. [3] 36.
[4] It may be desirable to repeat that such cognitive contact occurs, in my view, when the absoluteness of moral obligation is acknowledged, even though it is not recognized as contact with the God of religion.

an inference from these facts to the existence of God is the only reasonable explanation. I have rejected inference as a way of 'proving God', but I grant that the inference proposed by Owen can raise the question of God's existence in a particularly striking way. It will always remain *possible*, however, for someone to fall back on saying that the moral claim is just a brute fact. Inference of itself can never effect the passage from finite to infinite.

Let us now consider Owen's case in some detail. In the third chapter of *The Moral Argument for Christian Theism*, after stating the view that moral claims 'constitute an independent order of reality' (independent, that is, in that they can be recognized without knowledge of God), he offers 'five reasons for inferring God as their source or ground'. The first is that these claims are not self-explanatory. 'We feel their "pressure" ', he writes, '. . . but on the purely moral plane we are unable to give any further account of their existence. They just "are"—enigmatic entities in an uncharted sphere. Their enigma consists in the fact that, taken in themselves, they are *im*personal.'[1] Owen admits that to talk of a claim which has no personal ground cannot be shown to be a clear case of logical contradiction, but, since in our ordinary experience claims do refer to persons, the moral life becomes unintelligible unless they too receive this reference. If we are not prepared to accept this unintelligibility, we must explain the situation by reference to a personal God.[2] The secular moralist would remark that moral claims are sufficiently explained by reference to finite persons, but this will not account for their *authority*, as Owen proceeds to point out. He quotes a sentence of mine from *The Basis of Belief*:[3] 'moral obligation, as I see it, is so far from self-explanatory that if it were not made intelligible by being found in a metaphysical—and in fact a theistic-context— I should be greatly tempted to hand it over to the anthropologists and the psychologists'. The truth in this, he then comments, 'is that while naturalistic explanations of the moral law fail to account for its authority, they at least do justice to its *personal* character' (in their reference, that is, to the dictates of society). 'On the other hand', he continues, 'bare belief in an impersonal order of claims, while it is compatible with their absolute character, does not provide the personal basis which their imperatival quality requires.'

Owen's second reason is connected very closely with the first.

[1] 49. [2] 50. [3] 117.

He points out that *obedience* to the moral imperative offers an additional paradox if we leave God out of it. For these claims 'transcend every human person and every human embodiment', whereas 'we value the personal more highly than the impersonal....' Moreover (and this is the third reason) in human experience 'persons do not merely exemplify abstract claims. They exact claims in their own right because they are persons and not things'.[1] Owen proceeds to argue that belief in human dignity is not defensible in theory, although it may be tenable for a time in practice, 'unless it is derived from theistic premises'. 'Human persons cannot *in themselves* exert the absolute claim' of the moral imperative.[2] Fourthly, there are the phenomena of reverence, responsibility and guilt. It does not really mean anything to talk of 'reverencing an ideal' unless this refers to persons. We cannot be responsible except to persons, yet, as Owen puts it, 'we also speak of a responsibility when no human persons are in view. Thus a person who wasted his talents could be called "irresponsible" '.[3] The argument here is that one cannot be responsible to oneself in such a case and that the duty of using our talents is not owed to any human person. It could be suggested that it is owed to society at large, but the reply would be, as before, that society at large has no absolute authority over us. It seems to me that the inference proposed in this particular form is rather obviously more than an inference. We are being asked to acknowledge a personal but non-human claim made upon us. In fact we are being asked to make a discovery. What we are being asked to discover we may not identify with what is meant by God, but that, I hold, is what it is all the same.

Owen's final argument causes me a certain difficulty. He says that we find ourselves 'constantly frustrated by a self-centredness that we are powerless to eradicate' and asks: 'if our natures are defective, how can they be healed except by aid which is strictly *super*natural?' He does mention the difficulty—namely, that we are obliged to perform only those actions which lie within our power, but he does not here discuss it.[4] The facts to which he refers signify, I would say, our awareness of a perfect, absolute person to whom we cannot attain without his help.

Owen's arguments, then, in general, do present an impressive case against an interpretation of the moral claim on impersonal lines. And it seems to me all the more impressive when we

[1] 53.   [2] 55.   [3] 57.   [4] 59.

THEISM AND ETHICS

compare it, as he proceeds to do, with the interpretation attempted on those lines by Professor W. G. Maclagan in his book *The Theological Frontier of Ethics*. It must suffice to quote a few of Owen's extensive comments on Maclagan's book, preceded by a paragraph quoted by him from it:

'I readily concede [Maclagan writes][1] that to speak of an order of values is not to carry our thought to a point at which it may complacently rest. The concept is obscure and problematic in the highest degree. It challenges further enquiry which, if fruitful, might alter our language and thought almost beyond recognition— I wish I knew whether and how. But in default of this enquiry, in which I cannot claim to have made any headway myself, it appears to me that we can neither dispense with the concept—it must be taken as having anyhow a provisional validity—nor yet relate values in any helpful way to some Being supposedly more fundamental. The beginning of wisdom may here lie simply in getting used to the concept of values as a concept of what *is*, though not as temporal existents are.'

Owen comments on this remarkable passage: 'Since an independently existing order of values is inexplicable, and since (as Maclagan candidly concedes) their inexplicability is a philosophic offence, it would seem natural to accept a theistic explanation.'[2] Maclagan rejects any attempt to integrate God with values. Even if God is supposed to be the perfect exemplification of an order of values, still, Maclagan says, this order must be 'something other and apart from him, and it, rather than he, will be the true Deity'[3]. This provokes from Owen the very proper comment that 'the Christian theist cannot accept the view that God exemplifies an order of values . . . values have no existence outside his character and will'[4] (that is, he is their source).

Finally, it must be observed that although Owen insists on the unreasonableness of secular moralists he also insists that in the long run what settles the question is not discursive reason but what he calls 'the mind's capacity for intuiting God in (or contuiting him with) his effects'. 'The final intuition', he says, 'cannot occur unless there is at least some degree of spiritual experience. . . .'[5] I am in disagreement with Owen's position (apart from his use of the word 'intuition') only in so far as it

[1] 91–2.   [2] 82.   [3] Maclagan, 88–9.   [4] 82.   [5] 44.

separates spiritual experience and the moral sense from the apprehension of God. For me all these meet at a point. It is the main purpose of these discussions about theism and ethics to recommend that view.

Since it is a view which English-speaking philosophers do not often put forward, and this may cause a certain prejudice against it, I had better give some further indication at this point that it is, nevertheless, not one confined to the few individuals whom I have already mentioned or to the middle years of the present century. Mr P. F. Baelz some five years ago, in one of the Open Lectures of the Cambridge Divinity faculty entitled 'Is God Real?',[1] made no bones about appealing to 'the element of unconditional claim' in our moral experience as evidence of God. And he has pursued this topic in an important little book, *Christian Theology and Metaphysics*, published a year or two ago. A few quotations from it will show that his main conclusions about our knowledge of God are all of them in harmony with mine. 'It almost looks', he writes in his first chapter, 'as if those thinkers who have wanted to emphasize the person of Jesus Christ as the source of our knowledge of God to the exclusion of all other sources, whether in natural theology or in religious experience, have themselves paradoxically contributed to the rise of Christian atheism and what has been called the death of God'.[2] Baelz refers to 'the inescapable logical objection to all arguments for the existence of God which begin from premisses about the world and man'; which is 'If you start from what is other than God you cannot end up with God without making him other than God.'[3] 'Religious experience', he goes on (unconsciously echoing Price), 'is like coming to recognize the presence of something which has been present all the time but to the existence of which one has been blind. . . . It embraces and illuminates all other experiences. The religious object, correspondingly, is seen as the ground of all other objects. It is the transcendent in the midst. This is not to say that the discursive reason has no place in man's coming to believe.'[4] It is true that one formula employed by Baelz could of itself suggest a certain agnosticism: 'we apprehend the pressure of the other upon us rather than the other in its own being', but this is balanced by the further statement that 'it is the pressure of the other upon us which makes it possible

---

[1] Published by Collins, in *Faith, Fact and Fantasy* in the Fontana paperback series.   [2] 10.   [3] 99.   [4] 109-10.

for us to apprehend the other'.[1] This is precisely what I have been trying to say.

That this sort of appeal to our moral experience has been in fact a commonplace in the history of philosophy, although disregarded by so many contemporary philosophers, may be perhaps sufficiently indicated if I quote a remark of Professor Norman Kemp-Smith's from his Presidential Address of 1947 to the Aristotelian Society. 'Is not', he asked, 'the presence of the supra-natural or spiritual vouched for by what is characteristic of the moral life on all its levels—namely, by the feature of obligation?' Kemp-Smith, presumably, did not expect that all his hearers would be prepared to give that question an affirmative answer, but he did at least expect them to recognize it as a familiar one. It might be asked whether we must interpret Kemp-Smith's question in a theistic sense. In his British Academy lecture of 1931 ('Is Divine Existence Credible?'), Kemp-Smith concluded that 'Divine Existence is more than merely credible: it is immediately experienced; and is experienced in increasing degree in proportion as the individual, under the discipline and through the way of life prescribed by religion in this or that of its great traditional forms, is enabled to supplement his initial experiences by others of a more definite character.'[2] That seems to me admirably said, except that I would say 'mediately', not 'immediately', experienced. In this lecture, however, Kemp-Smith holds that 'the initial experience of the divine . . . has its own independent roots. It is out of them, not out of morals . . . that it has to grow.'[3] He is not thinking here, I take it, explicitly and in particular of moral *obligation*, a topic on which he does not directly touch in this earlier lecture and which he might seem, very curiously, simply to have overlooked. But in this lecture he disregards moral evidence of any kind and maintains that it is 'through and in connection with the *cosmic* setting of our human life, that we can alone experience that aspect of the Divine which is . . . required in order to give proper perspective to all our other assertions in regard to the Divine'. 'For', he says, 'by the Divine we must, at the least, mean that upon which all things rest.'[4] Perhaps, by 1947, Kemp-Smith had come to see that it is through our recognition of our own entire dependence on God that we come to see the world as dependent on him. At any rate he was well aware that this view has a very long history.

[1] 136.   [2] *Proceedings*, 234.   [3] 231.   [4] 233.

The writer whose work I am most anxious to emphasize, is, however, the late Professor G. F. Woods, whose book *A Defence of Theological Ethics* is particularly relevant to the specific question which is here engaging us, the question of the autonomy of ethics. His purpose in the book is to show that objections to a theistic interpretation of ethics, based on its alleged autonomy, are in fact without foundation; he is not concerned positively to press metaphysical claims but opens the way to them. In one sense, then, he does not so far as Owen does; in another sense, he goes further, because the conclusions to which he eventually comes carry with them at least the implication that ethics does not in any sense 'constitute an independent order of reality', as Owen would have it.

The first half of Woods's book is largely taken up with a discussion of what it means to talk about *standards*, with particular reference to moral standards. When we are talking about the metal bar known as the Royal Standard Yard, we have to remember that the bar is not the standard of measurement. It is 'no more than a physical expression or exemplar of the unit of length which at the material time is called a yard'. 'The standard itself', Woods points out, 'is elusive. It is not identical with any of its physical expressions but is somehow represented in them. This means that we are not speaking carefully in referring to physical standards because no standard is in itself physical.' And 'we may make the mistake of thinking that we can adequately understand the moral standard in terms of our misunderstanding of physical standards'.[1] We have also to realize that 'no standard is absolute in the sense of applying to no circumstances whatever. It is as useless as . . . a theatre ticket which applies to no particular seat . . . even a physical standard is not fully understood as applying *to* certain situations because in a sense the character of a situation effects its appropriate application.'[2] In other words, a standard must have both a certain independence and a certain relevance in regard to situations, and this applies both to moral and to physical standards. The notion of a 'standard' thus proves to be a complex and mysterious one even in its most down-to-earth instantiations.

When Woods turns to the topic of personal and professional standards he writes as follows:

'Those who believe that there is a genuine distinction between good and bad novelists are bound to believe that some kind of

[1] 30-1.   [2] 38.

standard is being or not being acknowledged or practised. This recognition does not imply, however, that any adequate expression of this standard is available or that its precise method of application is fully known. The manifest difficulties in applying many types of professional standards should not be taken as immediate proof that there are no standards to be expressed or applied. The fact that personal standards cannot be as conveniently operated as the physical standards which can be represented in some physical replica does not show that belief in personal standards must be an illusion'.[1]

And in a summary of this part of his argument Woods concludes that 'the relationship of a person to the standards of his being remains mysterious. He is not identical with their expression or their application, but in some way he is most himself in their true expression and true application.'[2]

Some would of course deny that it means anything to talk about the standards of being a person, and Woods's argument as so far described has been criticized as unconvincing for a positivist. But it has to be remembered that he is concerned not so much with positivists as with people who do accept unconditional moral claims although they reject a theistic interpretation of them.

Woods now turns directly to the autonomy of ethics. The expression, he reminds us, has sometimes been used with reference to the moral agent's autonomy in the exercise of moral freedom. But he is concerned with it in so far as it claims an autonomy for the moral standard applied by the agent and this, he says, 'cannot be autonomous in the sense in which a moral agent may be autonomous. The reason is that a personal being may have some kind of capacity to establish, to express and to apply some kind of standard expressed in some kind of legal form, but a moral standard which is itself devoid of any personal characteristic is incapable of establishing, or expressing, or applying itself'.[3] To say that a moral standard is autonomous expresses the conviction 'that this standard requires no extraneous support or approval....' 'For example', Woods goes on, 'if we witness a piece of wanton cruelty, we are all outraged. We naturally protest. We say that it is intolerable. We assert that it ought not to have been done; that it is simply not permissible for a human being to act in this way. If we speak in this way we are talking as though there were

[1] 61–2.   [2] 44.   [3] 80–1.

some kind of law against wanton cruelty. We are interpreting the operation of the moral standard as analogous to the operation of a human law. And we are affirming that the moral standard is autonomous, in the sense of being a law which we may disobey but never abrogate.' Woods considers that this is how people have come to describe the moral standard as autonomous and comments that he finds it 'a very awkward use of the word'.[1] He is surely right to find it so.

The argument to which this leads may be briefly expounded as follows. We are not merely registering a private opinion in protesting against the act of wanton cruelty, but saying, in effect, that nobody can abrogate the law in question. The moral standard has here an authority over all men. How are we to understand such a standard, bearing in mind the complexities to which the general notion of a standard has already given rise? 'It is', says Woods, 'in the sheer absence of any really satisfactory explanations of the nature of the moral standard that we may feel compelled to turn ... to a fresh examination of christian theological ethics.'[2]

He now takes up a topic which was mentioned also by Owen, that of moral failure. It is a fact, he points out, that people not only lapse into moral failures but also recover from them. There is not only the fact, adduced by Owen, that their moral autonomy has been interfered with as a result of their failure, but also the fact that their evil will has become once more a good one. This transition, Woods remarks, is a mystery. 'It is no simple autonomous act, because an evil will is not changed into a good will by the act of the evil will.'[3] This statement has been challenged on the ground that moral freedom precisely means that we can turn from good to evil and from evil to good. But that is to miss Woods's point. Moral evil does indeed mean this, but the question is: how does the evil will receive the power to change itself? This is a 'pointer' towards a theistic interpretation of the present matter. 'The whole process of repentance and forgiveness', Woods continues, 'even when we are not thinking of divine forgiveness, discloses problems which are not solved by any simple reference to the autonomy of the moral agent in the presence of an autonomous moral standard. There are depths of human experience which are not apprehended by any simple moralism.'[4] Again it must be remembered that Woods is here addressing those who believe in moral responsibility in the sense

[1] 82. [2] 84-5. [3] 86. [4] 87.

of moral *choice*—and not determinists like Professor Nowell-Smith.

So far Woods has hardly moved beyond Owen's position. He does seem to do so in the following passage: 'In our experience of the manifold character of personal being, I think we may have some slight insight into the character of ultimate being. In our own case, there is always a discrepancy between what we are and what we ought to be. And we have also here some sense of a discrepancy between our actual apprehension of what ought to be and what in truth we ought to be. The perfection of our being is beyond our full understanding and beyond our powers of execution. I believe that we can dimly conceive that this kind of discrepancy must be absent in God.'[1] This surely suggests that we have an apprehension of God and of who he is, however dim, *in* our moral experience. At any rate there is no suggestion that it is only a basis for *inferring* God's existence.

Woods now considers the objection that if what is willed by God is good this must be 'because it is in accord with the moral standard to which he is subject . . . God cannot be the explanation of what has authority over him'.[2] 'These puzzles', Woods comments, 'have been perennial', which is surprising since, as we have seen, a rather obvious answer has always been available, namely, that we know God as the source of goodness and goodness as that which has its source in him. Woods is content, for the moment, to hint at this as follows: 'It is an error to think of God as a finite person inhabiting a common world including an autonomous moral standard.' 'Even so,' he goes on, 'to discard a crude theology is only a step towards a more delicate interpretation of the being and activity of God.' The next step is this: 'To think of the moral standard is to think of the creative will of God. . . . The autonomy of the moral standard is here not simply affirmed without explanation but interpreted as a characteristic of what is ultimately the case,'[3] namely that God's will is 'morally sovereign over whatever exists'. And this, Woods adds, 'goes some way towards an elucidation of the curious ambiguity which is characteristic of the moral status of expressions of the moral standard. . . . All are useful but they are not all equally useful in all situations. All in some sense embody the moral standard but in every case the standard is neither wholly identical with its expression nor wholly other than the form in which it is expressed. It is at once transcendent and immanent in regard to its expressions.'[4]

---
[1] 97.   [2] 99.   [3] 102.   [4] 103.

A human will, Woods argues, is present in its expressions without being identical with any of them. He suggests that the will of God is related to the various expressions of the moral standard in a way analogous to that in which a human will is related to its expressions. This means, I take it, that the will of God for man, which is *for* man's good (which *is*, therefore, man's good), is reflected in the various expressions of the moral standard. The moral standard is 'relevant to human situations', and it applies to 'what is the case and what ought to be the case'.[1] The connection between facts and values, denied by Hume and his successors, is thus here established.

Woods develops the theme excellently: 'It is not only the case that a person is in the actual state in which he is at any particular time but it is also the case that his being essentially includes the personal standards in which he finds his true fulfilment. In dutiful submission to them, he may be said to be living in obedience to the will of his creator. But this is not submission to an alien tyranny nor is it capricious exercise of an irresponsible autonomy. It is a matter of being himself. Precisely for this reason, the creative will of God as it is more fully understood is found to be in accord with his reason and his conscience.'[2] 'Its presence within us,' Wood adds very usefully, '... should place under constant scrutiny the moral traditions which we receive.'

In the last section of his book Woods shows how the Christian interpretation of God's will as both a creative and a saving will throws light on the human situation: 'When the moral standard', he writes, 'is identified with some expression which is impersonal it offers no kind of assistance or hope to what is not in accord with the expressed standard.... There is clearly a greater possibility of interpreting the moral standard as a saving will if the standard is interpreted in terms of will.'[3] And to complete this rapid summary of Woods's argument I must quote the whole of his penultimate paragraph, which seems to me a fine piece of writing as well as good theology:

'When the moral standard is interpreted as the creative and saving will of God it is plain that such a will is never exhaustively manifested in any of its particular expressions or manifestations. Its fullest revelation is in a personal being in whom there is no inconsistency between what is the case and what must be the

[1] 105.   [2] 107–8.   [3] 125–6.

case. There could be no complete revelation through the medium of the impersonal. And the revelation is always imperfect in personal lives where the incongruity between what is and what ought to be has not been overcome. It is the christian claim that in Christ we see the truth of our nature. His significance is not fully appreciated if he is treated as an external example which we must strive to emulate. As a perfect but particular embodiment of the creative and saving will of God he is active in all men, disposing them towards moral perfection and striving to re-create them when they turn away from the perfection to which they are called. The quest for moral perfection is far more than a quest for private excellence. It involves the attainment of right relationships with God and with our fellowmen. And it includes a right relation of re-created humanity to the natural world. The consummation is set in eternity, which lies far beyond the range of profitable description.'[1]

There is one topic, which recurs from time to time in Woods's book, on which I want to comment. In discussing moral objections to theistic accounts of ethics he writes that they arise primarily in regard to 'the propriety of either receiving or giving divine grace' on the ground that, if the moral worth of an action depends upon the moral freedom of the agent, it is morally difficult to see how anyone can be entitled to help him or in what way he may be entitled to receive help. For 'it looks like the case of a schoolmaster surreptitiously giving help to one of his pupils who is sitting a public examination'.[2] Woods does point out that for the Christian it is 'taken to be an essential characteristic of the saving will of God that he is willing to save even those who do not strictly merit salvation', but he adds that serious problems arise when we try 'to reconcile the operation of grace with the autonomy of the moral agent' and declares at the end of the book: 'I know of no theory of divine grace which is not open to moral criticism.'[3] I shall not repeat what I have said already about these problems except to suggest that Woods's reference to 'those who do not strictly merit salvation' may be the clue to a possible misunderstanding about the relations in which God's creatures stand to him. There can be, as I have had occasion to say before, no question of our making any claims upon God for the simple reason that we receive everything from him. He will give us

[1] 130-1.   [2] 16-17.   [3] 130.

everything which we as individuals need, if we are prepared to take it, although this (the world being what it is) may involve suffering for us here and now. The language of 'merit' obscures these truths. And this way of looking at things does not abolish our autonomy. We remain responsible and, I have insisted, exclusively responsible, for refusing God's offers (he is omnipotent only as the source of all good). We remain genuine agents even, and especially, when we are accepting his offers unreservedly, for this is the way, as Woods himself has so admirably explained, in which we become truly ourselves. This is, if you like, the paradox of Christianity, but it is a paradox which lies at the heart of our experience and might even serve as the profoundest definition of it.

17. THE ETHICS OF PROFESSOR JOHN MACMURRAY (WITH A NOTE ON MISS IRIS MURDOCH)

The work of Professor John Macmurray will show a contrast (I hope, an illuminating one) to the view which I am proposing about the relationships between religion, Christianity, and morality. I have proposed that theism is identical with morality in its origin but that it goes beyond morality. Macmurray seems, at times anyhow, to identify Christianity with moral endeavour in the present world. And he constantly attacks all forms of 'dualism', especially that form of it which leads to what he calls 'mysticism'. I hope to make clear, eventually, the differences between a purely moralistic view of Christianity and the view which sees in it not only a moralism but above all a mysticism. At the moment, however, I must give some account of Macmurray's general position in philosophy as a preliminary to examining his views on Christianity.

He first attracted notice in a big way when he gave a series of broadcast talks published in 1932 under the title *Freedom and the Modern World*.[1] He had realized that the decade which had opened was one full of menace and his warnings made a very deep impression. The book is a defence of spiritual values which contain in germ the ideas which he has been developing for some forty years. One may say, I think, that its chief topic is the opposition behind thought on the one hand and feeling and action on the other which has been so often taken for granted in the history of

[1] Recently reissued as a paperback.

philosophy. Freedom, he ends by saying, means 'thinking and feeling, for ourselves, and expressing our own reality in thought and action'. And he adds the significant warning that 'we have to recapture the sense of beauty if we are not to lose our freedom'.

Macmurray's philosophical views were given definitive expression in his Gifford Lectures for 1953–4, published in two volumes, *The Self as Agent* (1957) and *Persons in Relation* (1961). The last pages of the second volume indicate his main conclusions in a convenient form. He tells us that 'the proper way of representing the relation between religion and science . . . is to say that religion is the expression and adequate apperception of our relation to the world, while science is the expression of a limited, partial, and therefore inadequate, apprehension. This is, of course, not a criticism of science.' Any impersonal conception of the world, Macmurray goes on, is inadequate. For 'we are elements of the world which we represent to ourselves and which in reflection we distinguish from ourselves; and all our activities are integral with the total activity of the world'.[1] 'If we are thought of as part of the scientist's world', Macmurray continues, 'then we cannot make mistakes or have illusions, not even the illusion that we are free to act.'[2] Here we have a critique of positivism which I can only applaud.

The following passage I also read with much satisfaction, mingled, however, as it went on, with a feeling of mystification: 'What is given immediately in action is the existence of the self and others in practical relation. In action, I know that I exist as an agent, and that the Other exists as resistance and support of my action. The rule by which I seek to determine the character of the Other is this: I must determine myself and the Other reciprocally, by means of the same categories. . . . Consequently, I must categorize the Other . . . as an agent acting intentionally in regard to me . . . the personal conception of the world is not the result of personifying what is first recognized as non-personal. The personal conception of the Other is original; and the conception of the impersonal is reached through a process of depersonalization. . . .'[3] What I find mystifying about this is not that the 'other' acquires a capital initial letter as the passage proceeds (for, if Macmurray means that we can make direct contact with God, of course I agree with him) but that there would seem to be a denial that we are aware of being immediately in

[1] 218.   [2] 220.   [3] 220–1.

contact with bodies, objects known as impersonal. To affirm this is what Macmurray calls 'dualism'. He tells us that we cannot accept an ultimate distinction between actions done by persons and events which just happen. We must say that 'what appears to be mere happening is really action', for 'we must . . . conceive the world . . . as the act of God, the Creator of the World, and ourselves as created agents, with a limited and dependent freedom to determine the future, which can be realized only on the condition that our intentions are in harmony with His intention, and must frustrate itself if they are not'.[1] We may indeed agree that God is acting in everything, but it is still true to say that there is a world which is itself impersonal. A created being is a being distinct from God, and some such beings are obviously *not* persons.

Our main question will be that of deciding what Macmurray means by 'God'. He rejects the suggestion that what he has just been saying is pantheistic. His conception of the world is not, he says, that of an organism. 'God', he asserts, 'as the infinite Agent is immanent in the world which is his act, but transcendent of it.'[2] Unfortunately that statement does not settle all the difficulties in his account of theism. They will appear very clearly if we now turn to his Forwood Lectures of 1960, published in the following year under the title *Religion, Art, and Science*. It is a great temptation to detail some of the excellent things which he tells us here about art and science, but I must resist it. He distinguishes religion from science in a way which we have already come across. It is the distinction between religion and art which calls for notice. According to Macmurray, 'contemplation' is the key word of art, whereas 'communion' is the key word of religion. 'Indeed', he writes, 'there is a fundamental sense in which contemplation excludes communion. Contemplation is inherently a solitary activity. It is the attitude of the spectator. One must stand aside to contemplate; one must not be personally involved. But a personal involvement is the core of communion.'[3] There is, however, I should want to point out, a form of contemplation which does carry with it not only one's own personal involvement but involvement also with other people.

Greek thought, Macmurray goes on to say, confuses art with religion, and this leads to a 'spiritualizing' of religion, resting upon 'the dualism of matter and spirit which identifies reality

[1] 222. [2] 223. [3] 43.

THEISM AND ETHICS

with the spiritual'. I agree, of course, that such an identification is a mistake. But I cannot agree with the further statement that 'the purely spiritual, unrelated to the material . . . is the purely imaginary'[1] unless perhaps if this were to be taken in some sense as true only of the human sphere, and, as we shall see, that is not the meaning of it. The second Forwood Lecture concludes: 'The belief that religion is grounded in mysticism, that it grows out of a commerce, real or imaginary, with the supernatural, is a form of the confusion which is very common at the present time. Mysticism is, in itself . . . an aesthetic rather than a religious experience.' So we are left wondering what religious experience will turn out to be.

The third of these lectures will tell us. What differentiates man from the rest of the animate world, the argument of it begins, is 'not speech itself, but the need which is served by speech—the need for communication'.[2] This is described as 'our only original adaptation to the environment into which we are born', on the ground that we are not provided with instincts sufficient to enable us to fend for ourselves but are wholly dependent upon others. And we grow as persons only by communicating with others. 'The self, the "I" is never the unit of personal life, but the "You and I".'[3] Many thinkers today, Christian and non-Christian, take that view in a more or less thorough-going way. It is surely something of a platitude, indeed, unless we take it so literally as to turn it into a paradox. Now it is this 'central field of experience', as Macmurray calls it, the field of personal relations, to which religion refers in his opinion. 'Its function', he writes, 'is . . . to deepen and develop human community. All valid forms of religion are conditioned by this function and can be understood through it.'[4]

At this point we might wonder whether God will come into the story at all. But the passage continues: 'This does not mean that in our religious activities we are aiming directly at this end. Religion is a mode of reflection, and it has its own reflective ends. . . . If someone wishes to assert that religion is concerned with the knowledge of God and communion with God, there is no need to dispute this. It is not an objection to what has been said, that the reference of religion is to the problematic of human relations. . . . The two assertions are not merely compatible. In the end they imply one another. Terms like communion and fellow-

[1] 44. [2] 51. [3] 52. [4] 54.

ship . . . are drawn directly from our experience of personal relationship and have a meaning for us only because of this.' I would say that a term like 'communion' should find its meaning for a theist not only in the experience of personal relationship among ourselves but also in the experiences of that relationship in which we stand to God, the super-person. Macmurray may seem to be saying that communion with God is a reflective activity which is meaningless except as deepening and developing human community. It is true that it will not be the genuine article unless it leads us to such a deepening and developing, but Macmurray has said that it is 'conditioned by this function and can be understood through it'. This may well suggest that it has no independent value. That conclusion I should absolutely reject.

That it is Macmurray's conclusion becomes still harder to doubt as we read on. 'Religious reflection', he says, 'in its primary and central expression, has the form of symbolic action, and this action is itself communal. It is at once a part of the common life of a group of persons and an expression or symbol of the common life as a whole. To put it otherwise, it has the form of ritual or ceremonial activity. . . . It involves thought, of course, and it involves emotion. . . . But since it is itself action, it unifies these as scientific and artistic reflection cannot do. These remain at the level of ideas and images. . . . The meaning of religion can only be unambiguously expressed in action.'[1] This is a point of view to which Christians in our time have been showing increasing sympathy, and it has led many of them, I fear, into professions of what must seem to be sheer atheism. It is perfectly true that 'the meaning of religion can only be unambiguously expressed in action'. Truly human acts are concerned not just with logic but with life, and the great value of Macmurray's work lies in his insistence on this. But human life does not mean just communion with other people; essentially, in my submission, it means communion with God.

Is Macmurray really denying it? A little later he writes: 'I can know you only if you reveal yourself to me, and you can reveal yourself to me only if I am prepared to do the same. This, then, is the ground of the religious truth that God can be known only by revelation.'[2] That sounds well enough, and it is true that God cannot be known unless he reveals himself, although I should want to add that the Christian revelation is, not indeed the only

[1] 55. [2] 56.

one, but in fact the definitive one. But it becomes difficult to believe that this is genuine theism when we read on the next page: 'What then is the invariant core of the meaning of a religious performance? So far as it can be expressed satisfactorily in ideas, we may formulate it thus: "We belong together in a common life, and we are glad of it." The participants are rejoicing in their fellowship. The performance is a celebration of communion. Because of this, it is also an act of worship; and these two aspects of the core of meaning are necessary to one another.' Who or what, we may ask, is being worshipped? Here religion does seem to be reduced to 'morality tinged with emotion'. It is a very fine morality (Macmurray speaks impressively of a 'perfect love which is a complete fullness of rationality'),[1] but it seems not to deserve the name of religion.

Macmurray now describes how this celebration of communion binds up the participants not only with one another but with the whole history, past and future, of the community and with the natural world. If we bear these things in mind, he goes on, 'it is not difficult to realize that only the worship of God can carry the full meaning that is required'. So once again we have to ask what he means by 'God', and this time we receive a fuller and, apparently, a much better answer. After all, it might appear, Macmurray is not really saying that men are just worshipping their own togetherness, for he now argues that, because 'all the members of the community are united in the same symbolic action', there must be 'the Other in relation to whom all find themselves in a complete self-transcendence'.[2] And this Other, we are told, 'can only be an infinite person, who is at once the Father of men and the Creator of the world. For the Other must be personal—since he is one term in a personal relationship. He must be infinite and eternal—because he must be the same for all persons at all times—the same yesterday, today and for ever. . . .' So surely we are now out of the wood.

Not quite, unfortunately, and in this matter a miss is as good as a mile. Macmurray continues: 'Since the ordinary experience of personal relation is necessarily a unity in co-operation, directed towards nature and upon nature, he [God] must unify the natural with the personal.' I am not sure what that means. But it rather suggests, when we consider its whole context, that God's function is simply to hold the world together, to make it a totality. Has

[1] 58.   [2] 59.

he then no life of his own? Since he has been called the Creator of the world, it would seem that he must have. But, if we bear in mind what has been said of him on various occasions, we cannot help suspecting that he is, after all, only a function of the world, that he has no meaning in himself over and above the meaning which he gives to the world. He is not, that is, genuinely transcendent. He belongs, so to say, essentially to the world.

The rest of this third lecture can only confirm our suspicion. We are told that 'to ask whether God exists is to ask an unnecessary and possibly a meaningless question'.[1] And all that we are told, apart from this, is that religion provides the basis for solving the problems of community. As it develops, it takes on the task of making real not just the total community but the community of all mankind, which is, in Macmurray's phrase. 'the correlate of monotheism'.[2] 'The function of a universal religion', he concludes, is 'to create the conditions' for the realization of this universal community. That is indeed a truth and one which peculiarly deserves the name of Catholic. But it is very far from being the whole truth for one who holds the Christian and Catholic faith. We seem forced back to the conclusion that, in Macmurray's view, God has no life of his own with which we are to be united, but is only a principle of life for the world which we now inhabit.

The fourth and last of these lectures certainly presents us with a purely this-worldly view of religion. It is concerned with 'the problem presented to Christianity for solution' at the present time. The statement of the problem is admirable so far as it goes, in its insistence, for example, that religious problems cannot be solved by political means because 'one can organize co-operation: one cannot organize love'.[3] But religion in these pages is concerned with the brotherhood of man, and with the Fatherhood of God only in function of that. Macmurray does here allow that there is 'an individual phase of personal relation' in religion, a 'necessary withdrawal into the self and so into solitariness', but this must be only temporary. 'A relation to God', he writes, 'which is not a relation to my neighbour is unreal.'[4] Yes, but is it nevertheless more than a relation to my neighbour? Religion, he also says, must not 'contrast the actual world of material existence with an idea or spiritual reality which lies beyond it',[5] and that seems plain enough. He especially discounts the view that 'religion is grounded in a belief in another world and in the immortality of

[1] 60.   [2] 61.   [3] 68.   [4] 69.   [5] 73.

the soul'.[1] No distinction between the natural and the supernatural is allowable.

But we have not yet reached the end of this story. A few years ago Macmurray, already in his seventies, became a member of the Society of Friends, and in 1965 he delivered the annual Swarthmore Lecture at the Friends House in London, taking as his subject 'The Search for Reality in Religion'. This was published in the same year as a book of some eighty pages remarkable for the attractiveness of its style and temper and containing an absorbing account of his formative years. This account throws some light on the significance of the rather puzzling statement of his religious position in the later stages of this extensive discourse. We learn that Macmurray, like so many distinguished men, was brought up in the atmosphere of Scottish Calvinism. When he went to Oxford in 1913 as a scholar of Balliol, he was, he says, still 'unable to question the reality of the religious experience of my parents, even when the forms of its expression, particularly in doctrine and belief, became more and more incredible to me'.[2] This has remained his position ever since. The experience of service in the Great War made him, he tells us, 'a confirmed realist'; and it made him 'deeply sceptical of the principles of the European civilization' in which he had been brought up.[3] In this connection he makes a most significant remark: 'There hangs about the official representative of religion an odour, not of sanctity, but of disingenuousness.' One knows all too well what he means. Macmurray, like so many other people, had not come across what I would venture to call authentic, genuinely traditional, Christianity. I am reminded of a remark made by David Daiches in his book on Milton that in Milton we find blended together all the great intellectual and artistic traditions of Western Europe with a single exception—its contemplative tradition.

Macmurray, then, was now opposed to 'idealism' by which he here means 'otherworldliness'. He still accepted, he says, the validity of Christianity, 'whatever Christianity might really be', and was 'committed to rediscover a Christianity which is non-idealist'.[4] It seemed to him that when Christianity became the religion of the Roman Empire it inevitably made a distinction between the spiritual and the material realms, and became a purely spiritual religion, relinquishing to the State the ordering of the material realm. And, he says, 'a purely spiritual religion is

[1] 75.   [2] 9.   [3] 22.   [4] 23, 27.

necessarily an idealist religion and so unreal. For the purely spiritual is the purely imaginary.'[1] Religion, he holds, was in its beginnings about the whole of life; it is so no longer.[2] There is truth in that. But it looks as though the Great War had so much impressed upon him the problem of universal brotherhood that he could no longer envisage as real any more far-reaching human problem. At one point he suggests that the similarity mentioned by Christ between the first and second commandments may be explained by the concern of primitive religion with the community not only between man and nature but between man and man.[3] This is not only an odd piece of exegesis but involves an interpretation of primitive religion which is very far from obvious.

But, as in the earlier lectures, another voice keeps breaking in and here becomes more insistent. We are told that in all religion there is 'the sense of an unseen presence, of something more in our experience which is somehow personal, which transcends our familiar experience of life in common'. 'In our own terms', Macmurray writes, 'it is the experience of the presence of God.'[4] He goes on to speak of the Old Testament and of a God who is certainly conceived of as having a life of his own. He puts in a footnote to warn us of the excesses of demythologizing, pointing out that 'it is the personal in our experience which points in the direction of God, and provides the most adequate language we possess for reference to God'.[5] And he speaks of 'the presence of Jesus Christ in and amongst the worshippers . . . this presence seems, as it were, to coalesce with, or join itself to the presence of God, in such fashion as to provide the image of God we need. This is *our* experience of His resurrection, and with it of His relation to God.'[6] What could be more satisfactory? But we are still warned against 'mysticism'. It is true, as Macmurray says, that 'Jesus came to proclaim, not a way of escape from the world, but the coming of the Kingdom of Heaven within it'.[7] His repeated denial that Christianity is concerned with a heavenly other-world is, however, unjustifiable. Christianity has always been concerned with a Kingdom to which this world is in progress, which not only comes into this world but raises it to what lies beyond it.

I shall now say something briefly about a writer whose system of thought is also ostensibly a moralism but whose assumptions are very different from Macmurray's. Miss Iris Murdoch is known

[1] 27. [2] 30. [3] 33. [4] 34. [5] 45.
[6] 53. [7] 59.

to a large public as a novelist whose work is obviously distinguished but becomes increasingly hard to evaluate, and to a smaller public as a moral philosopher with a special interest in the existentialists, Sartre in particular. Two years ago she delivered the Leslie Stephen Lecture in Cambridge, taking as her subject 'The Sovereignty of Good over Other Concepts'.

The title of the lecture intimates that the philosopher on whose thought it is based is Plato, the philosopher who, in Macmurray's eyes, has been so largely responsible for what he considers the unreality of traditional Christian thinking. Miss Murdoch simply presupposes, as she herself candidly avows, that there is no God in the traditional sense of the term (which sense, she adds, is perhaps the only one) and that human beings are naturally selfish. She proceeds to dismiss the typically 'romantic' notion, as she rightly calls it, that we create value by the exercise of our freedom, and remarks that 'if quality of consciousness matters, then anything which alters consciousness in the direction of unselfishness, objectivity and realism is to be connected with virtue'.[1] She gives a first instance of this, following a hint from the *Phaedrus*, by referring to the experience of art which 'affords us a pure delight in the independent existence of what is excellent'[2] and considers this to be more especially true of art which is non-representational. The arts, she says, show us 'the absolute pointlessness of virtue while establishing its supreme importance'. Macmurray would protest against this doctrine of pointlessness, and so should I if I could not interpret it as asserting the apprehension of absolute value, a value which does not point beyond itself. In other words, if this doctrine is not an implicit theism, then it seems to me quite baffling. Miss Murdoch insists that 'the pointlessness of art is the pointlessness of life itself', and at the same time that 'nothing in life is of any value except the attempt to be virtuous'. Value and pointlessness seem to be, if not identified, at least brought together with such a strange result that it would seem irrational to reject further inquiry into it.

As the lecture proceeds the language of religion becomes more and more pervasive. Still speaking of art, Miss Murdoch writes that 'we surrender ourselves to its *authority* [her italics] with a love which is unpossessive and unselfish' and that 'it pierces the veil and gives sense to the notion of a reality which lies beyond appearances'.[3] She goes on to say that 'there is a way of the intellect,

[1] 10.   [2] 12.   [3] 15–16.

a sense in which the intellectual disciplines are moral disciplines' and that 'they might be thought of as introductory images of the spiritual life'.[1] They are not 'the spiritual life itself'. To realize this we have to consider the concept of Good (this has a capital letter, we are told, to obviate the use of inverted commas). When we are faced with a conflict of desires, 'the difficulty is to keep the attention fixed upon the real situation and to prevent it from returning surreptitiously to the self' and 'the love which brings the right answer is an exercise of justice and realism and really *looking*'.[2] This, for me, rings all the bells at once. Yet, when we have just been told that human life is pointless, it is also very surprising. And at this point Miss Murdoch introduces 'God' into a list of 'trumped-up intermediaries invented by human selfishness to make the difficult task of virtue easier and more attractive'. 'True morality', she says, 'is a sort of unesoteric mysticism having its source in an austere and unconsoled love of the Good.'[3] This is the Kantian morality—you ought because you ought—on which I have already said what I have to say.

It remains to draw attention to certain later passages in which what is said about the Good is what I would say about God. Plato's great image of the sun is magnificently expounded and explicated. Miss Murdoch points out that 'the proper and serious use of the term [Good] refers us to a perfection which is perhaps never exemplified in the world we know'[4] ('there is no good in us', she quotes). Yet, she goes on, '"Good is a transcendent reality" means that virtue is the attempt to pierce the veil of selfishness and join the world as it really is.'[5] 'What is *that* world?', we must ask her. The world of the Good has been shown, plainly enough, to be beyond our world. Plato's *Republic* is then interpreted (correctly, in my opinion) as saying that 'we introduce order into our conceptions of the world through our apprehension of the Good'. Freedom, for example, now becomes 'not an inconsequential chucking of one's weight about, it is the disciplined overcoming of self'.[6] The moral values unify the whole of life. And Plato's famous words about the Good are then quoted: 'It is that which every soul pursues and for the sake of which it does all that it does, with some intuition and yet baffled. . . . It is the source of knowledge and truth and yet is something which surpasses them all in splendour.'[7] Still speaking of the sun-image

[1] 18.   [2] 20.   [3] 21.   [4] 22.   [5] 23.   [6] 26.
[7] *Republic*, 505.

of the Good, Miss Murdoch says that 'we do not and probably cannot know, conceptualize, what it [the Good] is like at the centre'. What can this be but our obscure awareness of God?

It would take too long to consider the illuminating commentary on Plato's allegory of the prisoners in the Cave (which contains something like a prophecy of Christ's Passion: 'If anyone endeavoured to set them free and carry them to the light, would they not go so far as to put him to death if they could only manage to get him into their power?').[1] But I must quote in full a particularly remarkable passage towards the end of the lecture. 'I think', Miss Murdoch writes, 'that there is a place both inside and outside religion for a sort of contemplation of the Good, not just by dedicated experts but by ordinary people: an attention which is not just the planning of particular good actions but an attempt to look right away from self towards a distant transcendent perfection, a source of uncontaminated energy, a source of new and quite undreamt-of virtue.'[2] And the paragraph concludes with these words: 'This is the true mysticism which is morality, a kind of undogmatic prayer which is real and important, though perhaps also difficult and easily corrupted.' Miss Murdoch ends by asking what more can be said about the Good: 'Is there not something about the conception of a refined love which is practically identical with goodness?'[3] One might think that the identification with theism of this morality, which has now become a metaphysic and a mysticism, would be inevitable. But Miss Murdoch says instead that 'good is the magnetic centre towards which love naturally moves' and that 'when we try perfectly to love what is imperfect our love goes to its object *via* the Good to be thus purified and made unselfish and just. The mother loving the retarded child or loving the tiresome elderly relation.'[4] This also, it must surely be clear, is to speak within the tradition of Christian theism. A Christian can only ask himself at this point with much searching of heart why Miss Murdoch does not recognize it for what it is.

18. CONCLUSION: RESPONSIBILITY AND THE SIGNIFICANCE OF ETHICS

In the course of this account of the evidence for God which, as I see it, is to be found fundamentally in our moral experience,

---
[1] *Republic*, 517.   [2] 35.   [3] 35.   [4] 35-6.

I have had to touch on a number of questions which have been treated in what may well have seemed a very casual way. I wanted to build up this account and compare it with others without complicating matters by detailed discussions of its various implications, and I have sometimes remarked that I should be considering later on some of these implications. This must now be done. The account may seem in the end an unacceptable one, even to those who have sympathy with it, if the general view of our moral life which is implied by it still seems exposed to important objections. The questions which are awaiting further discussions are all of them connected in one way or another with the topic of moral responsibility.

First, there is an objection made by determinists to the libertarian's case which needs further attention. It is that, on the libertarian's view, a morally free choice is an unmotivated one. On the determinist's view, when various courses of action present themselves for our choice, our choice is determined by our needs at the time and our needs are determined by our total situation, including what we call our characters, our habits and tendencies. This total situation results from the various influences brought to bear on us, our heredity, training, and so forth, taken in conjunction with the pressures of the moment. The choice is ours in that the decision is made consciously, after deliberation, not forced upon us against our wills but willed by ourselves. But there is in fact only one way in which we can choose, the circumstances being what they are. The libertarian denies this, and says that we could have acted otherwise in those same circumstances. And the determinist's objection to this is that it makes choice irrational. The libertarian must either give an account of the business in terms of motives in the sense of reasons for action (so the determinist will argue), in which case the motive will determine the choice, or he must say that there is no motive and then choice will be a sort of creation out of nothing, and quite unintelligible. It would be irresponsible—having no reason for what you do is surely what irresponsibility means. We can be responsible only if it is our characters which determine our actions.

The determinist's case, then, can be made to seem very plausible. It presupposes that, when a moral choice is made, the conflict of desires must always end with the victory of the most powerful. Two or more objects compete for our choice, and we have to decide which we really want. When we have found out as much about them as we reasonably can, it will become clear to us which of them is the most promising for our purposes (if not, we shall just have to toss for it), and we then take hold of it, rejecting the others. This description of a moral choice, although it will need to be considerably modified and expanded, is, I believe, perfectly sound in principle. The choice does involve a conflict of desires, and it does seem clear that the desire which wins *is* the strongest—that is to say, *when* it wins. What the determinist has overlooked is that it may not have been the strongest when the conflict started, that we can decide which is to be the strongest in the end. We do mean something by speaking of 'controlling' our desires. It is not just a way of saying that they fight it out among themselves, with ourselves as the battleground, not as participants.

But there are obvious difficulties about that account. 'What you are suggesting', the determinist may say, 'is that it is simply up to you to decide which motive is to win. But you must have a reason for doing so. If, for example, you believe in God and in heaven, and perhaps also in hell, then your desire to get to heaven or to avoid hell may have proved to be the strongest. In that case you have decided in consequence of your beliefs that some other desire must be disregarded, for you suppose that to promote it will be incompatible with your getting to heaven. And the desire to get to heaven or to avoid hell proved to be the strongest because you happen to have been brought up in a certain way and happened to think about it at just that moment. Anyway, whatever your state of mind may be, there must always be reasons to explain your choice, and, if they explain it, they also determine it. You feel that you could have chosen otherwise because, when you began to think about it, the matter was still undecided, and you made the decision yourself. But I have explained to you that this does not follow. What happened was that there were for the moment competing desires which neutralized one another—you were like the donkey presented with two equidistant carrots, or at any rate one desire was sufficiently strong to make others ineffective—but then for certain reasons which we need not go into in detail certain considerations invaded your mind, and one of your desires became in consequence the effective one. Your giving thought to the matter at all and the conclusion to which you eventually came were both equally determined by the total situation in which you were at the time.'

The libertarian may say at this point that he was simply aware of his power to decide the matter this way or that in the particular circumstances in which he found himself, that he simply *knew* that he *could* have chosen otherwise than in fact he did. To say only that he *would* have chosen otherwise if the circumstances had been different will not, he may maintain, fit the facts of the case. And this is, in my opinion, the right answer. But it may not seem acceptable until all the determinist's objections have been considered. And so the libertarian may take a further line. 'I disagree', he might say to his interlocutor, 'with your whole way of looking at this business of moral choice. You look at it as though it were a part of the natural world in which atoms bounce off atoms, billiard balls collide with billiard balls and so on. But the operations of human motives and human wills are quite different. They cannot be straightforwardly described, and one has to talk about them in metaphors. So, when I talk about throwing something into a scale when I talk about making up my mind, I must not be supposed to mean this literally. It is a way of saying that I can make a contribution of my own to the state of affairs, that I can alter it by a decision of my own and that the origin of this decision is just myself, my action at the present moment—it is not determined by my past actions or by anything else. Why should I not just do something on my own? Action is an ultimate fact which philosophers like you have forgotten about. It may seem scandalous that I should be in this sense creative, but you cannot analyse the fact of it away.' To this the determinist will no doubt reply that the operations of billiard balls and the operations of our wills are certainly different in important ways, but that if we are going to talk about motives for action at all (and surely we cannot avoid it) we must think of them as causes which are productive of effects. And he may go on to say that the picture of a 'self' which controls its desires implies a very odd sort of distinction between my desires and *me*.

I think that the determinist needs to receive another answer. My proposal is that we should accept his contention that we are moved to action by what we see as good, but that what we see as good will nevertheless depend on ourselves because we can shut our eyes to what is really good—with the result that we accept instead something which, though in itself some sort of good, is not in fact *our* good, the good which is summoning us here and now. We take *as* our good what is really opposed to it in the existing circumstances. If it were in no sense good, it could make no appeal to us. We would not be drawn to it, as we sometimes are, with the result (if we let ourselves be engrossed by it) that we shut out the real good, the good for us which has presented itself to us.

This ancient thesis (it goes back through St Thomas to the Greeks) may seem at first to be a mere playing with words and an attempt to analyse evil away. It has, indeed, analysed evil away in some of its forms in so far as it has failed to appreciate our own responsibility for moral failure as, for example, in the Socratic adage that no one is willingly evil. But in the form of it which I am proposing it will not be open to this objection. Let us consider the concrete facts. There are conflicting desires. All of them must somehow represent to us a possibility for our own self-fulfilment, which is surely what we mean by our good. You cannot, strictly speaking, desire your own annihilation, for to say this would be to talk about your non-existence as though it were a state of your existence; you can only desire the cessation of a certain state of frustrated existence. Even the most perverse and monstrous crimes must seem to their perpetrators some sort of positive enhancement of their natures. But these crimes will not represent the 'truth of their natures' (the phrase, it may be remembered, which Professor Woods used). In disregarding the rights of others, in performing actions which have negative effects, as in murder, theft and so on, they are also disregarding their own true status as persons, for, if they had acknowledged this status, they would have recognized that their own self-fulfilment was bound up with that of others—because, in acknowledging their own true value, they would be acknowledging, even without recognizing it, the infinite source of *all* value. The acknowledgement of value, so I have contended, is bound up with our awareness of ourselves as persons summoned absolutely, unconditionally, to the Good. This analysis is true to the facts of experience. We know perfectly well on occasion that a certain course of action (getting on with a job of work, let us say) represents the true good for us at the moment. We want to get it done, but the more immediate pressure of some other desire (going to a film or whatever) tempts us to concentrate on it to the exclusion of what we had once recognized as right, as the good for us now.

It is the turning away from the good in which moral evil consists. When it has certain negative consequences (as in murder, theft and so on), it is the more heinous, the less excusable, because it involves the rejection not only of one's own value but also that of others, and (normally, at least) it involves deliberateness in a relatively high degree. But moral evil in itself lies simply in the rejection of value. It may or may not result in physical evil, an absence of value.

It may be useful to recall at this point what Miss Murdoch told us about the concept of the Good. When we are faced with a conflict of desires, she said, 'the difficulty is to keep the attention fixed upon the real situation and to prevent it from returning surreptitiously to the self'—that is, I would interpolate, to the lower self, for we are now in a position to make the distinction, questioned by the determinist, between myself as a person summoned to infinite value and my relatively valueless desires for immediate enjoyment. Miss Murdoch went on to say that 'the love which brings the right answer is an exercise of justice and realism and really *looking*'. This is the discovery of value. If we suspect its presence, we shall find it if we go on 'really looking'. Unless we then stop 'really looking' we shall be accepting it. And, in so far as we accept the good, we are determined by it. When we fail to accept the true good, however, we are not being determined, although our failure results in our being determined by a lesser one. Failure itself, though real, something for which we are responsible, must nevertheless be described as a non-acting. This, as I tried to show earlier, is where the ultimate obscurity is found—in a fact of our experience, not in the decrees of God or in his government of the world, baffling though that may seem to us in its maintenance of the so-called 'laws' of nature with their frequently distressing but presumably inevitable results. It was in this connection that I first discussed the rejection of value. I have returned to it here not only to fill up the gaps in my first account, but also to emphasize its importance as being in itself evidence of God. It is the negative side, the reverse side, of our awareness that we are summoned by infinite value. We know ourselves as capable of the weird irrationality of turning away from a transcendent value which we had once glimpsed as such. We may not have called it anything. But it was 'other', and all-important. The awareness of moral freedom and the awareness of God are bound up with one another.

We shall not be certain of God until we recognize ourselves as knowers of the truth and summoned to know it at its fountainhead—and this is equivalently the recognition of our moral responsibility for knowing it or at least for 'looking' for it. Until we have accepted God we shall be in danger of letting truth slip through our fingers, of failing to grasp the measure of our responsibility and gradually lapsing into bafflement and indifference. We escape from relativism and determinism only by transcending both of them at once in the free assertion of our capacity for God, which is at the same time our discovery of him. In recognizing our negative capacity for evil we recognize at the same time our capacity for that positive freedom which consists in the service, the adoration, of God.

It seems to me, then, that, when we are discussing these ultimate issues, we cannot hope to reach any important results merely by the method of conceptual or linguistic analysis. Fr Patrick McGrath's recent book *The Nature of Moral Judgement*, although making some very effective criticisms of current theories on the subject, confines itself for the most part to these fashionable forms of analysis and comes to the conclusion that (human) 'rights constitute the ultimate criterion of morality'.[1] McGrath does not seem to take seriously the fact that some people simply reject the whole notion of a 'right' considered as something objective. A thinker like Nowell-Smith can give an explanation of our language about morals in non-metaphysical, naturalistic, subjectivist, terms which cannot be decisively rejected unless we substitute for it an explanation of our experience in theistic terms. In the last sentence of his book McGrath writes that 'one cannot coherently deny that one is morally obliged to respect the rights of others'. No, because to put it like that implies that they have rights to be respected. And this is not going to be granted by the positivist in the sense—we must call it, I think, a metaphysical sense—which McGrath intends. The notion that language rather than experience is the final court of appeal has had, I consider, a trivializing and sometimes even a stultifying effect upon English philosophizing for many years past. 'Rights' are indeed taken for granted in our Western society by public opinion as a whole. I doubt whether they will go on being taken for granted indefinitely in the (supposed) absence of a metaphysical foundation for them. It hardly needs saying that our century has already witnessed a

[1] 292.

large-scale disregard of 'rights' in actual practice. If the human individual is only a 'naked ape', it becomes easy to regard him as dispensable.

Let us consider for a moment Mr David P. Gauthier's *Practical Reasoning*, published in 1963; he denies that morality reduces to convention and self-interest, but he has nothing to say to anyone who thinks otherwise. The book, like McGrath's, is most useful as a criticism of certain current theories; for example, it is pointed out[1] that Nowell-Smith, who considers that 'I ought to do X' expresses a decision, also says that 'I ought to do X but shall not' expresses a prediction; but, Gauthier remarks, we cannot say that we are deciding to perform an action which we predict that we shall not perform: 'If I decide to do something, I may indeed fail to do it. But if I decide to do it, I cannot *expect* to fail.' That seems to be unanswerable. But when Gauthier gives his own account of 'ought', he simply lays it down that statements containing this word are grounded on statements which refer not only to the wants of the agent but also to those of others. This is indeed the case, but it remains that, to be convinced of objective 'rights', we need to reach certain metaphysical conclusions. Gauthier claims that it is rational to treat all rational agents as worthy of respect, but he admits that it cannot be proved. He calls it (rightly) the presupposition of moral as distinct from prudential and self-regarding judgements. But this is a presupposition which, according to him, we have to accept without further explanation. In other words, Gauthier believes in an autonomy of ethics.

I now turn to difficulties which may present themselves about the origins of human responsibility and about its definitive exercise from the metaphysician's and theologian's point of view. If I am right, the awareness of moral responsibility, which is also the awareness of God, is what constitutes the human being as such.[2] From the scientist's point of view certain sorts of behaviour seem to bear witness to the emergence of the human consciousness. For the metaphysician and the theologian, they may be bearing witness only to a penultimate stage in a process which has not yet reached its completion with the appearance of

[1] 15.
[2] Professor H. D. Lewis approaches the same conclusion in the fourteenth chapter, 'The Moral Status of Man', of his *Freedom and History* (Allen & Unwin, 1966).

the human person. It cannot therefore be made an objection to this way of looking at things that the first men had too rudimentary an intelligence for moral responsibility to be possible for them. The contention is that it is not until moral responsibility is present that *man*, strictly speaking, is present. We cannot, of course, pin down the moment when it becomes present, nor have we any need to do so.

But there may still be a feeling that when moral responsibility first made its appearance it must have been in so feeble a form as hardly to count for theological purposes; that is to say, it could not have carried with it more than a vague suspicion of God, so vague that it could not develop in the span of a lifetime into a definite awareness of him. I call this a feeling because there is in fact nothing rational about it. What people have in mind when they talk in this way is a picture of a general development from a mere acceptance of the totems and taboos of the local community to a recognition of absolute moral obligation. This recognition, they vaguely feel, could not have taken place in a flash. But if there is a real difference between these two states of affairs then this recognition must have started sometime. There was a time when it was not yet present and a time when it was. Either there is at least some suspicion of God, and of absolute moral obligation, or there is none at all. And there is no ground for saying that such a suspicion could not develop into a definite awareness in the course of one man's lifetime. There is also no ground for maintaining that there could not have been a definite awareness which was not preceded by a stage of mere suspicion. This irrational feeling that nothing can really happen is of course the same feeling which leads people to suppose that the whole evolutionary process is an affair of growth in which there are no definite moves from one level of existence to another level which is really different, really *new*. But this, if I may repeat it, is absurd. Things which were just not there before definitely turn up. Failure to appreciate this simple truth leads people to think that, because you can describe the visible process by which something emerges, you have said all that needs to be said about it.

There can be no disproof, then, of the proposals that a suspicion of God first arose on our planet at some definite moment and that the presence of such a suspicion constitutes a human being, or the further proposal, which we must now again consider, that such a being is destined to a definite awareness of God and to the eventual engagement of his full responsibility even if this occurs only at his death. The presence of the suspicion itself would seem to engage him in a certain responsibility, that of following it up, of trying to discover whether in fact it was a grounded suspicion. What he would be vaguely aware of would be God's summons, but he would not yet *know* that it was God's summons or any sort of summons. It could be an illusion. He would have, however, a responsibility for disregarding what might prove to be of supreme inportance for him. But we could not say that he was faced as yet with the alternative of accepting or rejecting God. He would not be sufficiently clear about things for that to apply to him. If man is destined to such a definitive choice, that would have to come later. But I can see no reason why the first man or the first men (if anyone wants to say that any number of them arose with absolute simultaneity) should not have been possessed at once of a knowledge of God such as to make possible that choice. It may be added that the first men remained ape-like, presumably, in appearance and in much at least of their visible behaviour. I am not suggesting that we need assign to them the picturesque attributes excogitated by medieval theologians for the state of primal innocence. Knowledge of God does not necessitate a special degree of culture or even (I venture to say) of linguistic expertise.

But what is more to the purpose is the difficulty which seems to face us when we consider how a definitive choice of God, which would appear to be necessary if in fact we are to attain to him, can be possible for all human beings in the present state of things. So many people lead lives which seem to by-pass the 'great option'. This is not necessarily to say that they acknowledge no responsibilities in any way or that they are wholly cut off from God, but that their acceptance of him has been so vague and half-hearted that, although they have not rejected him, they cannot yet be ready to be received into an unclouded and indefectible union with him. It is on this matter that Fr Ladislaus Boros's book *The Moment of Truth* is particularly valuable. His view that the moment of death is a moment of choice is by no means a new one. But it had been commonly thought of rather as a possible answer to a particular difficulty than as a general thesis following from principles both theological and philosophical. It had seemed a way of avoiding the awkward conclusion that the vast number of human beings who have died unbaptized in infancy must be consigned to a state of natural bliss (whatever that could be) in a sort of antechamber of heaven called Limbo (theologians at one time regarded it as a sort of antechamber of hell, a far more awkward conclusion). The proposed solution of a choice at the moment of death had met with two chief objections. First, this alleged choice would have to occur either in the last moment of *life*, when there is no ground for supposing some fresh knowledge of God which would enable an infant to make it, or when that moment is past, in which case there is, according to orthodox theology, no longer a possibility of choice at all—when we are dead, the time of choice is over. Secondly, an infant cannot choose God in any supposition. The answers which had been given to these objections were that the choice occurs neither before nor after the separation of soul and body but precisely *in* that process, and that the infant has a capacity for knowledge of God which may well be actualized when its life is being cut short by historical accidents—these were not willed directly by its Creator and must not be supposed to frustrate his designs upon us.

Boros takes over these answers, setting them in a far wider context. In the Introduction to this book he puts his position as follows (and in italics): 'Death gives a man the opportunity of posing his first completely personal act; death is, therefore, by reason of its very being, the moment above all others for the awakening of consciousness, for freedom, for the encounter with God, for the final decision about his eternal destiny.'[1] This is because the soul in parting from the body, becomes, according to Boros, fully awake to its own spirituality. 'In death', he writes, 'the spiritual movement of being is liberated from the alien element of non-personal temporality. The spirit's succession now becomes entirely interior, that is, determined wholly by the succession inherent in the exercise of its own being. This occurs in a total awareness and presence of being, and not in mere flashes which reach us only fragmentarily. Thus the soul is no longer swept along by an alien succession. It is able to realize fully the whole activity of its being, in one and the same act.'[2] We may find this language rather high-flown, and the reference to an 'alien' process of time may suggest a contempt for history and for the body. Boros is not intending this at all. His point is that the soul really comes into its own at this moment; after

[1] ix. [2] 7.

all, anyone who professes Christianity must view this world not indeed just as a vale of tears but certainly as a place of pilgrimage. Boros adds that the decisions of everyday life dispose us, favourably or unfavourably, for this final decision, so that this is not an encouragement to moral laxity in the meanwhile.

The philosophical argument for Boros's conclusion draws upon Blondel, Maréchal, Bergson and Marcel. 'Since', he writes, 'freedom . . . derives from the actual, fully realized, expanse of the mind, this latter becomes completely free only when it grasps its infinite expanse—a reality always there as given—that is to say, in death. In reality, therefore, the case is the opposite of what Plato declared in his *anamnesis* theory: knowledge is in no sense a remembering of the thinker's timeless contemplation exercised in a pre-existent state; it is an anticipatory clutching at a possession—a holding—whose light can shine forth only in death. Death is really a *dies natalis*, a day of birth for our mind. . . .'[1] And another passage reads: 'Our first possibility of acting out our love fully is given us in the moment of death when our whole existence is exposed and surrendered.'[2] I am not suggesting that the details of this description are always acceptable, but I do suggest that Boros has put his finger on an important principle, that the act of dying is something that we *perform*, our really definitive action, and that conditions in which we perform it are significantly different from any others. Here I should point out that, just as the scientist's definition of man may be different from the theologian's, because the scientist is judging only by outside appearances whereas the theologian has his metaphysical conclusions to guide him, so the moment of death from the doctor's point of view is not necessarily the same as it is from the theologian's. There can be no disproof of the claim that this (theological) moment is always a conscious one. Physiology can lay down no rules for the presence or absence of consciousness in these unique circumstances.[3]

In the second part of his book Boros develops a theological argument in support of his position, showing how it throws light on Christian doctrines which might otherwise remain puzzling. One of them is the doctrine that we reach through death a definitive state. Why, he asks, does the time for the possible

[1] 35. [2] 83.
[3] That is, there can be an awareness of God in conditions which, *from a medical man's point of view*, may rule out consciousness altogether.

revising of our decisions end with our death? It would seem to be a purely arbitrary decree on God's part—except on the hypothesis that we must make our decision at this moment of clarity because we are now fully capable of doing so. This final decision, in Boros's words, 'realizes all at once the whole plenitude of a man's dynamism of existence and exhausts at one stroke, therefore, all future possibilities of making decisions'.[1] Again, it becomes possible to say, on Boros's view, that salvation is attained by personal fellowship with Jesus Christ in all cases, for, according to him, it is God in Christ whom we encounter at the moment of death, and that may not have been possible for so many in the course of their lives. And it will be obvious that, on the basis of this view, much light can be thrown on the death of Christ, which is his victory and so our redemption. But this is not the place for embarking on that supreme subject. I have only wished to show that a serious case can be made out for the full exercise of our moral responsibility at the time of death. I am not convinced that Boros is right when he maintains that it is never possible at any other time.

It is perhaps not without interest to remark that the reception of Boros's book in the English version (from which I have been quoting these inevitably odd-sounding sentences) was in general a very enthusiastic one but that there were dissentient voices—these were the voices of men brought up on a combination of scholasticism and the linguistic analysis current in the English-speaking universities, and they complained of vague speculations and of ambivalent or even meaningless language. They had, I think, a certain excuse for it. But the point here is that there are two sorts of theologian—the speculative sort and the unspeculative. It is hardly necessary to say that my sympathies belong with the former sort, and this will become, if possible, still more evident in the second volume.

[1] 166.

INDEX

Abelard, 111, 114
Alexander, S., 70
Allen, G., 156
Anselm, St, 205-6
Aristotle, 36, 37, 43-4, 51, 52, 117, 134, 201
Augustine, St, 28, 97, 127, 156, 190, 192
Austin, J. L., 73 n
Ayer, A. J., 51-52, 77, 79

Baelz, P. F., 222-3
Baillie, J., 159-65, 209
Banez, 150-2
Barfield, O., 50-1
Barth, K., 161, 163, 171
Baum, G., 60
Bell, D. R., 19-22, 25, 29, 49-50
Bergson, H., 252
Berkeley, G. 45, 80
Berlin, I., 24-5, 63-4
Bevan, E., 155-9
Blondel, M., 27-8, 125-38, 148-51, 160, 187, 191, 192, 252
Boedder, B., 111-12
Boros, L., 250-3
Bouillard, H., 129 n
Bradley, F. H., 23
Browning, R., 153
Brunner, E., 171, 215
Buber, M., 99-100
Bultmann, R., 98

Campbell, C. A., 32-4
Casserley, J. V. L., 196, 197
Clarke, N., 181-2
Cousin, V., 111
Croce, B., 65

Daiches, D., 237
Descartes, 28, 29, 34, 38-9, 41, 44, 49, 143
Dewart, L., 58-61
Dubarle, D., 191
Duméry, H., 129 n

Eliot, G., 208
Eliot, T. S., 122, 215
Emmet, E. R., 24-6, 29, 49
Ewing, A. C., 36, 57, 64

Farmer, H. H., 99, 101, 216
Farrer, A., 123 n, 196, 197-8
Flew, A., 123 n, 182 n
Freud, S., 210

Garrigou-Lagrange, R., 117
Gasparri, Cardinal, 159
Gauthier, D. P., 248
Geffré, C,-F., 186
Gray, C., 153-4
Guenther, A., 111, 113
Gunderson, K., 181

Häring, B., 130
Hartland-Swann, J., 54-6
Hartshorne, C., 181
Hawkins, D. J. B., 31-2, 35, 36, 43-4, 46-8, 54, 72, 73, 75, 195-8
Hegel, G. W. F., 17, 19, 192
Heidegger, M., 28, 128, 171-2
Hepburn, R. W., 23-4, 99-103, 212-16
Hick, J., 110, 118, 147-8
Hirst, R. J., 18-19, 23, 24, 37
Hügel, F. von, 121 n
Hugo, V., 149
Humani Generis, 118, 130
Hume, 31, 45, 49, 81, 208, 214, 227

Irenaeus, St, 116

Kant, 52, 192, 200, 206, 208, 214, 240
Kemp-Smith, N., 223
Kneale, W., 56-7
Kierkegaard, S., 27, 28, 161, 192
Kovesi, J., 26

Leibnitz, G. W., 184
Lewis, C. S., 110-12

Lewis, H. D., 32, 40-1, 95 n, 165-9, 201, 202, 209-12, 248 n
Locke, 44-5, 50 n
Loisy, A., 138
Lonergan, B., 59-60
Lovejoy, A. O., 109-10
Lubac, H. de, 118, 129-30, 196

McGrath, P., 247
Maclagan, W. G., 221
Macmurray, J., 230-8
Macquarrie, J., 97-9, 170-7, 181 n
McTaggart, J. McT. E., 36
Malcolm, N., 74-5, 77-9
Malebranche, N. de, 143
Mansel, H. L., 158
Marcel, G., 23, 27, 159, 191, 215, 252
Maréchal, J., 252
Maritain, J., 151, 159, 166
Marx, K., 210
Mascall, E. L., 148, 167, 196, 201-6
Merleau-Ponty, M., 193-5
Milton, 237
Molinists, 143, 150
Moore, G. E., 162
Morris, D., 31 n
Most, G. M., 151 n
Murdoch, I., 238-41, 246
Murray, G., 164

Nédoncelle, M., 218
Newman, J. J. H., 28, 138, 183
Nowell-Smith, P., 213, 214, 227, 247, 248

Osborne, H., 157
Otto, R., 168-9
Owen, H. P., 217-22, 224, 226-7

Pascal, B., 28, 128, 180, 186
Penido, M. T.-L., 122
Petter, D. de, 61, 63, 184-6

Plato, 22, 28, 34, 43, 52, 97, 108, 134-5, 177, 239-41, 252
Pontifex, R. M., 146 n, 196, 201
Porter, B. P., 216-17
Price, H. H., 177-82, 187, 222

Rahner, K., 29, 128-9, 171
Ramsey, I. T., 76-7
Ramsey, P., 212
Robert, J.-D., 186-95
Robinson, J., 93
Rosmini, A., 114
Royce, J., 155
Ryle, G., 32-4, 39, 52

Sartre, J.-P., 27, 82, 127, 194, 239
Schillebeeckx, E., 60-3
Sertillanges, A.-D., 117, 141-3
Sillem, E., 195, 199-200
Smith, J. E., 49
Socrates, 245
Somerville, J. M., 126 n
Strawson, P. F., 40

Teilhard de Chardin, P., 126
Thomas Aquinas, St, 37, 109-10, 115, 116-17, 122-4, 134, 151, 176, 185, 187, 195, 199-200, 201-6, 245
Thomists, 42, 90, 112, 115, 117, 134, 141-4, 146, 150-2, 166, 185, 189, 190
Tillich, P., 161, 167, 171

Voltaire, F., 149

Walgrave, J.-H., 183-4
Walsh, W. H., 23, 37-40
Whitehead, A. N., 177
Whiteley, C. H., 103-6
Wicker, B., 60
Wilhelmsen, F., 59
Wisdom, J., 75
Wittgenstein, L., 37-8, 66, 75
Woods, G. F., 224-30, 245